T0301031

49

January
2007

ECONOMIC POLICY

Published in association with the European Economic Association

Blackwell Publishing Ltd for Centre for Economic Policy Research,
Center for Economic Studies of the University of Munich, and
Paris-Jourdan Sciences Economiques (PSE)
in collaboration with the Maison des Sciences de l'Homme.

PANEL

49

January 2007

STATEMENT OF PURPOSE

Economic Policy provides timely and authoritative analyses of the choices which confront policy-makers. The subject matter ranges from the study of how individual markets can and should work to the broadest interactions in the world economy.

Economic Policy is a joint activity of the Centre for Economic Policy Research (CEPR), the Munich-based Center for Economic Studies (CES) and the Paris-based Maison des Sciences de l'Homme (PSE). It offers an independent, non-partisan, European perspective on issues of worldwide concern. It emphasizes problems of international significance, either because they affect the world economy directly or because the experience of one country contains important lessons for policy-makers elsewhere.

All the articles are specifically commissioned from leading professional economists. Their brief is to demonstrate how live policy issues can be illuminated by the insights of modern economics and by the most recent evidence. The presentation is incisive and written in plain language accessible to the wide audience which participates in the policy debate.

Prior to publication, the contents of each volume are discussed by a Panel of distinguished economists from Europe and elsewhere. The Panel rotates annually. Inclusion in each volume of a summary of the highlights of the Economic Policy Panel discussion provides the reader with alternative interpretations of the evidence and a sense of the liveliness of the current debate.

Economic Policy is owned by the Maison des Sciences de l'Homme, CEPR and CES. The 43rd Panel meeting was held in Vienna and was hosted by the Österreichische Nationalbank. We gratefully acknowledge this support, without implicating any of these organizations in the views expressed here, which are the sole responsibility of the authors.

CONTENTS

Editors' introduction

The four papers published in this issue were among those presented in draft form at the panel meeting hosted in April 2006 by the Austrian National Bank in Vienna. In this introduction we place their contribution in the context of wider debates.

FISCAL DECENTRALIZATION

Poorly coordinated, time-inconsistent policy decisions can defeat their own purposes, and credible commitment devices are valuable in many contexts. In the monetary policy area, a credible commitment to low inflation avoids self-fulfilling inflation expectations. Similarly, tax policy can benefit from constraints preventing the kind of *ex post* exorbitant taxation that, eliminating *ex ante* incentives to invest and produce income, would lower revenue yields. Tax competition between independent fiscal constituencies is one such constraint. It has been argued that investors should expect taxes to be low in countries where tax-setting powers are decentralized, and that such countries should therefore be able to attract foreign direct investment (FDI) flows more easily than centralized countries. Sebastian G. Kessing, Kai A. Konrad and Christos Kotsogiannis make a forceful theoretical and empirical case against this line of reasoning. They point out that in exactly the same situations where *ex ante* tax expectations affect tax bases – that is, when taxable income results from forward-looking investment decisions – 'horizontal' tax competition between the regions or states of federal countries is ineffective in keeping *ex post* taxes low: once investors have allocated projects irreversibly to a specific location within a country, there is no competition between that and other constituencies, and fiscal decentralization cannot eliminate each region's temptation to exploit its tax power. A similarly simple mechanism may in fact deliver the opposite prediction. If income produced in a specific geographical location within a federal country is subject to taxation by more than one level of government, lack of 'vertical' coordination between numerous such layers

Economic Policy January 2007 pp. 1–4 Printed in Great Britain
© CEPR, CES, MSH, 2007.

of tax-setting decisions may lead investors to fear more intense *ex post* tax pressure in more decentralized countries. Kessing, Konrad and Kotsogiannis confront this insight with empirical evidence, and uncover strong evidence that more numerous layers of government are associated with smaller inward FDI flows. The panel was keenly interested in the panel draft's theoretical and, especially, empirical results, but voiced some doubts as to the latter's statistical strength. This encouraged the authors to clarify further the relationship between their theoretical reasoning and unavoidably imperfect and incomplete empirical information. A wide variety of specifications allows the published version of the paper to establish that the correlation between 'vertical' decentralization and FDI flows is an empirically robust fact that will need to be taken into account by the policy debate on the allocation of tax powers. The many countries that are considering or implementing fiscal decentralization should not do so in the hope of fostering FDI-friendly tax competition and, to prevent 'vertical' multiplication of tax pressure from discouraging investment, should carefully coordinate tax- and base-setting decisions at different levels of their government structure.

The next paper also explores institutional influences on cross-country investment evidence, albeit from a different, labour-market oriented perspective.

WAGE INEQUALITY

Everybody knows that involuntary unemployment can result from institutions that prevent wages from falling so low as to make it profitable for employers to hire workers, and it is widely thought that collective bargaining, minimum wages, and welfare benefits are the reason why low-skill workers are not employed in many European countries. Employment patterns, however, are not the only consequence of institutional constraints. Firms choose not only how many and which workers to hire, but also how much to invest, and how. While some types of equipment can substitute low-skill workers, others can make such workers more productive. In a 'frictional' labour market, where firms cannot easily replace their employees with unemployed workers, investing in ways that increase incumbent workers' productivity can be an attractive option, and all the more attractive if rigid wages prevent those workers from appropriating that investment's returns. Winfried Koeniger and Marco Leonardi assess the empirical relevance of this channel comparing employment and investment patterns across countries, over time and across industries. Their data come from Germany, where wage floors are binding, and from the US, where labour markets are flexible. Over time, their data span a period when manufacturing equipment became cheaper. The paper's regressions establish that industries employing unskilled workers tend to invest more in Germany than in the US in the available sample. Thus, the data support the view that firms react to institutions which imply high, rigid, compressed wage structures not only by reducing employment, but also by investing so as to boost the productivity of workers above binding minimum-wage floors. The paper's careful and extensive empirical work and findings make an important contribution to the broader and evolving literature that studies interactions between capital costs, capital accumulation, and the labour market opportunities of differently skilled workers. As the discussants' comments make clear, data limitations have so far prevented this literature from offering a coherent and robust picture to policy makers and public opinion, and the paper by Koeniger and Leonardi is also unable to offer conclusive evidence on the relevant issues. But the paper will remain a relevant reference for work on more detailed data as they become available, and usefully reminds policy-makers that investment patterns are one of the many consequences of institutions that interfere with labour market equilibria: while no way out of the standard 'equity vs efficiency' trade-off, investments that boost the productivity of low-skill workers are another way in which profits and competitiveness are reduced in countries where institutions aim at slicing the pie in favour or less advantaged individuals.

SENIORITY

The growing importance of information technology in modern economies has prompted fears that some groups of workers may be increasingly disadvantaged, because of inadequate skills. One group of workers about whom particular concern has been expressed is older workers. There is evidence of poor labour market performance of older workers, and evidence that an ageing workforce can become a burden for some kinds of firm. Francesco Daveri and Mika Maliranta investigate this question by providing evidence on the relation between age, seniority and experience, on the one hand, and the main components of labour costs, namely productivity and wages, on the other, for a sample of plants in three manufacturing industries (forestry, industrial machinery and electronics) in Finland during the IT revolution in the 1990s.

They uncover evidence of a significant divergence between the wage and productivity profiles of more senior workers – that is, those who have been a long time with the same employer. It is this group rather than older workers *per se* who are most at risk of becoming a burden on firms in IT-intensive sectors. In 'average' industries – those not undergoing major technological shocks – both productivity and wages keep rising with the accumulation of either seniority (in the forestry industry) or experience (in the industry producing industrial machinery). In electronics, however, the seniority–productivity profile shows a positive relation first and then becomes negative as one looks at plants with higher average seniority. This body of evidence is consistent with the idea that fast technical change brings about accelerated skill depreciation of senior workers. The authors cannot rule out, however, that their correlations are also simultaneously produced by worker movements across plants. The seniority–earnings profile in electronics is instead rather similar to that observed for the other industries – a likely symptom of the prevailing Finnish wage bargaining institutions which tend to make seniority one essential element of wage determination.

In the end, seniority matters for labour costs, not age as such. But only in high-tech industries, not in the economy at large. This is well tuned with previous research on gross flows of workers and jobs in the US and other OECD countries which unveiled the productivity-driving role of resource reallocation between plants. To improve the employability of the elderly at times of fast technical change, the authors argue that public policy should divert resources away from preserving existing jobs and lend more attention to the retraining of old workers to ease their reallocation away from less productive plants (or plants where they have become less productive) into new jobs.

Discussion at the panel focused on whether the undoubted statistical association between seniority and declining productivity was more likely to reflect a decline in productivity among older workers, or a sorting process by which less productive workers were less likely to leave their employers and join new firms. The existing data do not allow this question to be answered with any confidence, but it remains an important issue for future research.

ECOSYSTEMS

As public debate and public policy focus increasingly on the protection of environmental resources it is becoming important to find rigorous methods for valuing environmental assets such as ecosystems whose future may be threatened by economic change. The paper by Edward Barbier explores two methods for valuing such ecosystems by valuing the services that they yield to various categories of user and that are not directly valued in the market. It applies these methods by way of illustration to the valuation of mangrove ecosystems in Thailand. The first method is known as the production function approach and relies on the fact that ecosystems may be inputs into the production of other goods or services that are themselves marketed, such as fisheries. Barbier discusses issues that arise in measuring the input into fisheries, particularly those due to the fact that the fishery stock is changing over time, and the shadow value of the ecosystem consists in its contribution to the maintenance of the stock as well as its contribution to current output. The second method is known as the expected damage approach and is used to value the services of storm protection in terms of the reduction in expected future storm damage that the ecosystem can provide. These two methods are shown to yield very different valuations of ecosystems from those that would be derived by the methods typically used in cost–benefit analyses. The author argues that they represent a significant improvement on current practice.

The panel was somewhat divided on the appropriateness of the methods proposed, largely because current practice was widely felt to be highly unsatisfactory, and opinions differed as to how much improvement could reasonably be expected of methods that could be implemented in practice. Both the production function and the expected damage approach leave out many potential benefits from ecosystems, so the fact that they also correct for unsatisfactory assumptions made in existing valuation methodologies was not thought by all panellists to be enough reason to recommend their widespread adoption. However, most panellists agreed that important policy decisions might turn on issues of valuation of precisely this kind, and that urgent attention needs to be given to refining methods of measurement and valuation for use in the future.

Fiscal decentralization
VERTICAL, HORIZONTAL, AND FDI

SUMMARY

Both in the developed and developing world, decentralization of fiscal policy is frequently argued to foster investment, because allowing investors to choose between competing locations should make it difficult for each jurisdiction to tax the investment's returns. We point out that this 'horizontal' dimension of decentralization cannot eliminate ex post incentives to tax investments once they are irreversibly located in a jurisdiction, and that the negative ex ante investment effects of such 'hold up' problems are actually stronger when decentralization inevitably leads to multiple levels of taxation power in each location. Empirically, we detect significant negative effects on FDI of the 'vertical' dimension of decentralization, measured by the number of government layers, in a data set containing many countries and many suitable control variables. Indicators of overall fiscal decentralization do not appear to affect the investment climate negatively per se, but our theoretical arguments and empirical results suggest that policymakers should consider very carefully the form and degree of government decentralization if they aim at improving the investment climate.

— Sebastian G. Kessing, Kai A. Konrad and Christos Kotsogiannis

Economic Policy January 2007 Printed in Great Britain
© CEPR, CES, MSH, 2007.

Foreign direct investment and the dark side of decentralization

Sebastian G. Kessing, Kai A. Konrad and
Christos Kotsogiannis

Wissenschaftszentrum Berlin für Sozialforschung (WZB); Wissenschaftszentrum Berlin für Sozialforschung (WZB) and Freie Universität Berlin; University of Exeter and Athens University of Economics and Business

1. INTRODUCTION

Countries differ in their government architecture. Some countries are characterized by a high degree of concentration of fiscal, administrative, judicial, executive and lawmaking powers, whereas others have decentralized many functions and responsibilities of government to different jurisdictions and various levels of government. The cross-country differences in the organization of government are also not static but have been subject to substantial change in many countries. The co-existence of different organizational patterns of government has created an important debate regarding the determinants of particular government structures as well as questions regarding the optimality of different forms of organization.

We are grateful to Nils Herger and Steve McCorriston who have allowed us to make use of the data set they use in their work on cross-border mergers and acquisitions and institutional quality. We also thank them for many discussions, comments and advice during the preparation of the first draft of this paper. Likewise, we thank Daniel Treisman for providing us with his decentralization data. For very helpful comments we thank our discussants and the Panel as well as Johannes Becker, Thiess Büttner, Michael Devereux, Bruno Frey, Clemens Fuest, Achim Wambach, and seminar participants at research seminars and conferences in Berlin, Bonn, Copenhagen, Cyprus, Cologne, Frankfurt, Hanoi, Munich and Warwick. The usual caveat applies.

The Managing Editor in charge of this paper was Giuseppe Bertola.

Economic Policy January 2007 pp. 5–70 Printed in Great Britain
© CEPR, CES, MSH, 2007.

We aim at contributing to this debate by analysing the role of decentralized governance for attracting foreign direct investment (FDI). Decentralized governance, understood here as institutional rules which allocate some governmental decision rights in a country to independent regional governments of non-overlapping territories inside the country, has important effects on the potential of countries to attract FDI. We offer a number of theoretical considerations in this regard, and highlight various effects of the degree of decentralization on FDI that we believe have not been sufficiently recognized. Our main contribution, however, is empirical in nature as we empirically assess the effects of decentralization on FDI.

We point out that, in theory, decentralization of government operates along both a *horizontal* and a *vertical* dimension. Consider first the *horizontal* dimension. Decentralization comes along with the partitioning of the state territory into smaller districts or regions with some autonomy in governmental decision making. The local governments are 'closer' to their constituency, both physically and in terms of accountability. Also, potential competition and benchmarking between the regions becomes feasible whereas this is not feasible under a unified central government. In the policy debate, these aspects of horizontal segregation play an important role. In the traditional view it is argued that horizontal disintegration may also have some disadvantages, as it becomes more difficult for the disintegrated entities to cope with inter-regional spillovers and economies of scale in the public sector. But it is frequently maintained that the beneficial effects that stem from inter-regional competition dominate, in particular with respect to attracting FDI. Horizontal segregation 'permits a degree of institutional competition between centres of authority that can . . . reduce the risk that governments will expropriate wealth' (World Bank, 2004, p. 53). To a large extent, this reasoning is rooted in the view that bureaucrats and politicians are not purely benevolent but they may try to use their power to tax in order to extract revenues, and investment projects that are owned by foreigners may be welcome targets for extractive activities. Competition between jurisdictions for mobile factors of production makes opportunistic behaviour of bureaucrats and politicians more difficult (see Weingast, 1995; Qian and Weingast, 1997), a view that can be traced back to Hayek (1939) and Tiebout (1956). That inter-jurisdictional competition may serve as a welcome supplement to inadequate constitutional constraints and imperfect political institutions has also been emphasized by Brennan and Buchanan (1977, 1980). Also, it is argued that the competition between horizontally segregated regional governments may alleviate some time consistency problems of taxation that emerge even if politicians pursue the welfare of their citizens (Kehoe, 1989).

Complete horizontal disintegration and competitive governmental decision making on the regional level is the implication of decentralization, if decentralization is meant to be a complete break up of a nation into many small and fully independent nations. However, such a complete break up typically does not happen, and should not happen from an efficiency point of view: scale effects and difficulties with the internalization of inter-regional spill-over effects or global public goods suggest that only some, but not all decision rights should be allocated to local or regional governments. Some decisions will continue to be made on more aggregate levels, for example, by the district level government, by state level government, or by the federal government, depending on the architecture of government layers that is chosen. The creation of local governments and the process of horizontal segregation are typically accompanied by a process of *vertical* disintegration. A firm owner who is located in a particular city deals with the governmental decision making of governments of the city, the district in which this city is located, the state in which this district is located and the federal government. When choosing locations, investors should accordingly take into account that they will be subject to the jurisdiction of all such government tiers. An exclusive focus on the benchmarking, competition and accountability features of inter-regional competition that may result from horizontal segregation fails to acknowledge this other side of decentralization.

Our analysis identifies the vertical disintegration of governmental decision making as a major source of disadvantages of decentralization. If the private sector has dealings with several tiers of government, this will potentially create problems of rivalry between the different tiers, coordination failures, free-riding incentives between government decision makers from different government tiers, common pool problems between them when making independent tax and expenditure decisions, problems when it comes to the enforcement of implicit contracts between the government and private investors, and moral hazard problems from joint accountability of politicians from different vertical tiers. These problems affect a country's attraction as a location for FDI in several ways. Suppose governments are tempted to extract revenue from existing investment projects that are owned by foreigners. If governments from several tiers are able to extract revenue from the same investment project a common pool problem emerges that may increase the amount of extractive activity. Governments may also subsidize or make bids for attracting investment projects that are future targets for extractive policy or benefit the host-country in other ways. If local, regional and federal governments can make such bids, they may free ride on one another.

At the end of the day, only empirical evidence can tell whether decentralization, and its different dimensions, has positive or negative effects on the level of FDI inflows. Our econometric analysis provides novel evidence in this respect. Introducing measures of decentralization in a 'knowledge-capital' model and using firm data on cross-border acquisitions, our findings suggest, in line with our theoretical perspective, that a one-dimensional and positive view of decentralization is not appropriate. Employing various decentralization measures in our empirical work, we derive insights as to which aspects of decentralization are conducive to FDI and which turn out to be rather problematic.

The vertical dimension of decentralization, measured by the number of government tiers in a country, is found to affect FDI negatively. On the other hand, fiscal decentralization can have significant positive effects. Expenditure decentralization is found to be correlated with more FDI, while revenue decentralization appears to have a negative influence on FDI.

Our results are highly relevant for policy makers as policy reforms that change the degree of decentralization of governance have been high on the policy agenda both for the developed and the developing world. Poor economic performance of many developing countries is often attributed to the failure of centralized bureaucracy and centralized decision making, and many consultants advocate decentralization of policy-decision making as a way to sustain or increase growth and prosperity. Decentralization is also a frequent advice given by international organizations. Substantial resources have been geared towards programs that promote decentralization of policy decision making. Recently, for instance, the OECD, the World Bank, the Council of Europe, the Open Society Institute (Budapest), the UNDP and USAID have joined forces and introduced the Fiscal Decentralization Initiative to assist developing countries in carrying out intergovernmental reforms (OECD, 2002). The prime objectives of this initiative are to encourage local democracies to improve the capacity of local governments to plan and administer expenditures and raise revenues, and to support local governments in their efforts to become more responsive and accountable. This tendency is expected to continue well into the future.

Practitioners and academics have not been unaware of potential pitfalls of decentralization. For example, the World Bank states that 'sub-national governments are not immune from governance problems – and in some contexts may be more vulnerable to them than national authorities' (World Bank, 2004, p. 53). Similarly, Bardhan and Mookherjee (2000, 2005) discuss the incidence of corruption in centralized and decentralized systems. From our perspective, the question whether local or central governments are more corrupt, easier captured, better informed, etc. is only one aspect of the decentralization debate, albeit an important one. Still, our argument is that this view remains incomplete. It is not sufficient to consider just the incentives and capabilities of each *individual* government. We stress that the *distribution* of power, responsibilities and accountability across different government levels within a federal system has important effects. These effects interact and typically reinforce the governance problems that exist at each individual level of government. This paper is not the first to highlight problematic aspects of decentralization, and that tries to single out more precisely the specific conditions and institutional provisions that are necessary for federalism to unleash its potential for improving the countries' economic performance. For instance, an important feature of the usual efficiency argument for decentralization is that it is developed in a system within which there is a clear division of powers between the different government tiers, in which all spillovers, including vertical fiscal externalities are absent by assumption or are contracted away (Riker, 1964). Vertical fiscal externalities have recently been identified as a source of inefficiency in the context of tax competition (see, for instance, Wrede, 1997, 2000; and Keen and Kotsogiannis, 2002, 2003, 2004) and it has been argued that they are difficult to avoid, even if seemingly different tax bases are assigned to different tiers of government, and regardless whether politicians and bureaucrats are assumed to be benevolent or perfectly selfish.

Treisman (1999a, 1999b, 2000b, 2003) has put forward a number of further arguments why decentralization may lead to a less satisfactory performance, and Cai and Treisman (2005) show that the disciplinary effect of inter-regional competition, even where it could be at work in principle, may lead to adverse effects if regions are asymmetric, making some of them drive out all mobile capital and specialize on a high level of oppression. This and other consequences of a federal structure may also reduce FDI.

2. DECENTRALIZATION AND FOREIGN DIRECT INVESTMENT

The analysis of the benefits and costs of decentralization has generated a number of important general insights. We provide a brief overview in Box 1. While the conclusions from this work also have a bearing on countries' ability to attract FDI, we seek to go beyond these established results and to dwell deeper into the specific relationship between decentralization and the attractiveness of host countries for potential foreign investors. In particular, we focus on two questions. First, can the potentially beneficial effect of inter-regional fiscal competition really unfold its effectiveness on FDI? Second, are there potentially harmful effects of the vertical dimension of decentralization on FDI and how do they operate?

2.1. The nature of FDI and the hold-up problem

Consider the timing of decision making between the investor and the government that has jurisdiction in the location in which the FDI takes place, which creates what is called the *hold-up problem* in the context of FDI[1]: an investor can freely choose where to locate its FDI. Once the investment is made, some share of it is sunk and irreversible. The host government which has the jurisdiction in this location can now choose how much to demand from the investment returns, and may even choose to appropriate the investment completely. These incentives arise if the government is simply revenue maximizing, but also if the government is benevolent or acts in the interest of the citizens in the host country for political reasons, simply because the owners of the FDI that occurs in a host country are foreigners in that country by definition. If foreign investors anticipate this extractive behaviour, they will invest too little or not invest at all. Even investment projects that yield a very high gross return and would be highly profitable in the absence of the threat of confiscatory taxation do not take place. Unless the government can credibly commit not to make use of the opportunities to extract, or can compensate investors upfront, investors will not invest if they anticipate that the whole returns on their investments are confiscated.

---

[1] For a characterization and some essential aspects of this problem see Eaton and Gersovitz (1983), Janeba (2000), Konrad and Lommerud (2001) and Schnitzer (1999).

Box 1. Arguments for and against decentralization

Decentralization of fiscal responsibility to sub-central government is thought to change the public sector's *allocative efficiency*, and the policy makers' *accountability* to their constituencies.

Oates (1972, 1999) suggested that decentralization allows local preferences to be reflected more sensitively in the decentralized provision of local public goods. One of his arguments is rooted in the view that the central government is relatively poorly informed about local tastes for public goods and about the cost of producing them, pointing to the problem of discovering local preferences. Also, he suggests a tendency of the central government to choose local public goods uniformly across different regions. Mobility of labour across jurisdictions has been suggested as a solution to this information problem in a decentralized context. If citizens feel discontent with the pattern of local taxes and spending in their own locality, they may express this discontent by 'voting with their feet' and may move to other jurisdictions they find more suited to their preferences. In the limit one can conceive a situation in which citizens sort themselves across localities in such a way that the allocation of resources is entirely efficient: no reallocation is possible such that citizens' welfare increases. This view, that labour mobility alone is enough to secure efficiency in the pattern of local public expenditure, is known as the Tiebout hypothesis (see Tiebout, 1956).

Decentralization may change the accountability of government that stems from the existence of local elections in decentralized structures (see, e.g., Seabright, 1996). With decentralized policy decision making, and separate elections in each locality, politicians are elected on the basis of their performance on the local policies and not on 'an average' measure of performance as it would be under centralization (see, among others, Besley and Smart, 2003, and Kessler *et al.*, 2005). There is a variety of considerations pointing to centralized policy decision making. With the risk of over-simplification these considerations can be divided into two broad categories: *efficiency* and *administration*. As regards efficiency, the mobility of factors of production may generate inefficiencies in the allocation of resources due to fiscal externalities in the context of tax competition between localities for a mobile tax base. Possible remedies to this problem are multilateral reforms that coordinate taxes, or, inside a federation with a central government, Pigouvian subsidies for the localities, 'presumably administered by a higher level government' (Wildasin, 1989). As regards administration, decentralization entails duplication of certain fiscal activities. As Oates (1972, p. 201) notes, this may suggest that the optimal degree of centralization is a function of country size.

This picture alludes to an empirically important investment obstacle. Full expropriation may be less likely to be the outcome in reality, because the actual returns that accrue from an investment depend, to a considerable extent, on other factors of production (such as the amount of workers employed, or managerial effort) that are chosen by the investor at the point when the host government(s) made their choices on taxes and other extractive efforts.[2] This ability to adjust production activity *ex post* will generally lead to less than full confiscation. The relationship between the anticipated level of confiscatory taxation and overall revenue that accrues will typically follow a 'Laffer' curve. The overall tax burden in the equilibrium depends on the governance structure, and we may ask whether the hold up problem of FDI is mitigated or aggravated by (a) horizontal competition between independent regions, and (b) the vertical organization of governance. We turn, starting with the former question, to this next.

2.2. The benefits of horizontal competition

Federalism and decentralization of authority comes along with horizontal and vertical disintegration. Consider first the aspect of a horizontal split up of a unitary country into regions with independent governments. Kehoe (1989) highlighted an important aspect of inter-regional competition. He addressed a time consistency problem in capital income taxation that is related to the hold-up problem in FDI and had been discussed by Kydland and Prescott (1980). They considered the choice of savings of private households if they have to invest their savings within one country with a unitary government. The government chooses its future tax system time consistently. It minimizes the excess burden that is caused by the taxes at the point in time when the taxes are chosen. In such a single unitary country, households anticipate that their savings will constitute a fully immobile tax base in the future and that the government will try to make use of this non-distortionary source of taxes. But if the households anticipate that their savings will be taxed quite heavily, or even completely confiscated, they will not save. Kehoe (1989) suggested that this problem of time consistent capital income taxation can be solved if there are many countries or many regions with local governments who choose their tax policy independently, if the private households can choose in which country to locate their savings at a point in time when the countries have already chosen their capital income tax rates. Even though the total amount of savings is given when the countries or regions choose their tax policy, governments still have to consider that the owners of capital may relocate its existing stock from a country that chooses high tax rates to low tax countries, and in the equilibrium, this drives down the tax rates chosen by the different governments.

Formally, decentralization of single countries into many small regions is not needed to implement this type of competition. International capital mobility may be sufficient.

---

[2] Charlton (2003) argues that only a share in the total assets, that constitute an FDI project, consists of fully immobile property plant and equipment.

But this mechanism may function even better for the competition between regions, as the transaction cost of shifting capital from one region to another may be lower than for shifting capital across country borders.

Applied to FDI, the competition between the governments in different regions could be to the benefit of foreign investors who can choose their investment location, as they can choose the most attractive offer, and competition between the regions is likely to drive down the rents that can be appropriated by the regional government and its citizens. This competition aspect is emphasized by many writers on federalism and FDI. As a prominent example Weingast (1995, pp. 5–6) expresses this view in the following statement:

> [i]f a jurisdiction attempts to confiscate the wealth of an industry, the mobility of capital implies that firms will relocate. The mobility of resources thus raises the economic cost of those jurisdictions that might establish certain policies, and they will do so only if the political benefits are worth these and other costs. Federalism thus greatly diminishes the level of pervasiveness of economic rent-seeking and the formation of distributional coalitions.

This view is quite influential in the policy debate. However, it is important to note that inter-regional competition of the kind underlying Kehoe's (1989) argument addresses the problem of savings well, but it is not suitable to address and solve the hold-up problem in FDI. One of the implicit preconditions for Kehoe's mechanism to work in the FDI context is that the investors or capital owners are able to relocate their capital between regions or countries at a point of time when the politicians or bureaucrats have made their policy choices. To some extent, this may also be true for some FDI, and, but to a different degree, for different types of investment.[3] Also, if the existing stock of investment and future investment has to be treated equally and uniformly, competition for future flows of FDI may make the aggregate stock of FDI that accumulates over time more elastic with respect to how foreign investors are treated once the investment has been made and is sunk. Still, much of the investment in a specific FDI project, and most notably the physical capital is fixed and tied to the local region in which it is installed, and cannot react further to changes in taxes, regulation and bureaucratic demands.

For the beneficial effects of competition between localities for investors to unfold it is required that this competition opens up alternatives for investors at the point of time when a locality has chosen how investors are treated in terms of taxes and public services. Only if investors can easily adjust their activities by moving from one locality to another as a reaction to this treatment, the threat to do this will discipline the policy makers and give them incentives not to exploit investors. If, at some stage, the investors have irreversibly made investments in a locality that are sunk, moving these investments into another locality is no longer an option, and the investors are at the mercy of the decision makers who have jurisdiction over the particular locality in which they are locked.

---

[3] For instance, the share in property plant and equipment in total assets that is used in Charlton (2003) is a rough measure for how immobile a given foreign direct investment is.

2.3. Harmful effects of vertical disintegration

Consider now how the vertical dimension of decentralization bears on investment and taxation decisions. (For a formalization and extensions of the following reasoning, readers should refer to Kessing *et al.*, 2006a.)

Delegation of some governmental choices to lower tiers of government, without complete disintegration of the top level of government, leads to a situation in which an investor who made a decision to build a plant in, say, Munich has to deal with several governments: with the city government of Munich, with the district government in the district in which Munich is located, with the government of the State of Bavaria in which Munich is located, and with the federal government of Germany, as Munich also belongs to Germany. If one considers the European Union as another level of government, since Germany is a member of the European Union, and the Union's decisions affect most firms in important ways, there is even a fifth level.

To the extent that the investment is fixed and irreversible, the investor is subject to all these governments' policies, whereas the existence of other cities or states and their different jurisdiction becomes unimportant for the investor. This joint responsibility of several government tiers is an inevitable consequence of federal decentralization and can have a significant effect on the attractiveness of a locality for FDI. The argument put forward in this paper is that the various governance problems that exist between a host government and a foreign investor, and in particular the severity of the hold-up problem, may depend on whether an investor who has chosen a given investment location has to deal with few or many vertical layers of government.

2.3.1. The common pool problem.   Suppose that an investor contemplates investing in one of two countries: a hierarchically organized one (federal), denoted by F, and one where there is only one level of government (unitary), denoted by U. Suppose also that in both countries governments cannot credibly commit to not making use of the opportunity to extract revenue from the investor's project, and that investment is irreversible: its cost cannot be recovered, and production activities cannot be relocated.

Consider first the choices open to an investor who is vulnerable to *ex post* expropriation. In both countries, governments' inability to commit not to expropriate (and the resulting weakness of private property rights) implies lower incentives to invest. Once investment has been made, and to the extent that production uses variable factors and effort as well as irreversible physical assets, it also bears on the amount of production and profits resulting from a given investment. More intense extractive efforts (higher tax rates) lead to lower production, so that the relationship between the overall rate and the overall tax revenues is an inverted-U 'Laffer curve'. Revenues are zero for a zero tax rate, and also zero if taxes approach a 100% confiscatory rate.

Consider next the choice of the tax rate by the two types of government. For simplicity assume that governments maximize tax revenue that can be extracted from the foreign direct investor. A unitary country will choose a confiscatory tax rate that generates the maximum overall tax revenue. It chooses the peak of the Laffer curve. In a decentralized country, several governments can try to appropriate from the same source of revenues, and typically do. They may also choose their appropriation activities non-cooperatively and extract from a common pool. Because of the presence of vertical fiscal externalities the resulting joint tax rate will be excessive. The country F therefore will end up with an overall tax on the wrong side (i.e., the right-hand side) of the Laffer curve. The actual tax revenue will not be larger than in a unitary country, but the marginal tax burden will be higher. When investors consider where to invest, they anticipate this behaviour and this makes the federal country with many government tiers a less attractive place as an investment destination.

Countries are typically decentralized to some degree in the sense that economic power and responsibility are shared between interdependent levels of government. This is likely to create fiscal interdependencies between the different levels of government. A clear-cut instance in which vertical interdependencies arise is when there is commonality of tax bases between the central government and lower-level governments (in the sense that several levels of government tax the same tax base).

Tax base commonality creates a common pool problem (with the fiscal decisions of each level of government inducing responses that affect the common tax base) that gives rise to negative vertical fiscal externalities. It generally leads to excessive taxation. Note that the common pool problem cannot be alleviated by an increase in horizontal competition between regions. Once the investment is sunk, and has taken place in a particular locality, say S, the existence or behaviour of other local governments which do not have jurisdiction over investors in locality S is not relevant for the resulting common pool problem. The common pool problem emerges because of the vertical dimension of decentralization, that is, because there are several government tiers who all have some independent jurisdiction over investments made in S, and which have independent policy objectives that are not perfectly aligned.

Of course, in a larger picture tax policy is not completely targeted towards a single investment project. Hence, some tax policy will affect a stock of projects that cannot be relocated in reaction to the tax policy, and the flow of new projects. The larger or more important is this latter share, the more important becomes the dimension of horizontal tax competition and the closer become the results to the standard results on the interaction between horizontal and vertical tax competition for a generally mobile tax base.[4]

The common pool problem could be avoided if the ability to expropriate revenues from the foreign direct investor could be attributed to one of the government tiers. This is often assumed to be the case in the literature on federalism, and sometimes

[4] There is a growing literature on vertical externalities. Johnson (1988), Dahlby (1996), Boadway et al. (1998), Wrede (2000), Keen and Kotsogiannis (2002, 2004) provide, among others, a treatment of vertical externalities when the policy makers are benevolent. For a treatment of the case in which policy makers are revenue-maximizing Leviathans see Wrede (1996), and Keen and Kotsogiannis (2003). For an early survey on vertical externalities see Keen (1998).

even included in the definition of what ideally constitutes federalism. However, it is extremely difficult or impossible in reality. Different tax bases are (implicitly) inter-dependent with similar incidence effect. The different levels of government might have formally different tax bases, but these may overlap in real terms through general equilibrium effects. Taxes on labour income and VAT taxes, or the corporate income tax and local business taxes may, for instance, be governed independently by different government tiers. As these pairs of taxes have very similar tax incidence, the common pool problem emerges, despite the nominal independence.

2.3.2. The free-rider problem in the subsidy game. A further disadvantage that decentralized countries with disintegrated vertical government tiers face, vis-à-vis unitary countries, emerges when locations can compete for foreign direct investors by offering them economic favours in a process that has been described by the term 'bidding for firms'. Bidding for firms (and to pay a firm upfront what the firm will have to pay in terms of confiscatory taxation in later periods) is one way to cope with the hold-up problem. Central ('federal') and lower-level ('regional') governments may engage in either active or defensive incentive strategies aimed at attracting FDI in competition with other locations. Bids offered by governments to foreign investors may be direct cash payments or indirect in the form of offering cheap or subsidized investment ground, or of special deals when taking over existing plants and equipment or consumer relations in the context of foreign direct investment that takes place as a joint venture.

Turning to the difference between unitary and federal countries in the bidding process, the bid of a unitary government internalizes the country's full benefits of the foreign direct investment and in particular the full tax revenues that will emerge from this investment. If the bid is made by a government which belongs to a hierarchical system of governments then, in the absence of full cooperation between the govern-ments at all levels of hierarchy, it will only take into account the benefits that accrue to its own sphere of responsibility. This, as a consequence, results in the government bidding less aggressively for the foreign investor if the government belongs to a federation. In the bidding competition between various countries with various degrees of decentralization the investment is therefore more likely to be attracted by the country that has fewer government levels.

2.3.3. Interaction between common pool and free-riding problems. The free-riding problem in bidding for firms reduces the equilibrium bids of a government that belongs to a federation, compared to a government in a unitary state for the same, given total benefits that accrue to the country as a whole from attracting the FDI project. The common pool problem suggests that the total gross benefits that accrue from attracting an FDI project are smaller in the federally structured country than if the country is governed by a unitary government. Reconsider, for instance, the Laffer curve analysis. If the federal country chooses an aggregate tax rate that exceeds the tax rate that maximizes total tax revenue, the total amount of taxes obtained by all government tiers is smaller than in the unitary country, and each tier receives only a share of this smaller amount, with all shares adding up to this smaller amount. Accordingly, the government of each tier has a smaller gain from attracting the FDI than the government in a unitary government, and even all governments in the federal country taken together have a smaller willingness to pay to attract the FDI project than the government in the unitary country. This shows that the two problems compound and mutually enforce each other. Not only is the government in a federation unwilling to bid according to the whole benefits that accrue to this country if it attracts the FDI project, in addition, this total amount would be smaller in the federally organized country.

2.3.4. Multiple tiers weaken implicit contracts. The preceding analysis has emphasized the possibility that hold-up problems in FDI may be more severe in decentralized government structures with many government tiers. This then raises the question how 'likely' it is for these countries to develop institutions that credibly commit to pre-announced policies and, hence, do not resort to confiscatory taxation or to other extractive activities *ex post*. Given the interaction between the hold-up problem and the common pool problem, countries with more government tiers have more to gain from developing such 'credible' institutions. If such institutions are successfully implemented, foreign direct investors can more safely invest in these countries, and as a consequence the number of government tiers becomes less important as an impediment to FDI.

The term 'institutions' may, but need not be meant in a literal sense. An important 'institution' in the interaction between economic agents is the implicit contract that may be enforced and enforceable by repeated interaction. Previous work on the hold-up problem in FDI (see, for instance, Eaton and Gersovitz, 1983; Thomas and Worrall, 1994) has stressed that the main element that prevents governments from expropriation and confiscatory taxation is the prospect of future benefits from repeated investment. Kessing *et al.* (2006b) show that it may be more difficult to develop such implicit institutions and to sustain an equilibrium with 'tacit collusion' in a country with a federal structure with several tiers of governments than in a unitary country.

Consider an investor who invests in a decentralized host country infinitely repeatedly. The sequential nature of the relationship means that 'players' (the government levels and the investor) can adopt strategies that depend on behaviour in previous interactions. The returns to investment accrue in every period for which investment takes place, and the taxation of these returns is subject to the common pool problem identified earlier. Similar to the discussion of tacit collusion in oligopoly theory, governments may collude in the sense that they all abstain from excessive taxation and share in the continued flow of benefits of tacit collusion, because a deviation from the collusive outcome by any of the players would be 'punished' by all players by reversion to an equilibrium in which no investment takes place and, hence, no tax revenue at all occurs in all future periods. Each government may also decide in a given period to deviate and extract more than the share that it should receive according to the collusive outcome, and, in the period in which a government makes use of this opportunity, its payoff is higher. However, it will be punished for this in all future periods. Tacit collusion is feasible if a government's additional period benefit from deviating does not exceed its present value of the sacrifice in future periods. Both the gain and the loss from deviating depend on the number of governments. In particular, the potential to punish a deviating government is reduced with an increase in the number of governments. This provides the intuition for why vertical decentralization reduces the range of feasible implicit contracts with 'tacit collusion'. First, with a larger number of governments the spoils of cooperation for each government is lower than with a smaller number of governments and so is the punishment (loss of future tax revenues if punished). Hence, the future losses from deviating decrease in the number of governments. Second, it is also the case that it is more rewarding for each of the government players to defect from the agreed cooperation if the number of government layers is larger. Both identified effects make cooperation more difficult to be sustained in more decentralized government structures. The situation is largely analogous to the possibility of sustaining collusion between firms. The more firms are operating in a given market, the more difficult it becomes to sustain collusion.

2.3.5. Multiple tiers and joint accountability. The issue of accountability in federal systems can be analysed in a political economy context in which politicians are elected and, among other things, care about re-election. These studies typically compare the politicians' and voters' choices for a case in which decentralization simply means that a given territory is governed by one government, or broken up into two completely separate countries with independent governments (see, for an example and further references, Hindriks and Lockwood, 2005). Due to the higher measurability of a politician's performance, and possibly due to benchmarking, accountability may increase by this break up. But as discussed, the horizontal separation of a country into regions is only one side of decentralization. Decentralization also leads to vertical disintegration. As a result of decentralization, many relevant economic performance measures for a region will depend not only on the decisions and the competence of the local politician, but also on the decisions of the politicians on the higher government tiers that join in the jurisdiction of a given local region. Compared to unitary government, this joint responsibility leads to joint accountability. In turn, this may generate problems similar to those that have been discussed in other contexts as the problems of moral hazard in teams, sabotage in team work production etc. An aspect that makes this reasoning less straightforward in the context of FDI is the fact that there may be a conflict of interests and an accountability problem not only between the government(s) and its citizens, but also between the citizens and the foreign direct investors, where citizens have the right to vote and foreign investors do not.

2.3.6. The importance of property rights and other institutions. The discussion of feasibility of tacit collusion as a function of the number of tiers already
shows that the ability of countries to attract FDI should depend on institutions. Of
course, vertical disintegration is a potentially important institutional aspect, but not
the only institutional aspect that matters. In addition, some other institutional
features may interact with the aspect of vertical disintegration, and may lighten up
or further darken this dark side of federalism.

Any government strong enough to protect property rights can also use this strength
to coerce (e.g., North and Weingast, 1989). When illustrating the dark aspects of vertical
decentralization, we focused on governments which do not have the appropriate
institutions to restrain themselves from using their strength to enforce high confiscatory taxes. More generally speaking, governments may use their power for extracting
rents, including the means of expropriation, and this caused the hold-up problem in
FDI. As discussed, even a benevolent government that acts on behalf of its citizens
or politicians who are motivated by prospects of re-election would like to attract FDI
first and then, once the investment has been made, would like to extract revenue from
the investor. Good institutions that endow the government with the power to commit
not to extract an excessively large share in the returns *ex post* are therefore very
desirable.

Countries differ both in the quality of institutions that restrain government from
using its power to coerce and in the degree of vertical disintegration. A natural
question to ask now is how the vertical dimension and the protection of property
rights interact. No clear answer, however, can be given from a theoretical point of
view. As a starting point it is useful to think about two extreme cases. First, if property
rights protection is perfect, that is, if governments do not resort to confiscatory taxation at all, there should be no effect of increasing the extent of vertical disintegration.
If government actors do not affect the investors' profits, increasing their number does
not have any effect. On the other hand, if property rights protection is completely
absent, that is, if any single government would completely appropriate the investors'
profits, there would also be no additional effect of further vertical disintegration.
Increasing the number of government actors does not have an additional effect, if the
entire investment is taken anyway. For levels of property rights protection in between
these two extreme cases there will be an additional effect of increased vertical disintegration, but it is not clear *a priori*, whether this effect will be stronger for high or low
levels of property rights protection. If property rights protection is low, there may be little
scope for further worsening the effect on FDI, but the interaction may compound the
effect sufficiently. On the other hand, for higher levels of property rights protection,
the interaction may not have such strong compounding effects, but there is more
scope for reducing the level of FDI. The bottom line of this reasoning is that we
expect a non-monotonic relationship regarding the interaction of the level of property
rights protection and the vertical dimension of decentralization. It should be zero at
the two extremes and positive in between, potentially displaying an inverted U-shape.

Before we turn to the empirical analysis, we should mention that there are potential further channels through which vertical decentralization can negatively affect FDI, and that those other channels are typically related to some other dimension of governance. While we have focused on the governments' incentives to extract revenue from the investment, similar arguments should hold for the regulatory framework an investor is facing, for example. The commonality problem will typically result in over-regulation, possible mismatch of regulatory activity and an excess of red tape the investor faces.

3. EMPIRICAL ANALYSIS

3.1. The main hypothesis

Our theoretical perspective suggests that vertical decentralization impinges negatively on the amount of FDI inflows. We can accordingly state our main hypothesis:

> **Hypothesis 1**: An increase in the amount of vertical decentralization of a host country has a negative effect on the amount of FDI that is attracted by this host country.

Our discussion has acknowledged that federalism affects a country's performance along several dimensions and also has beneficial effects. We would expect that the negative relationship between FDI and the measure of decentralization is strongest for measures of decentralization that are closest to measuring the aspect of vertical disintegration. We will be able to draw on a variable that is closely related to the vertical dimension of decentralization when we test hypothesis 1.

As discussed, other dimensions of decentralization may improve or worsen the climate for FDI. On *a priori* grounds, decentralization measures that quantify other aspects besides vertical decentralization may therefore have a positive or a negative impact on the size of FDI in the empirical analysis. Introducing such variables is interesting and important for at least two reasons. First, to some degree they allow to disentangle the effects of vertical decentralization (for which we have a fairly good measure) from these other effects. Second, the quantitative effects of these decentralization variables are of interest for policy making.

3.2. Empirical strategy

Our empirical strategy to test our hypothesis and to reveal the effects of decentralization on FDI is straightforward. We add decentralization variables to the 'knowledge-capital' model.

3.2.1. The 'knowledge-capital' model.
The 'knowledge-capital' model has solid theoretical foundations from the theory of the multinational firm and has emerged over recent years as the workhorse for analysing international FDI flows. Multinationals are typically distinguished in 'horizontal' firms which produce the same goods

and services in multiple countries, and 'vertical' firms, which geographically fragment production by stages. The 'knowledge-capital' model, developed by Markusen *et al.* (1996), and Markusen (1997), is a framework that nests both horizontal and vertical motives for FDI into a unified framework. It assumes that 'knowledge' (or 'knowledge-based' assets) is (a) skilled labour intensive relative to production, (b) geographically mobile, and (c) a joint input to multiple production facilities and so has a public-goods character in that it can be supplied to additional facilities at very low cost. The latter assumption implies there is a market size motive if there are plant scale economies and so gives support to horizontal FDI. The first two assumptions relate to differences in relative factor endowments, and these consequently give rise to an incentive for vertical fragmentation of production. The proper treatment of relative factor endowments in the estimation of the model has spanned some considerable controversy, see Carr *et al.* (2001, 2003) and Blonigen *et al.* (2003). We avoid this debate and employ a variant that has become popular recently among scholars of international economics. It circumvents some of the problems involved in the earlier formulations and has been proposed by Markusen and Maskus (2002), and employed by Buch *et al.* (2005) and Herger *et al.* (2005). This version possesses the following structure. The amount of FDI from source country i to host country j is a function of

- the sum of source and host country's GDP, ΣGDP
- the square of the difference in source and host country GDP, $(\Delta GDP)^2$
- measures of proximity between source and host country
- measures of trade costs between source and host countries[5]
- measures of investment costs in the host country
- three interaction variables ($INT1$, $INT2$, $INT3$).

These interaction variables relate to the different incentives for vertical and horizontal fragmentation of production. They interact factor endowments with relative country size and market size. The first interaction we introduce, $INT1 = \Delta SKILL * \Delta GDP$, if $\Delta SKILL > 0$, 0 otherwise, captures vertical fragmentation. Horizontal motives are captured in the second and third interaction variables $INT2 = \Delta SKILL * \Sigma GDP$, if $\Delta SKILL > 0$, 0 otherwise, $INT3 = -\Delta SKILL * \Sigma GDP$, if $\Delta SKILL < 0$, 0 otherwise, where $\Delta SKILL$ captures the skill endowment difference between the source and the host countries. The theoretical foundation and the relationship of this specific formulation to its theoretical foundation are summarized in Markusen and Maskus (2002).

---

[5] The original formulation of the 'knowledge-capital' model asks for the specification of trade costs in the host and the source country separately. The availability of such measures for individual countries is limited, so that, because we are interested in having a large cross-section of countries, we use bilateral trade costs proxies instead.

3.3. Data

To measure international direct investment flows we use a recent data set on international cross-border mergers and acquisitions (CBAs) provided by the SDC platinum database of Thomson Financial. These data appear to be currently the only ones that allow us to (a) cover a large number of host countries that differ in their degree of decentralization, (b) embed our analysis in the 'knowledge-capital' model which requires bilateral FDI flows, and (c) increase the power of our analysis by using a large cross-section of source countries which substantially increases the number of country pairs. This database is increasingly employed in the analysis of international capital flows, see, for instance, Di Giovanni (2005), Rossi and Volpin (2004), and Herger et al. (2005). The former two contributions have focused on the values of CBAs whereas the latter also considers counts of CBAs constructed from the original dataset. These CBA counts are constructed by counting the number of firms acquired by buyers from a source country i, in a host country j in a given year t. Only deals in which the acquiring firm acquired a controlling share of at least 50% are counted.[6]

In our analysis we consider both types of aggregate measures, in terms of values and of counts, since arguments can be made in favour of both measures. Using counts of CBAs may be justified by three reasons. The first is the limited coverage of the value of the deals in the original data set. For the OECD countries, for instance, for less than 50% of all deals the value of the transaction paid by the acquiring firm is reported. For developing countries this number is lower and in some instances well below 15%.[7] Second, the focus on the value of acquisitions might introduce a particular bias in the analysis as some major deals, which were particularly observed in the stock market rally of the late 1990s, may dominate the aggregate values (see Herger et al., 2005). Third, the literature on FDI, typically, refers to the decision of the mother company in the source country to invest (or not) in a host country rather than to the value of the investment. On the other hand, there are also good arguments in favour of considering the values of the investments. First, the values contain information on the size of the investments which obviously also depends on the investment conditions in the host country. Moreover, most factors that determine the profitability of an investment should determine the price actually paid for acquiring a given firm and therefore, we should be interested in the effect of decentralization on the value of the transactions. Using both measures gives justice to both sides of the argument and insures that the results do not hinge on the particular way of measuring FDI. It turns out that the results are very similar for the two measures, which is not surprising given that the number of CBAs for a particular year country pair and the aggregate value of these deals are closely correlated. Considering only the deals where the value is reported in the original data, the correlation coefficient between them is 0.79.

---

[6] The count data set has been assembled by Herger et al. (2005), from the original data, for the time period 1997–2003.

[7] For the total sample around 57% of completed CBAs have no reported deal value.

The coverage of the data is extensive. Our original sample reports yearly CBAs counts and yearly values in US$ millions for the period 1997–2003. It contains information on CBAs from 67 source countries to 147 host countries.[8] Table 1 gives an overview of the most important host countries for CBAs. Table 2 lists the host countries that are actually included in our study. Developed countries experience more CBAs, in total value and in numbers. There are, however, a large number of developing countries that are experiencing substantial amounts of CBAs, with, important for our purpose, substantial variation among these countries.

There are also some potential problems with using CBAs as a measure of FDI. They are only an imperfect measure of total FDI activity, since not all FDI takes the form of CBAs. However, CBAs comprise a substantial part of world FDI which makes them suitable for such an analysis. UNCTAD (2001) has recently reported that, by around 2000, CBAs' share of all FDI was around 80% in value of the investment. CBAs play an increasingly important role in developing countries too: with the share of CBAs being around 40% in the late 1990s, up from around 10% in the late 1980s. This tendency is most likely to continue in the future (UNCTAD, 2001).

One must notice that, because CBAs only comprise a part of all FDI, albeit an important one, there are potential composition effects caused by our variable(s) of interest, which could give rise to invalid inference. In particular, if an increase in vertical decentralization leads to an increase or decrease in the share of CBAs in total FDI, this will affect the estimations that consider only the number of CBAs. From our theoretical perspective, however, we expect green field investment to be more strongly negatively affected by the vertical dimension of decentralization. Thus, this will make it even harder to detect a negative effect of vertical disintegration using data on CBAs, and our estimations are likely to underestimate the negative effect of vertical decentralization on total FDI.[9]

3.3.1. Measurement of decentralization and intergovernmental overlap.

For the main variable of interest to test our hypothesis regarding the negative effects of the vertical dimension of decentralization, we consider the number of government tiers in the host country. This variable has been constructed by Daniel Treisman (see Treisman, 2000a). It measures particularly well the vertical dimension of decentralization. The theory aspects identified in Section 2 are conceptually directly related to the number of tiers of government. This is because what is decisive for the amount and the success of foreign direct investment is (a) the number of rival decision makers that potentially try to appropriate their share after an investor has irreversibly

---

[8] In the actual estimations the number of the source and host countries will reflect the availability of the control and the decentralization variables.

[9] A similar argument holds with respect to CBAs induced by bad governance and hold-up problems. To escape the bad governance, locals sometimes own their own firms through some foreign holdings, and that inflates the number of CBAs even if it is just disguised local investment. However, since we expect a negative correlation between vertical disintegration and local property rights security, such induced CBAs bias the results against our main hypothesis.

Table 1. CBA host countries

Rank	Host country	# CBA	Fraction of CBA in %	Value in US$ millions
1	United States	6939	14.9	1 178 252.8
3	Germany	3259	7.0	446 918.3
5	Canada	2447	5.2	189 863.8
6	China	1537	3.3	87 190.8
7	Australia	1512	3.2	92 411.2
8	Netherlands	1389	3.0	158 434.2
9	Italy	1229	2.6	152 145.5
10	Spain	1189	2.5	62 169.4
11	Sweden	1172	2.5	117 019.1
12	Switzerland	944	2.0	64 707.9
13	Brazil	888	1.9	66 594.9
14	India	876	1.9	8641.0
15	Hong Kong, China*	827	1.8	30 136.1
16	Belgium	780	1.7	71 391.7
17	Poland	725	1.6	15 186.6
18	Norway	652	1.4	52 621.7
19	Argentina	618	1.3	48 055.4
20	Denmark	613	1.3	29 090.7
21	Finland	597	1.3	32 931.9
22	Mexico	559	1.2	40 786.0
23	Singapore	559	1.2	18 605.1
24	Korea, Rep.	554	1.2	55 608.8
25	Czech Republic	535	1.1	16 355.0
26	Japan	529	1.1	40 492.2
27	Austria	509	1.1	20 333.3
28	New Zealand	451	1.0	17 585.8
29	Ireland	449	1.0	24 707.7
30	Thailand	432	0.9	9143.8
31	Malaysia	412	0.9	4292.6
32	South Africa	407	0.9	24 594.7
33	Indonesia	365	0.8	13 496.3
34	Hungary	354	0.8	6206.3
35	Russian Federation	311	0.7	4076.3
36	Portugal	309	0.7	9127.1
37	Israel	285	0.6	14 234.8
38	Chile	268	0.6	21 863.6
39	Romania	255	0.5	4360.2
40	Philippines	250	0.5	7333.5
41	Bulgaria	215	0.5	3362.7
42	Estonia	196	0.4	733.4
43	Lithuania	168	0.4	1644.3
44	Turkey	160	0.3	3372.3
45	Slovak Republic	158	0.3	4247.2
46	Ukraine	138	0.3	866.0
47	Luxembourg*	133	0.3	26 452.3
48	Colombia	129	0.3	6522.7
49	Peru	128	0.3	6543.9
50	Venezuela, RB	124	0.3	7424.1
51	Greece	119	0.3	4327.5
52	Croatia	113	0.2	2357.1
53	Latvia	103	0.2	846.6
54	Egypt, Arab Rep.	83	0.2	4514.2
55	Vietnam	77	0.2	620.2

Table 1. *Continued*

Rank	Host country	# CBA	Fraction of CBA in %	Value in US$ millions
56	Bermuda	76	0.2	21 573.9
57	Puerto Rico	70	0.1	5367.9
58	Kazakhstan	59	0.1	4204.8
59	Slovenia	53	0.1	1554.9
60	Uruguay	52	0.1	619.2
...	...	...	...	...
All		45 168	100	4 162 966

Note: Countries marked with * not included in the analysis for lack of available control variables.

Table 2. Decentralization variables

Country	Tiers	Exp.-decentralization	Rev.-decentralization
Angola	4		
Albania	3	0.20	0.02
United Arab Emirates	3		
Argentina	3	0.38	0.32
Armenia	3		
Australia	3	0.41	0.28
Austria	4	0.30	0.27
Azerbaijan	3		
Burundi	3		
Belgium	4	0.12	0.06
Burkina Faso	4	0.03	
Bangladesh	5		
Bulgaria	4	0.19	0.16
Belarus	4	0.30	0.28
Bolivia	4	0.18	0.18
Brazil	4	0.34	0.25
Botswana	3		
Canada	4	0.57	0.52
Switzerland	3	0.51	0.46
Chile	4	0.08	0.06
China	5		
Côte d'Ivoire	5		
Cameroon	6		
Colombia	3	0.29	0.19
Costa Rica	4	0.03	0.03
Czech Republic	3		
Germany	4	0.41	0.35
Denmark	3	0.44	0.31
Dominican Republic	3	0.03	0.01
Algeria	4		
Ecuador	4		
Egypt, Arab Rep.	4.5		

Table 2. *Continued*

Country	Tiers	Exp.-decentralization	Rev.-decentralization
Spain	4	0.24	0.15
Estonia	3	0.27	0.21
Ethiopia	5	0.02	0.02
Finland	3	0.39	0.32
France	4	0.19	0.12
United Kingdom	4	0.25	0.13
Georgia	4		
Ghana	6		
Guinea	4		
Greece	4.5	0.04	0.03
Guatemala	4	0.04	0.05
Guyana	3		
Honduras	3		
Croatia	3		
Haiti	5		
Hungary	3	0.21	0.12
Indonesia	5	0.11	0.03
India	5	0.46	0.33
Ireland	3	0.24	0.09
Iran, Islamic Rep.	4	0.03	0.04
Iceland	2	0.23	0.23
Israel	3	0.11	0.07
Italy	4	0.22	0.07
Jamaica	2		
Jordan	3		
Japan	3		
Kazakhstan	4		
Kenya	6		
Kyrgyz Republic	4		
Cambodia	4		
Korea, Rep.	4		
Kuwait	3		
Lebanon	4		
Sri Lanka	4	0.03	0.04
Lithuania	3	0.29	0.22
Latvia	3	0.23	0.19
Moldova	3		
Madagascar	5		0.05
Mexico	3	0.20	0.20
Macedonia, FYR	2		
Mali	4		
Mongolia		0.37	0.27
Mauritania	4		
Mauritius	3	0.04	0.01
Malawi	4		
Malaysia	3	0.19	0.16
Namibia	3		
Niger	4		
Nigeria	4		
Nicaragua	4	0.07	0.08
Netherlands	3	0.25	0.07
Norway	3	0.33	0.22
Nepal	3		

Table 2. *Continued*

Country	Tiers	Exp.-decentralization	Rev.-decentralization
New Zealand	3		
Oman	3		
Pakistan	4.5		
Panama	4	0.02	0.02
Peru	4	0.18	0.07
Philippines	4		
Poland	3	0.23	0.15
Korea, Dem. Rep.	4		
Portugal		0.10	0.07
Paraguay	3	0.04	0.03
Romania	3	0.13	0.09
Russian Federation	4	0.38	0.40
Rwanda	4		
Saudi Arabia	3		
Sudan	4		
Senegal	6		
Singapore	1		
Sierra Leone	4		
El Salvador	3		
Suriname	3		
Slovak Republic	4		
Slovenia	2		
Sweden	3	0.36	0.33
Swaziland	4		
Togo	4		
Thailand	5	0.08	0.05
Tajikistan	4		
Turkmenistan	4		
Trinidad and Tobago	2	0.04	0.03
Tunisia	4	0.05	0.02
Turkey	4		
Tanzania	6		
Uganda	6		
Ukraine	4		
Uruguay	2	0.09	0.10
United States	4	0.44	0.40
Uzbekistan	4		
Venezuela, RB	4	0.00	0.00
South Africa		0.24	
Congo, Dem. Rep.	5		
Zambia	3	0.04	0.05
Zimbabwe	5	0.19	0.17

Note: Baseline regressions without decentralization variables also include Benin, Bosnia-Herzegovina, Congo, Fiji, Morocco, Mozambique, Papua New Guinea, Syria, Chad, Vietnam, and Yemen as host countries. Expenditure and revenue decentralization are 1980–95 averages of the ratio of sub-national government expenditures to total government expenditures and the ratio of sub-national government revenues to total government revenues, respectively.

invested in the host country, and (b) the amount of implicit or explicit (tax) overlap between these government players. The tax overlap is difficult to assess in a unified measure that can be compared across countries. The number of decision makers, however, is approximated quite well by the number of government tiers.

One can argue that the number of government tiers should be corrected for some measure of country size, such as population or area. This would be in line with the insights of Oates (1972) in his classic study of federalism, where the optimal degree of decentralization is related to the size of the country in terms of population.[10] Of course, any normalization carries the danger of inducing spurious correlation, if FDI is correlated with the variable used for the normalization. We consider the unadjusted number of government tiers as our main variable of interest to avoid these potential problems, but also report some results for the number of government tiers adjusted by population.

We also consider the effects of fiscal decentralization in the host country. As empirical measures of fiscal decentralization we employ the ratio of sub-national tax revenues to total government revenues, and the ratio of sub-national government expenditures to total government expenditures. Of course, the ratio of sub-national tax revenues to total government revenues could be low because there is little fiscal autonomy at the sub-national level (and so minimum tax base overlap), or because there is a lot of fiscal autonomy (with tax base overlap effects) but tax competition between sub-national governments has resulted in low tax revenues at sub-national level. The same applies to the other fiscal decentralization measure, the ratio of sub-national government expenditures to total government expenditures. These share measures, however, do pick up some aspects of decentralization, such as the power distribution between the central government and lower levels of government within the host country. By the same token one may regard these measures as measuring 'closeness' of the government to its people and firms. Given their distinct focus on government revenues and expenditures, they also allow additional qualitative insights into the nature of decentralization and its effects on governments' behaviour and the consequences of these for firms.

To avoid potential endogeneity problems and to increase the cross-section of host countries, we use the 1980–95 average of the fiscal decentralization variables. An overview of the values of tiers, and the fiscal decentralization variables of the host countries present in our study, are presented in Table 2. Before we turn to our estimations, we have a first cursory look at the data. Figures 1–4 plot the decentralization

---

[10] Oates (1972, pp. 200–1) writes: 'one important factor influencing the extent of centralization should be the size of the nation in terms of population . . . In a relatively small country, for example, there are likely to be real cost-savings in centralizing a substantial portion of the activity in the public sector. As a nation becomes larger, however, it becomes efficient for decentralized jurisdictions, because of their own significant size, to provide their own outputs of a wide range of public services. Moreover, as a country grows in size, central administration becomes more difficult and is likely to result in a less effective use of resources within the public sector. For these reasons we would expect the degree of fiscal centralization to vary inversely with the size of a country.'

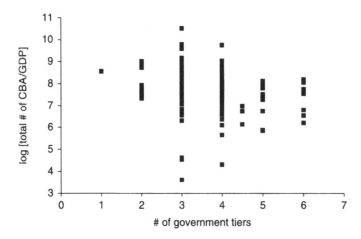

Figure 1. Number of government tiers and log of # of CBA over GDP

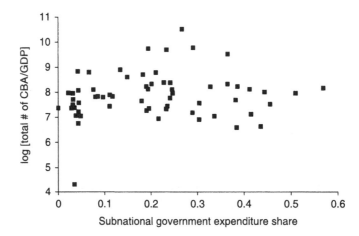

Figure 2. Average (1980–1995) expenditure decentralization and log of # of CBA over GDP

variables against the log of the number of acquired firms by foreigners over average host country GDP for the entire period 1997–2003. These figures are quite illustrative and partly foreshadow the results of our more formal analysis. Figure 1 suggests a negative relationship between the number of government tiers and FDI. On the other hand, average expenditure decentralization and average revenue decentralization appear to be somewhat positively correlated with incoming CBAs. Also, we see that the differential effect of average expenditure and average revenue decentralization is positively correlated with CBA inflows.

3.4. Estimation

We employ two different econometric techniques in our estimations depending on whether we consider the count or the value of CBA. To explain the number of firms

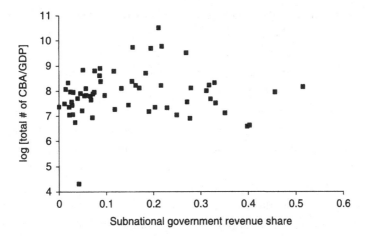

Figure 3. Average (1980–1995) revenue decentralization and log of # of CBA over GDP

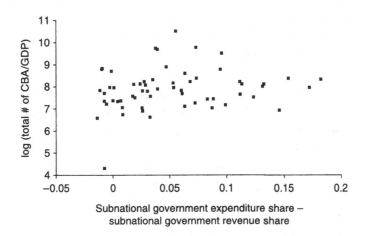

Figure 4. Average (1980–1995) differential fiscal decentralization and # of CBA over GDP

acquired by buyers from source country i in host country j in a given year t we use a negative binomial model for count data. The conditional expected number of CBAs from country i to country j in year t is specified as a non-linear function of the vector of control variables, the decentralization variable(s), and the parameter vectors to be estimated. The details of this model are spelled out in Appendix 1. To explain the aggregate value of all CBAs from source country i to host country j in a given year t we run Tobit regressions, thus accounting for the fact that the left-hand side variable is zero for many country pairs in many years.

Our basic control variables are the key factors for estimation of the 'knowledge-capital' model: the sum of source and host country GDP, the squared difference of source and host country GDP, and the three interaction variables (explained above) *INT*1, *INT*2, and *INT*3. Furthermore, we control for the costs of starting a business in the host country, taken from Djankov *et al.* (2002): the number of days it takes to start a business which we call duration, the number of procedures to complete, and the costs of setting up business as a percentage of per capita GDP. The variables measuring the proximity of source and host country and the ease of trade between them are dummy variables regarding the existence of a common language and the existence of a common border, respectively, and a dummy on the existence of an agreement on trade in services, a dummy that captures the existence of a free trade agreement, and a dummy that captures the existence of a customs union. We also use the distance between the capitals of source and host countries. Di Giovanni (2005) has emphasized that capital market deepening is an important determinant of FDI flows. To capture this, we include domestic stock market capitalization relative to GDP. Furthermore, we include the real exchange rate, since changes of the real exchange rate alter the price of CBAs. Finally, we include variables for the size of the host country, as a country's size may systematically influence capital inflows. In particular, decentralization ('tiers') is systematically correlated with these variables, so including them avoids that the tiers variable picks up the effects of country size. The host country size variables are the surface area of the host country and the population of the host country. We also use the inverse and the square of both of these variables to make sure that the decentralization variables do not pick up existing non-linear relationships between country size and FDI inflows. All estimations with yearly data also contain time dummies. A description and the sources of all variables used in our analysis can be found in Appendix 2.

Although the tiers variable and past average fiscal decentralization are constant over time, we use panel estimations including all observations from all 7 years from 1997–2003 to exploit the variance in the controls over time. Given that some of the controls are not available for all years the panel is unbalanced. We also report the estimation results using the pure cross-section of averages to make sure that the significance of our results regarding the number of tiers are not driven by the increased sample size or the unbalanced nature of the panel.

3.5. Results

3.5.1. Benchmark model with count data.
In Table 3 we report the results of estimating negative binomial models using the count data on cross-border acquisitions. We first estimate a benchmark 'knowledge-capital' model without any decentralization variables. The results are given in column (1) of Table 3. The signs of the estimated coefficients are by and large in accordance with the theoretical predictions. The theoretical foundations of the 'knowledge-capital' model predict a positive coefficient of the sum of host and source country GDP, and a negative coefficient of the squared difference of the two countries' GDPs. The negative signs of the first and the third

interaction variables are also perfectly in line with the 'capital-knowledge' model. The positive coefficient of the second interaction variable indicates evidence for vertical FDI. Several variables measure proximity between host and source countries, either physically, as in the case of distance and the existence of a common border, or culturally as in the case of a common language. Higher proximity implies larger FDI flows between host and source countries. In line with the findings of Di Giovanni (2005), domestic stock market capitalization in the source country plays a significant positive role, and also the real exchange rate affects CBAs significantly. The existence of a free trade agreement, a customs union, or an agreement on trade in services all affects bilateral investment flows positively. The costs of setting up a business, as measured directly by the setup costs, or indirectly by the number of procedures to be fulfilled, affects investment negatively. Thus, all control variables are significant with signs that can be theoretically justified, except for the duration to set up a business.[11] Not surprisingly, these results are broadly consistent with the results of Herger *et al.* (2005), who use a slightly different set of control variables. The control variables for the size of the host country are also found to be significant determinants of FDI flows.

To the benchmark model we subsequently add the decentralization variables we are interested in. Column (2) of Table 3 reports the results of individually adding tiers. The number of government tiers has a significant negative effect on inward CBAs. If the sub-national expenditure share and the sub-national revenue share are added individually, they both are found to have a significant positive impact on the number of CBAs (results not displayed). Column (3), which includes both fiscal decentralization measures, shows that this finding is spurious regarding the degree of revenue decentralization. The positive effects found for revenue share is due to the high correlation between expenditure decentralization and revenue decentralization.[12] Expenditure decentralization affects investment positively, whereas revenue decentralization affects it negatively. This is also confirmed by the estimation reported in column (4) of Table 3 which includes all three decentralization variables, and by column (5) which replaces 'tiers' with 'tiers normalized by population size'.

3.5.2. Benchmark with CBA values.   Table 4 shows the results for the specification with values. By and large, they are very similar to the analysis using CBA counts. We report the estimates of the baseline model without decentralization variables in column (1). The findings are mainly analogous to the count data model with the exception of two of the interaction variables. Interaction variable 1 is now positive, but insignificant, and interaction variable 2 is now negative and significant. The latter

---

[11] The positive sign of the coefficient may reflect better institutions in developing countries that are positively correlated with the duration of setting up a business. In fact, estimates we report below show that when we re-estimate the model using only OECD host countries, duration is found to have a negative coefficient. Alternatively, the costs of setting up a business may be more important for green field investment, and the positive sign may reflect a substitution effect from green field investment to mergers and acquisitions.

[12] The correlation coefficient between them is 0.92.

Table 3. Benchmark estimations counts

	(1)	(2)	(3)	(4)	(5)
ΣGDP	1.31	1.27	1.07	1.06	1.03
	(0.07)***	(0.07)***	(0.07)***	(0.07)***	(0.07)***
$(\Delta GDP)^2$	-0.09	-0.09	-0.08	-0.08	-0.08
	(0.01)***	(0.007)***	(0.01)***	(0.01)***	(0.01)***
INT1	-0.03	-0.03	-0.003	-0.001	-0.001
	(0.01)***	(0.01)***	(0.01)	(0.01)	(0.01)
INT2	0.02	0.02	0.000	-0.001	-0.001
	(0.01)**	(0.01)**	(0.007)	(0.006)	(0.01)
INT3	-0.01	-0.01	-0.01	-0.01	-0.005
	(0.002)***	(0.002)***	(0.002)***	(0.002)***	(0.002)**
POP	0.003	0.004	0.004	0.004	0.002
	(0.001)***	(0.001)***	(0.002)**	(0.002)***	(0.002)
POP^{-1}	-1.39	-1.92	-1.04	-0.96	1.65
	(0.31)***	(0.49)***	(0.32)***	(0.26)***	(1.05)
POP^2	$-2.99*10^{-6}$	$-3.63*10^{-6}$	$-4.19*10^{-6}$	$-5.03*10^{-6}$	$-3.2*10^{-6}$
	$(7.54*10^{-7})$***	$(8.2*10^{-7})$***	$(1.45*10^{-6})$***	$(1.47*10^{-6})$***	$(1.53*10^{-6})$**
AREA	$3*10^{-4}$	$2*10^{-4}$	$2*10^{-4}$	$2*10^{-4}$	$1.71*10^{-4}$
	$(4*10^{-5})$***	$(4*10^{-5})$***	$(4*10^{-5})$***	$(4*10^{-5})$***	$(4.26*10^{-5})$***
$AREA^{-1}$	0.98	0.38	-3.14	-3.69	-2.1
	(0.17)***	(0.18)**	(0.94)***	(0.98)***	(1.17)*
$AREA^2$	$-1.92*10^{-8}$	$-1.74*10^{-8}$	$-1.34*10^{-8}$	$-1.39*10^{-8}$	$-1.36*10^{-8}$
	$(2.47*10^{-9})$***	$(2.4*10^{-9})$***	$(2.65*10^{-9})$***	$(2.63*10^{-9})$***	$(2.64*10^{-9})$***
DISTANCE	-0.13	-0.13	-0.12	-0.12	-0.12
	(0.01)***	(0.01)***	(0.01)***	(0.01)***	(0.01)***
COMMON BORDER	1.26	1.19	0.88	0.81	0.8
	(0.14)***	(0.14)***	(0.15)***	(0.15)***	(0.15)***
COMMON LANGUAGE	1.31	1.31	1.51	1.5	1.51
	(0.1)***	(0.11)***	(0.13)***	(0.13)***	(0.13)***

Table 3. Continued

	(1)	(2)	(3)	(4)	(5)
DOM. MARKET CAPITALIZATION	0.77 (0.04)***	0.78 (0.05)***	0.83 (0.06)***	0.84 (0.06)***	0.83 (0.06)***
REAL EXCHANGE RATE	-0.38 (0.05)***	-0.38 (0.05)***	-0.58 (0.06)***	-0.6 (0.07)***	-0.63 (0.07)***
FREE TRADE AGREEMENT	0.45 (0.12)***	0.42 (0.13)***	0.43 (0.16)***	0.41 (0.16)**	0.42 (0.16)**
SERVICE AGREEMENT	0.81 (0.17)***	0.8 (0.17)***	0.63 (0.19)***	0.61 (0.18)***	0.56 (0.18)***
CUSTOMS UNION	0.38 (0.19)**	0.36 (0.19)*	0.44 (0.2)**	0.4 (0.2)**	0.4 (0.2)**
SET UP COSTS	-0.01 ($2{\times}10^{-3}$)***	-0.005 ($2{\times}10^{-3}$)***	-0.002 ($4{\times}10^{-4}$)***	-0.002 ($4{\times}10^{-4}$)***	-0.002 ($3.7{\times}10^{-4}$)***
DURATION	0.002 (0.002)	0.003 (0.002)*	0.002 (0.002)	0.002 (0.002)	0.002 (0.002)
PROCEDURES	-0.11 (0.01)***	-0.11 (0.01)***	-0.07 (0.02)***	-0.07 (0.01)***	-0.07 (0.01)***
TIERS		-0.39 (0.06)***		-0.14 (0.08)*	
TIERS/POPULATION					-1.16 (0.54)**
SUBNAT. EXPENDITURE SHARE			5.28 (0.82)***	5.46 (0.84)***	5.61 (0.82)***
SUBNAT. REVENUE SHARE			-3.38 (0.88)***	-3.57 (0.87)***	-3.45 (0.86)***
Obs.	49 969	44 464	22 103	21 355	21 355

Notes: Panel estimates (1997–2003) including all countries as given in Table 2. Dependent variable is the count of yearly CBA for source-host country pairs. Standard errors are clustered by country pair. All estimations include year dummies.

Table 4. Benchmark estimations: Values

	(1)	(2)	(3)	(4)	(5)
ΣGDP	2683.21	2680.02	2818.87	2824.73	2775.78
	(68.96)***	(71.54)***	(101.19)***	(103.47)***	(102.61)***
$(\Delta GDP)^2$	−174.91	−174.04	−196.04	−200.09	−188.96
	(7.91)***	(8.27)***	(11.61)***	(11.92)***	(11.84)***
$INT1$	2.79	3.74	19.86	21.17	19.51
	(3.5)	(3.61)	(4.52)***	(4.57)***	(4.58)***
$INT2$	−23.72	−24	−36.56	−36.63	−35.89
	(3.68)***	(3.79)***	(4.61)***	(4.65)***	(4.66)***
$INT3$	−33.17	−34.42	−27.62	−27.29	−24.37
	(2.5)***	(2.57)***	(3.5)***	(3.54)***	(3.57)***
POP	8.13	10.43	15.78	17.86	9.37
	(1.52)***	(1.65)***	(3.11)***	(3.26)***	(3.36)***
POP^{-1}	−3287.46	−4465.09	−2958.07	−2706.5	9436.5
	(355.73)***	(426.2)***	(494.54)***	(480.1)***	(1878.05)***
POP^2	−0.007	−0.008	−0.02	−0.02	−0.01
	(0.001)***	(0.001)***	(0.003)***	(0.003)***	(0.003)***
$AREA$	0.81	0.8	0.7	0.74	0.7
	(0.06)***	(0.07)***	(0.09)***	(0.09)***	(0.09)***
$AREA^{-1}$	2875.63	1622.73	−6312.7	−7569.11	162.39
	(314.45)***	(356.01)***	(2750.35)**	(2835.11)***	(2949.99)
$AREA^2$	−50.6*10^{−6}	−49.8*10^{−6}	−51.1*10^{−6}	−54.2*10^{−6}	−51.7*10^{−6}
	(4.57*10^{−6})***	(4.71*10^{−6})***	(6.18*10^{−6})***	(6.29*10^{−6})***	(6.28*10^{−6})***
$DISTANCE$	−240.15	−254.5	−286.68	−297.75	−311.97
	(15.72)***	(16.69)***	(22.92)***	(23.34)***	(23.66)***
$COMMON\ BORDER$	1758.3	1662.41	922.16	841.73	797.27
	(238.8)***	(251.48)***	(322.69)***	(329.82)**	(330.81)**
$COMMON\ LANGUAGE$	3024.16	3141.96	4213.66	4253.85	4229.62
	(162.89)***	(176.5)***	(252.7)***	(255.71)***	(256.64)***
$DOM.\ MARKET\ CAPITALIZATION$	1477.41	1523.91	1875.11	1899.4	1884.63
	(75.06)***	(80.18)***	(110.87)***	(113.42)***	(113.93)***

Table 4. Continued

	(1)	(2)	(3)	(4)	(5)
REAL EXCHANGE RATE	-913.32	-936.2	-1578.58	-1656.73	-1762.96
	(85.24)***	(90.62)***	(125.88)***	(130.15)***	(131.89)***
FREE TRADE AGREEMENT	1618.99	1505.43	1296.09	1229.98	1206.81
	(253.02)***	(274.93)***	(357.62)***	(363.1)***	(360.91)***
SERVICE AGREEMENT	1611.84	1683.79	1580.78	1524.66	1374.28
	(316.71)***	(335.57)***	(411.26)***	(417.94)***	(415.16)***
CUSTOMS UNION	2318.9	2291.06	1642.69	1572.42	1550.55
	(368.18)***	(389.61)***	(472.49)***	(481.28)***	(478.86)***
SET UP COSTS	-9.99	-7.6	-3.16	-2.87	-2.87
	(0.87)***	(0.89)***	(0.85)***	(0.87)***	(0.85)***
DURATION	5.56	7.14	-0.98	-2.47	0.75
	(2.38)**	(2.57)***	(4.01)	(4.08)	(4.11)
PROCEDURES	-258.99	-259.17	-173.58	-166.13	-178.69
	(22.42)***	(23.75)***	(32.06)***	(32.39)***	(32.56)***
TIERS		-845.02		-310.19	
		(101.01)***		(176.67)*	
TIERS/POPULATION					-5619.96
					(890.34)***
SUBNAT. EXPENDITURE SHARE			13410.68	14073.75	13685.89
			(1831.28)***	(1914.77)***	(1887.85)***
SUBNAT. REVENUE SHARE			-10441.19	-10884.59	-9952.08
			(1949.9)***	(1975.54)***	(1988.2)***
Obs.	48212	42901	21330	20608	20608
Uncensored obs.	3771	3584	2834	2786	2786
Pseudo R^2	0.09	0.09	0.08	0.08	0.08

Notes: Panel estimates (1997–2003) including all countries as given in Table 2. Dependent variable is total yearly value of CBA for source-host country pairs. All estimations include year dummies.

findings would be in line with the horizontal model of FDI (Markusen and Maskus, 2002).[13]

Adding decentralization variables to the baseline model gives a set of results that entirely parallel the results of the count data specification. Adding tiers shows a significant negative effect. Again, both fiscal decentralization variables have a positive effect if added individually (not shown). However, if both enter the estimation simultaneously, as reported in column (3), only expenditure decentralization is found to influence investment positively, whereas revenue decentralization affects investment negatively. Analogously to the count specification, the positive coefficient of expenditure decentralization is larger in absolute value than the coefficient of revenue decentralization, suggesting that a simultaneous increase in expenditure and revenue decentralization has a net positive effect. If tiers and the fiscal decentralization variables are added at the same time the significance of tiers drops to the 10% level, analogously to the count data model. This drop in significance may be caused either directly by the fiscal decentralization variables, or it may be due to the reduction in the sample that is caused by lower availability of the fiscal decentralization variables. Re-estimating the model using only tiers for the reduced sample reveals that the main factor is the effect of the fiscal decentralization variables, since tiers are found to be significantly negative in that specification (not shown). However, we demonstrate in the next section that the low significance of tiers in the joint specification results from controlling insufficiently for the quality of governance in the host country.

3.5.3. Governance quality.

We now extend our analysis to allow for additional measures of governance quality. This is interesting from a theoretical point of view, because we have highlighted potential relationships between several dimensions of governance quality, in particular in the form of property rights protection, and the vertical dimension of decentralization. Thus, we ask, whether the significance and the size of the effects of decentralization variables we have found in our benchmark estimation are changed by the inclusion of governance variables. This is also an important check of the robustness of our findings. In particular, in the raw data there are some countries from sub-Saharan Africa with a high number of government tiers. Therefore we need to inquire whether our findings regarding the number of government tiers are possibly spurious and only driven by a potential correlation with important governance variables.

Not only property rights protection, but also other dimensions of host country governance are likely to be important determinants of foreign investment flows, and likely to be linked to government architecture. Corruption, for example, has been

---

[13] It may be possible to explain these differences between the estimations using the counts and the values of the investment respectively by the average size of the investment. A plausible conjecture would be that horizontal investments are larger in size on average and therefore the horizontal investment motive dominates if we consider the value of the overall investments, whereas the pure count could be dominated by the vertical motive. We do not analyse these questions further, since they are beyond the scope of this analysis.

shown to negatively influence FDI (see, for example, Wei, 2000). Corruption has also been related to government structure, see Shleifer and Vishny (1993). Thus, the effect of tiers we find in the baseline specification without governance variables may be picking up the importance of corruption which deters foreign investors. Similar arguments are likely to hold for other dimensions of governance. Therefore, we employ a large set of governance variables. These are voice and accountability, regulatory quality, corruption, government effectiveness, rule of law, political stability, and property rights protection. The latter variable is measured by the Heritage Foundation property rights index. All other governance variables are taken from Kaufman et al. (2005).[14]

Table 5 presents our estimation results when the governance variables are included in the specification. We use CBA counts as well as their value as our dependent variable. Columns (1)–(3) present the count specification. Column (1) includes only tiers. Column (2) includes the fiscal decentralization variables and tiers, and column (3) includes both fiscal decentralization variables and tiers divided by population. Column (1) of Table 5 shows that all governance variables with the exception of the rule of law are found to be significantly important for the determination of foreign investment. Except for corruption, all have the expected positive sign, that is, better quality of governance in the host country increases the amount of foreign investment inflows. The effect on the tiers variable is a drop in its coefficient to around 0.3. In the specification with all decentralization variables, rule of law is found to be significant, but regulatory quality is insignificant in this case. The more important message of column (2), however, regards the tiers variable. The inclusion of the governance variables results in an increase in the significance level of tiers to 1%. Thus, tiers are a significant negative determinant of CBAs. This specification also returns a coefficient of 0.27, which is very close to the estimate without the fiscal decentralization variables. Columns (4)–(6) report the same specifications for the Tobit estimations using the values of yearly CBAs as the dependent variable. The evidence on the significance of the various governance variables mirrors the findings of the count specification. In both estimations, nearly all are significant, and only corruption has the wrong sign. Column (4) indicates that, including these variables, the coefficient of tiers is reduced in absolute magnitude, just as in the count specification, but in case of the joint specification shown in column (5), the effect of tiers is increased compared to the estimation that does not include the governance variables. However, the evidence on the tiers variable in column (4) shows again, that, controlling for governance quality raises dramatically the significance of tiers in the joint specification.[15]

Finally, we also consider interaction effects between the level of property rights protection and the number of government tiers. As argued above, our theoretical perspective

[14] The Heritage Foundation index is available on a yearly basis. It ranges from 1 to 5 (with integer values only) and we use it in inverse scale, so that higher values imply better property rights protection. The other governance variables range from −2.5 to 2.5. It is available on a bi-annual basis from 1997–2003, and we use linearly interpolated values for the three intermediate years.

[15] To achieve this effect it is already sufficient to include only property rights protection as an additional governance variable.

Table 5. Governance

	(1)	(2)	(3)	(4)	(5)	(6)
...	•	•	•	•	•	•
VOICE AND ACCOUNTABILITY	0.6	0.3	0.41	1295.38	610.85	910.2
	(0.07)***	(0.12)**	(0.12)***	(162.47)***	(318.24)*	(316.87)***
REGULATORY QUALITY	0.34	0.03	0.18	1222.76	530.21	1134.32
	(0.09)***	(0.1)	(0.09)**	(221.54)***	(299.8)*	(314.11)***
CORRUPTION	-0.92	-0.95	-0.94	-1987.69	-1745.26	-1934.17
	(0.14)***	(0.17)***	(0.17)***	(315.38)***	(464.95)***	(470.94)***
RULE OF LAW	-0.03	0.56	0.4	15.47	1104.47	1076
	(0.17)	(0.22)**	(0.22)*	(368.77)	(650.85)*	(643.93)*
GOVERNMENT EFFECTIVENESS	0.92	0.37	0.35	1912.9	376.92	142.36
	(0.13)***	(0.14)***	(0.14)**	(298.6)***	(441.56)	(443.84)
PROPERTY RIGHTS PROTECTION	0.18	0.35	0.28	238.22	881.97	572.91
	(0.06)***	(0.07)***	(0.08)***	(145.75)	(222.51)***	(225.8)**
TIERS	-0.3	-0.28		-648.1	-628.62	
	(0.05)***	(0.07)***		(106.07)***	(187.2)***	
TIERS/POPULATION			-1.48			-6748.28
			(0.51)***			(925.89)***
SUBNAT. EXPENDITURE SHARE		3.33	3.77		8339.83	8721.67
		(0.98)***	(0.95)***		(2276.86)***	(2262.66)***
SUBNAT. REVENUE SHARE		-2.28	-2.04		-7758.7	-6457.94
		(0.95)**	(0.95)**		(2163.79)***	(2192.63)***
Obs.	42 994	21 126	21 126	41 483	20 387	20 387
Uncensored obs.				3553	2782	2782
Pseudo R²				0.09	0.08	0.08

Notes: Panel estimations (1997–2003) including all controls as displayed in Table 3 and Table 4. Dependent variable in (1), (2), and (3) is the count of yearly CBA for source-host country pairs. Dependent variable in (4), (5), and (6) is total yearly value of CBA for source-host country pairs. Standard errors of (1), (2), and (3) clustered by country pair. All estimations include year dummies.

Table 6. Interaction between tiers and property rights protection

	(1)	(2)	(3)	(4)
. . .	•	•	•	•
VOICE AND	0.6	0.32	1269.32	641.08
ACCOUNTABILITY	(0.07)***	(0.12)***	(162.91)***	(319.3)**
REGULATORY QUALITY	0.35	0.07	1183.85	567.27
	(0.09)***	(0.1)	(222.46)***	(300.46)*
CORRUPTION	−0.94	−0.94	−1903.93	−1758.75
	(0.14)***	(0.17)***	(318.78)***	(464.78)***
RULE OF LAW	−0.1	0.51	−40.45	1065.28
	(0.17)	(0.22)**	(369.79)	(652.44)
GOVERNMENT	0.91	0.34	1934.72	338.78
EFFECTIVENESS	(0.13)***	(0.14)**	(298.74)***	(442.76)
PROPERTY RIGHTS	0.41	0.98	−381.38	1617.85
PROTECTION	(0.19)**	(0.25)***	(380.52)	(653.25)**
TIERS	−0.08	0.38	−1231.46	142.18
	(0.17)	(0.24)	(348.91)***	(668.72)
TIERS*PROPERTY	−0.06	−0.17	170.67	−200.53
RIGHTS PROTECTION	(0.05)	(0.06)***	(97.0)*	(167.08)
SUBNAT. EXPENDITURE		2.85		7864.05
SHARE		(0.99)***		(2316.78)***
SUBNAT. REVENUE		−1.83		−7266.2
SHARE		(0.96)*		(2207.28)***
Obs.	42 994	21 126	41 483	20 387
Uncensored obs.			3553	2782
Pseudo R²			0.09	0.08

Notes: Panel estimations (1997–2003) including all controls as displayed in Table 3 and Table 4. Dependent variable in (1) and (2) is the count of yearly CBA for source-host country pairs. Dependent variable in (3) and (4) is total yearly value of CBA for source-host country pairs. Standard errors of (1) and (2) clustered by country pair. All estimations include year dummies.

does not exclude the possibility of interaction between the number of tiers and governance variables such as property right protection. However, theoretically, it is *a priori* not clear which way such interaction effects should point. Columns (1) and (2) of Table 6 report count estimations with only tiers and with tiers and the fiscal decentralization variables, respectively, where we have added an interaction variable between property rights protection and tiers in both specifications. Columns (3) and (4) report the same exercise for the Tobit model using the values. Here we encounter the rare instance of differences between the count and the value specification. The count specification finds no evidence of interaction if the fiscal decentralization variables are left out, and a significant negative interaction effect if they are included. The value specification, however, indicates a positive interaction effect without the fiscal decentralization and no interaction, if the fiscal decentralization variables are included. These conflicting results are in line with our perspective that has argued in favour of an ambiguous prediction for the direction of potential interaction effects.

3.5.4. Non-linear relationships.
Thus far we have included the number of tiers as such into our estimations. However, this may be insufficient for at least two

reasons. First, the specification of the count estimation implies that a reduction or an increase in the number of government levels has the same proportional effect on the amount of FDI received by a particular host country regardless of its given number of government levels. Similarly, the value specification implies a constant marginal effect of a change in government tiers. Second, also from a theoretical perspective, it may be that there is something like an optimal amount of vertical decentralization and one should expect inverted U-shapes regarding the optimal amount of decentralization. Of course, such an optimal degree of decentralization will also depend on several other characteristics of countries, in particular their size in terms of population or area.

Since we found the governance variables to be important determinants of foreign investment, we use our benchmark specification enlarged with the set of governance variables as the baseline in all further specifications. We add quadratic and cubic terms of tiers to assess whether there are signs of such non-linear structures in the data. Similar to the analysis of the interaction terms, the results are somewhat different depending on whether all decentralization variables are included or whether the decentralization variables are being left out.

Columns (1) and (3), and (2) and (4), respectively, of Table 7 show the result of adding quadratic and cubic terms of tiers to the specification including only tiers and to the specification including all decentralization variables for the count specification. In both cases there is strong evidence of a non-linear relationship regarding tiers and FDI. However, the nature of this relationship appears quite different in the two specifications. Without the fiscal decentralization variables, tiers and its cubic term are found to have a significant negative coefficient and the quadratic tiers term has a positive significant coefficient (column (3) of Table 7). In the specification that includes expenditure and revenue decentralization shown in column (4), however, all the signs of these terms are reversed. This effect appears to be driven by the reduced sample of countries for which the fiscal decentralization variables are available, since estimating the same specification for this reduced sample, but without the fiscal decentralization variables, gives very similar results.

It is interesting to characterize the estimated third degree polynomials more closely. In the case of the estimation without the fiscal decentralization variables, column (3) in Table 7, FDI is decreasing in the number of tiers over the entire relevant range of the tiers variable between 1 and 6 tiers. With the fiscal decentralization variables, column (4), the polynomial has a more volatile shape over this range. FDI is decreasing in the range of 3 and 4 tiers only, where, however, most of the observations are located. The estimated parameters are more sensible in the former estimation as we discuss below when we consider the quantitative importance of our results. The Tobit estimates for the values show an analogous picture, again indicating that non-linearity is important, and that the form of the non-linearity is quite dependent on the controls added and sample that is being used. In summary, there is evidence of non-linear patterns regarding the effects of tiers on FDI, but its specific form depends on the

Table 7. Non-linearity in tiers

	(1)	(2)	(3)	(4)	(5)	(6)	(7)	(8)
TIERS	0.23	−2.74	−2.39	19.07	993.28	−7167.85	−11388.39	277751.7
	(0.23)	(0.65)***	(1.1)**	(3.11)***	(622.16)	(1643.68)***	(2831.4)***	(8861.52)***
TIERS²	−0.07	0.34	0.61	−5.77	−209.58	912.51	3021.56	−8921.87
	(0.03)**	(0.09)***	(0.29)**	(0.88)***	(78.63)***	(228.4)***	(727.21)***	(2445.09)***
TIERS³			−0.06	0.56			−268.73	899.94
			(0.02)**	(0.08)***			(60.37)***	(221.55)***
SUBNAT. EXPENDITURE SHARE		3.67		1.42		9404.4		5357.98
		(1.0)***		(1.13)		(2277.4)***		(2477.2)**
SUBNAT. REVENUE SHARE		−2.48		−1-28		−8334.01		−5898.21
		(0.94)***		(0.99)		(2162.53)***		(2241.39)***
Obs.	42 994	21 126	42 994	21 126	41 483	20 387	41 483	20 387
Uncensored obs.					3553	2782	3553	2782
Pseudo R²					0.09	0.08	0.09	0.08

Notes: Panel estimations (1997–2003) including all controls as displayed in Table 3 and Table 4, and including all governance controls as given in Table 5. Dependent variable in (1), (2), (3) and (4) is the count of yearly CBA for source-host country pairs. Dependent variable in (5), (6), (7), and (8) is total yearly value of CBA for source-host country pairs. Standard errors of (1), (2), (3) and (4) clustered by country pair. All estimations include year dummies.

specific sample of countries and the added control variables. Also the non-linear estimates suggest that there is a negative relationship between tiers and FDI, at least over the most relevant range.

3.5.5. Quantitative importance.
The estimated coefficients can be interpreted quantitatively. The estimated negative coefficient of tiers somewhere between −0.25 and −0.3 implies that reducing the number of government tiers will increase the number of CBAs per year by around 30%. This is a large number and should be treated with care. The estimations using also squared and cubic tiers, suggest different magnitudes. These estimations do not assume that the effects of reducing the number of tiers are independent of the number of existing levels. The estimated third degree polynomials suggest that moving from 4 to 3 levels of government increases the number of firms acquired by about 5% in the estimation without the fiscal decentralization variables, see column (3) in Table 7, whereas the estimation with the fiscal decentralization variables (see column (4) in Table 7), suggests an increase by 120%! However, the change from 5 to 4 levels or from 3 to 2 levels is found to reduce CBAs substantially in that latter specification.

The Tobit estimates also suggest substantial magnitudes of the effects of the number of tiers. The coefficient of the tiers variable imply that an increase in the number of tiers by 1 in all countries will result in a reduction of the average value of yearly CBA flows between any two countries in the sample by US$61 million.[16] This is again a high number in relation to the average yearly CBA flow of US$170 million, but is quite in line with the results from count data. The total marginal effect can be split up into the effect of increased investment for those country pairs that are already experiencing CBA inflows (−18 million) and in the effect of those country pairs that will seize to have positive flows, as the number of government tiers in the host country are reduced (−43 million). Again, these numbers should not be taken at face value. The significance of the non-linear specification as shown in Table 7 underlines that the simple linear specification using tiers is open to challenge, and that its estimated quantitative implications are subject to substantial qualifications.

We can also consider the quantitative effects of the estimated coefficients for fiscal decentralization. The estimated coefficients such as from the count specification given in Table 5, column (2), indicate that an increase in average expenditure decentralization by one percentage point would have, on average, increased the number of CBAs by about 3%. An increase of revenue decentralization by one percentage point would have resulted in a reduction of CBAs by about 2%. This implies that a joint increase in expenditure and revenue decentralization would have increased CBAs by about 1%. The Tobit estimates, such as reported in column (5) of Table 5, imply that an increase in average expenditure decentralization by one percentage point would have resulted in an increase of the average value of CBA flows by about US$8

---

[16] These calculations assume that the errors are normally distributed.

million, compared to an average flow of US$170 million. An increase in average revenue decentralization by one percentage point would have resulted in a reduction by US$7.5 million. Thus, joint fiscal decentralization of expenditure and revenue would have resulted in an average net increase of about US$0.5 million. These magnitudes of the effects of fiscal decentralization appear plausible and give an indication of the size of the potential gains from fiscal decentralization on the investment climate, although it should be stressed that the actual magnitudes will vary largely for different host countries.

In summary, the effects of the vertical dimension of decentralization are found to be substantial. We find that the size of the effects for the number of government tiers can be quite large. However, different specifications leave us with a substantial range of the effects, which imply that the results should not be taken at face value but must be treated with care. With regards to fiscal decentralization, the results are also found to be substantial and quite plausible in size.

3.6. Extensions and robustness

We have seen that the magnitude of the effects of the decentralization variables and their significance are somewhat sensitive to the inclusion of appropriate control variables. To ensure that our findings are sufficiently robust, we carry out a number of robustness checks. These exercises also generate further qualitative insights and important qualifications regarding the validity of specific policy recommendations that can be derived from our analysis. Again, all robustness and sensitivity checks are carried out including the full set of all governance variables.

3.6.1. Poor countries, rich countries. Rich countries are different from poor countries. It is, therefore, conceivable that the motivations of firms to invest are different for these groups of countries. Our approach of imposing one model with constant parameters may be too restrictive, and could be a source of potential bias. Furthermore, the effects of the different forms and the degree of decentralization on FDI could be different across these two groups of countries.

To investigate these possibilities, we split up the sample of our host countries into OECD and non-OECD countries. The latter group consists mainly of developing countries, although it also contains a few countries which have a relatively high level of per capita income. Table 8 reports results for the non-OECD countries, Table 9 the analogous estimations for the OECD host countries. For both groups of host countries we again use the evidence from the negative binomial model using count data, as well as the Tobit estimates using values. The conjecture that FDI in OECD countries may be structurally different from FDI in the developing world is reflected in the findings regarding the coefficients of the 'knowledge-capital' model. For instance, the estimations for the OECD countries (Table 9) show a negative coefficient for the second interaction variable, consistent with the theoretical implications of horizontal

Table 8. Non-OECD host countries

	(1)	(2)	(3)	(4)	(5)	(6)	(7)	(8)
INT1	−0.05	−0.05	−0.05	−0.05	−15.10	−17.62	−17.51	−17.55
	(0.01)***	(0.01)***	(0.01)***	(0.01)***	(1.63)***	(2.85)***	(2.86)***	(2.85)***
INT2	0.03	0.02	0.02	0.02	5.53	1.85	1.81	1.79
	(0.01)***	(0.01)***	(0.01)***	(0.01)***	(1.54)***	(2.65)	(2.65)	(2.65)
INT3	0.08	−0.16	0.17	−0.15	23.78	−81.86	−83.45	−80.36
	(0.03)**	(0.11)	(0.11)	(0.11)	(9.85)**	(39.27)**	(39.34)**	(39.25)**
TIERS	−0.27	−0.02	6.48		−119.04	−25.3	1416.57	
	(0.05)***	(0.09)	(4.53)		(19.92)***	(45.06)	(2097.84)	
TIERS²			−1.91				−420.66	
			(1.32)				(613.26)	
TIERS³			0.18				39.65	
			(0.12)				(58.55)	
TIERS/POPULATION				−0.62				−357.1
				(0.5)				(280.27)
SUBNAT. EXPENDITURE SHARE		2.18	1.07	1.99		1931.52	1690.44	1856.64
		(1.82)	(2.2)	(1.79)		(744.8)**	(827.7)**	(746.1)**
SUBNAT. REVENUE SHARE		3.78	4.6	3.88		−376.26	−192.69	−289.54
		(2.1)*	(2.3)**	(2.13)*		(941.21)	(995.86)	(938.75)
Obs.	32 498	12 970	12 970	12 970	31 357	12 517	12 517	12 517
Uncensored obs.					1483	989	989	989
Pseudo R²					0.12	0.1	0.1	0.1

Notes: Panel estimations (1997–2003) including all controls as displayed in Table 3 and Table 4, and including all governance controls as given in Table 5. Dependent variable in (1), (2), (3), and (4) is the count of yearly CBA for source-host country pairs. Dependent variable in (5), (6), (7) and (8) is total yearly value of CBA for source-host country pairs. Standard errors of (1), (2), (3) and (4) clustered by country pair. All estimations include year dummies.

Table 9. OECD host countries

	(1)	(2)	(3)	(4)	(5)	(6)	(7)	(8)
⋮								
INT1	0.01	0.00	0.00	0.00	26.07	19.20	18.46	21.20
	(0.00)	(0.00)	(0.00)	(0.00)	(6.12)***	(7.00)***	(6.99)***	(6.98)***
INT2	−0.00	−0.01	−0.01	−0.01	−37.67	−45.99	−48.80	−48.43
	(0.02)***	(0.00)***	(0.00)***	(0.00)***	(5.70)***	(6.41)***	(6.42)***	(6.43)***
INT3	−0.00	−0.00	−0.00	−0.00	−27.70	−23.14	−23.40	−24.73
	(0.00)***	(0.00)*	(0.00)**	(0.00)**	(4.14)***	(4.97)***	(4.96)***	(4.96)***
⋮								
TIERS	−0.31	−0.87	−481.67		−720.37	−3513.56	−16 03464	
	(0.1)***	(0.2)***	(65.0)***		(343.69)**	(731.26)***	(222 641)***	
TIERS^2			125.11				414 195.6	
			(16.90)***				(57 907.32)***	
TIERS^3			−10.69				−35 160.19	
			(1.44)***				(4952.38)***	
TIERS/POPULATION				−14.28				−45 880.33
				(1.88)***				(6746.13)***
SUBNAT. EXPENDITURE SHARE		−3.19	12.31	4.93		−24984.02	32454.57	6116.66
		(2.61)	(3.55)***	(2.27)**		(7531.24)***	(11151.14)***	(7650.78)
SUBNAT. REVENUE SHARE		1.5	−10.19	−3.9		13616.22	30110.81	−5966.92
		(1.98)	(2.73)***	(1.9)**		(6130.12)**	(8857.86)***	(6676.02)
Obs.	10 496	8156	8156	8156	10 126	7870	7870	7870
Uncensored obs.					2070	1793	1793	1793
Pseudo R^2			0.07	0.07	0.07	0.06	0.07	0.06

Notes: Panel estimations (1997–2003) including all controls as displayed in Table 3 and Table 4, and including all governance controls as given in Table 5. Dependent variable in (1), (2), (3) and (4) is the count of yearly CBA for source-host country pairs. Dependent variable in (5), (6), (7) and (8) is total yearly value of CBA for source-host country pairs. Standard errors of (1), (2), (3) and (4) clustered by country pair. All estimations include year dummies.

FDI, whereas the estimations for the non-OECD hosts (Table 8) find a positive coefficient for that variable, consistent with vertical FDI (Markusen and Maskus, 2002). This implies the possibility that decentralization may impact differently on FDI in these countries for two reasons. The different nature of FDI may make certain investments more or less vulnerable to the problems originating from multiple layers of government. On the other hand, the lower level of socio-economic development and the development of the institutional framework in these countries may change the nature and the magnitude of the effects of decentralization on FDI.

The results for the non-OECD countries are mainly in line with the findings of the overall sample (see Table 8). Including tiers as the only decentralization variable shows a significant negative effect and the size of the coefficient is very similar to the results using the full sample. In the specification using tiers and the fiscal decentralization variables, however, the coefficient of tiers remains negative but is no longer significant, either in the specification using the values or using the counts. If tiers divided by population is used in this joint specification, we also find it not to be significant, although significance is substantially increased. Regarding the fiscal decentralization, we find that in the count estimation (see columns (2)–(4)), only the sub-national revenue share is found to be significant, and, contrary to the full sample, has a positive coefficient. However, the estimates using the values, columns (6)–(8), show results that are analogous to the full sample, with a significant positive effect of expenditure decentralization and a negative effect of revenue decentralization, although the latter is not significant.

For the OECD countries (see Table 9) we find that tiers have a significant negative effect on FDI inflows in all specifications. Without the fiscal decentralization variables, the estimated coefficient of 0.3 is slightly bigger than in the full sample. In the count specification, the fiscal decentralization variables are not significant, but they are in the specification using the values. However, if one considers also non-linear specifications, see columns (3) and (7), the results are highly significant and very similar to the results in the overall sample, with expenditure decentralization affecting FDI positively and revenue decentralization affecting it negatively.

In summary, decentralization appears to be important for OECD and non-OECD hosts. Tiers have a significant negative effect in both groups of countries. However, for the non-OECD hosts the effect is no longer significant, if fiscal decentralization variables are added. This finding indicates that for poorer countries the problem of government overlap may be less of a problem. One alternative explanation of this finding could be that in less developed countries the formal existence of a government level does not imply the existence of a government actor that can affect the profitability of a foreign investor's investment. In other words, the measurement error in tiers may be systematically correlated with the development level of a country. In developing countries, the number of government levels as counted from the constitutional rules of each country, may overstate the number of actual levels that hold effective power in reality.

3.6.2. Excluding countries with extreme values of tiers. It may appear that our results on the negative effects of vertical decentralization are driven by the extreme values in our sample. For example, Singapore is the only country in our sample with only one government level and this country had a relatively strong record of attracting FDI. On the other hand, there are several countries from sub-Saharan Africa with 5 or 6 levels of government, and most of these countries did not receive sizable amounts of foreign investments. Therefore, we ran our regressions including only those countries which have either 3 or 4 level of government. This is also a necessary exercise to understand better the results of the estimations that include the fiscal decentralization variables. These estimations suffer from the reduction of the sample, which leave very few observations with less than 3 and more than 4 levels of governments. These outliers may then affect the results strongly. Columns (1)–(4) of Table 10 report the results of the count data as well as the Tobit specifications. We find that the negative effect of tiers is robust, but the fiscal decentralization variables lose their significance in both specifications.

3.6.3. Taxes. Our theoretical perspective has stressed the fiscal externalities that arise between different levels of government in the hold-up problem. This makes it potentially interesting to consider whether our findings are robust to the inclusion of measures of tax burden on the investment. Columns (5)–(8) of Table 10 report results for specifications that use the statutory corporate tax rate of 2002 as reported by Ernst & Young (2002) as an additional control variable. The statutory tax rate is found to have a negative effect on FDI. This is in line with existing results in the literature (see De Mooij and Ederveen, 2003, for a survey and a meta-analysis). We also see that the results for the decentralization variables are hardly affected by the inclusion of this additional variable.[17]

3.6.4. Regions. As a further robustness check, we consider estimates for particular regions only. Given that the regions need to comprise a certain minimum number of countries for cross-sectional analysis we focus on three regions, Europe, Asia and Africa. Only for Europe does it make sense to also consider estimations that include the fiscal decentralization variables. We report the results in Table 11. The results from the full sample are broadly confirmed by the estimates for Europe, columns (7)–(10), and Africa, columns (1) and (2), which shows significant negative effects for tiers on FDI. In the case of Asia, however, we either find an insignificant negative effect of tiers for the CBA counts, column (3) or even a significant positive effect for the values, column (4). This conflicting result appears to be driven by several large economies in Asia that have received large amounts of FDI over recent years. This is confirmed by results using tiers divided by population. In the count specification, column (5), we now find

---

[17] If one uses data for 2002 only, the significant negative results for tiers can still be found, but the reduction in the sample causes the significance of the fiscal decentralization to drop below common significance levels.

Table 10. Countries with 3–4 government tiers / Inclusion of corporate taxes

	(1)	(2)	(3)	(4)	(5)	(6)	(7)	(8)
···								
CORP. TAX RATE	•	•	•	•	−0.03	−0.01	−45.05	−15.95
					(0.007)***	(0.01)	(12.33)***	(17.02)
TIERS	−0.37	−0.8	−668.53	−1742.58	−0.36	−0.31	−740.41	−740.9
	(0.08)***	(0.11)***	(172.19)***	(264.22)***	(0.05)***	(0.07)***	(112.55)***	(192.94)***
SUBNAT. EXPENDITURE SHARE		−0.77		641.32		2.36		6065.72
		(1.31)		(2909.81)		(1.01)**		(2402.58)**
SUBNAT. REVENUE SHARE		0.07		−2183.05		−1.48		−6595.74
		(1.05)		(2490.23)		(0.98)		(2273.64)***
Obs.	33 632	18 186	32 453	17 551	34 199	19 545	32 998	18 862
Uncensored obs.			3025	2512			3365	2693
Pseudo R²			0.09	0.08			0.09	0.08

Notes: Panel estimations (1997–2003) including all controls as displayed in Table 3 and Table 4, and including all governance controls as given in Table 5. Dependent variable in (1), (2), (5), and (6) is the count of yearly CBA for source-host country pairs. Dependent variable in (3), (4), (7) and (8) is total yearly value of CBA for source-host country pairs. Standard errors of (1), (2), (5) and (6) clustered by country pair. All estimations include year dummies.

Table 11. Regions

	(1)	(2)	(3)	(4)	(5)	(6)	(7)	(8)	(9)	(10)
	AFRICA	AFRICA	ASIA	ASIA	ASIA	ASIA	EUROPE	EUROPE	EUROPE	EUROPE
... TIERS	-0.28 (0.16)*	-55.49 (33.71)	-0.01 (0.2)	185.21 (65.77)***			-0.3 (0.09)***	-1102.67 (305.6)***	-0.33 (0.19)*	-1585.01 (593.99)***
TIERS/POPULATION					-0.67 (1.83)	-1168.84 (509.07)**				
SUBNAT. EXPENDITURE SHARE									-0.94 (1.65)	-6508.89 (5285.28)
SUBNAT. REVENUE SHARE									2.33 (1.4)*	7926.13 (4316.341)*
Obs.	10 141	9785	10 307	9943	10 307	9943	12 765	12 315	10 038	9686
Uncensored obs.		117		684		684		1721		1556
Pseudo R^2		0.14		0.13		0.13		0.08		0.07

Notes: Panel estimations (1997–2003) including all controls as displayed in Table 3 and Table 4, and including all governance controls as given in Table 5. Dependent variable in (1), (3), (5), (7), and (9) is the count of yearly CBA for source–host country pairs. Dependent variable in (2), (4), (6), (8), and (10) is total yearly value of CBA for source–host country pairs. Standard errors of (1), (3), (5), (7) and (9) clustered by country pair. All estimations include year dummies.

a negative but insignificant effect, and the value specification, column (6), shows a negative and significant effect.

3.6.5. The role of country size.

Our analysis has shown that appropriately controlling for governance variables is important to detect the effects of decentralization on FDI. Controlling for country size is equally important, since large countries can be expected to feature higher decentralization. But country size itself may be an important determinant of FDI, so the specification of our regression's functional forms is very delicate and debatable.

We have included tiers unadjusted for country size in most of our regressions. However, since tiers is itself systematically correlated with country size, it is essential to include sufficient controls to ensure that our tiers variable does not pick up FDI effects that should be accounted for by the effects of country size. Columns (1)–(6) of Table 12 show what happens if a reduced number of country size controls are used. The estimations of columns (1) and (2) do not control for the squared terms of area and population, columns (3) and (4) display the results of using only area and population as controls, and, finally, (5) and (6) show what happens if there are no controls at all for country size. The size of the coefficient of tiers decreases, and the significance of tiers also drops as we take out the controls for country size. Without any country size controls tiers is found to have a significant positive impact on CBAs in the values specification. This demonstrates that appropriately controlling for country size is very important. We should stress, however, that all the country size controls we use are typically found to be significant in our estimations, at least when we use the full sample, as can be seen from Tables 3 and 4.

3.6.6. Estimates using averages.

As our final robustness check we consider estimating the model using averages. Since our variable of government tiers and our fiscal decentralization measures do not change over time, estimating a panel may be regarded as an unjustified inflation of the sample size. We therefore collapse all time varying variables to their 1997–2003 averages. For the count data model, we consider how these averages determine the total number of acquired firms of a given country pair. The Tobit specification also uses the average yearly value as the dependent variable. The results are displayed in Table 13. The coefficient of tiers is negative and significant in all specifications, and of a magnitude that is similar to the estimated coefficients in the panel model. The fiscal decentralization variables are, however, no longer found to be significant.

4. DISCUSSION

Our empirical analysis has detected a dark side of decentralization. Its vertical dimension, measured by the number of government tiers in the host country, has a negative effect on foreign FDI inflows into the host country. This finding is robust in the type of FDI data used as the dependent variable: count or aggregate values. It is also quite robust to the division of the sample into particular subsets of countries.

Table 12. Sensitivity with respect to country size variables

	(1)	(2)	(3)	(4)	(5)	(6)
POP	$91.16*10^{-5}$ $(20.25*10^{-5})$***	2.56 (0.36)***	$74.5*10^{-5}$ $(20.89*10^{-5})$***	2.51 (0.36)***		
POP^{-1}	-2.87 (0.56)***	-6339.61 (450.19)***				
POP^{2}						
AREA	$7.34*10^{-5}$ $(1.2*10^{-5})$***	0.24 (0.02)***	$9.39*10^{-5}$ $(1.25*10^{-5})$***	0.29 (0.02)***		
$AREA^{-1}$	0.58 (0.21)***	1687.8 (407.27)***				
$AREA^{2}$						
TIERS	-0.31 (0.05)***	-603.59 (104.34)***	-0.14 (0.05)***	-204.4 (87.53)**	-0.06 (0.05)	158.25 (81.81)*
Obs.	42 994	41 483	42 994	41 483	42 994	41 483
Uncensored obs.		3553		3553		3553
pseudo R^2		0.09		0.09		0.09

Notes: Panel estimations (1997–2003) including all controls as displayed in Table 3 and Table 4, and including all governance controls as given in Table 5. Dependent variable in (1), (3), and (5) is the count of yearly CBA for source-host country pairs. Dependent variable in (2), (4), and (6) is total yearly value of CBA for source-host country pairs. Standard errors of (1), (3), and (5) clustered by country pair. All estimations include year dummies.

Table 13. Averages

	(1)	(2)	(3)	(4)	(5)	(6)
TIERS	-0.34	-0.25				
	(0.05)***	(0.08)***				
TIERS/POPULATION			-1.83	-289.68	-335.24	-2159.5
			(0.36)***	(69.97)***	(135.47)**	(669.52)***
SUBNAT. EXPENDITURE SHARE		1.71	1.77		423.14	707.35
		(0.99)*	(0.98)*		(1742.54)	(1741.96)
SUBNAT. REVENUE SHARE		-0.48	0.21		-658.75	-218.34
		(0.94)	(0.95)		(1628.1)	(1648.08)
Obs.	5923	3340	3340	5740	3237	3237
Uncensored obs.				1291	959	959
Pseudo R^2				0.08	0.07	0.07

Notes: Cross-section of 1997–2003 averages. Dependent variable in (1), (2), and (3) is count of total 1997–2003 CBA for source-host country pairs. Dependent variable in (4), (5), and (6) is 1997–2003 average yearly value of CBA for source-host country pairs.

Finally, this finding is robust to the inclusion of variables that control for governance as well as for other variables. Interestingly, the inclusion of governance variables is found to increase the significance of the results. The results are quantitatively important, although the magnitudes of the effects are sensitive to the specification and set of control variables included in the estimation.

We have found robust evidence of the negative effects of the vertical dimension of decentralization, very much in line with our Hypothesis 1. The importance of the different channels through which these negative effects are working is difficult to be identified. We have suggested several of such channels in our conceptual analysis in Section 2, but, with our data, it is not feasible to evaluate which of these channels is most important. Further evidence for the operation of the various mechanisms identified could be obtained with better availability of comparable cross-country data, as well as from individual case studies. We have used a large set of governance variables as controls and still identified a significant negative effect of tiers, although the inclusion of governance variables reduced the size of the effects of tiers. This latter finding relates to the results of Dreher (2006), who considers the effects of decentralization on various indicators of the quality of governance. He finds a negative effect of the number of government tiers on various measures of governance. More specifically, he finds a negative effect of the number of tiers on the rule of law, as measured by the Kaufman *et al.* (2005) index. These interdependencies point at potential endogeneity of several important variables in our analysis, including not only the governance variables, but potentially, also the decentralization variables. This may call for a modification of our econometric approach. However, there appear to be many channels through which tiers affect CBA, and it is not clear how to select among these, and what an adequately specified multi-equation model should look like. As regards the potential endogeneity problems of our decentralization variables, these are likely to differ between them. Our main variable of interest, the number of government tiers, is typically determined at the constitutional level. Further, since the tiers variable is treated as constant and relates to the beginning of our sample period, it can be regarded as exogenously given for our period under consideration. For the case of fiscal decentralization the possibility of endogeneity is more important. If the foreign investment generates substantial tax revenue, and if this revenue accrues differently to the various levels of government compared to other tax revenues, then the amount of FDI clearly affects the revenue ratio. Again, we may argue that the tax revenues stemming from a CBA in a given year will only arise in later years, and this implies that contemporaneous fiscal decentralization is exogenous to the number and the value of CBA inflows. However, since we use past average fiscal decentralization, our estimates do not suffer from this potential endogeneity problem.

The empirical analysis also showed that unlike vertical disintegration, fiscal decentralization may have positive effects. First, it should be noted that they do not contradict our theoretical perspective, but highlight that decentralization policy has several dimensions. Where the tiers variable is most suitable for measuring the vertical dimension, fiscal decentralization measures may account for other effects. They may relate more closely to the horizontal dimension of federalism, and therefore can be seen, for instance, as measuring 'closeness' of the government to firms and individuals.

We have not provided an explicit theoretical perspective on the potential aspects captured by the fiscal decentralization variables, and an interpretation of the findings on the fiscal decentralization measures is of an exploratory nature. However, it is still feasible to link them to various theoretical arguments made in the literature and we can also square them with several empirical results that have been obtained by previous research. First, we can relate our findings on the research that has been carried out on the direct relationship between decentralization and governance. Fisman and Gatti (2002) and Treisman (2000b) have considered the effect of decentralization on corruption. Fisman and Gatti (2002) consider the fiscal decentralization variables only, and find that more fiscal decentralization reduces the level of corruption. Such potential positive effect of fiscal decentralization on governance in the host countries may be an additional channel that explains the positive findings of fiscal decentralization on FDI. Conversely, Treisman (2000b) considered federalism (proxied by a dummy variable) and did not find an effect on corruption. Dreher (2006) also finds a positive effect of revenue decentralization on governance variables. This is in line with reduction in the magnitude of our estimated effects when governance variables are included, but we should stress that fiscal decentralization still has significant effects when we control for the quality of governance.

Another explanation for the increased attractiveness to foreign investors caused by fiscal decentralization can be found in the argument of Keen and Marchand (1997). They suggested that competition between cities or regions will result in a distortion of the mix of public goods provided by the regions and cities. In particular they will over-invest in infrastructure. This effect is likely to be stronger, if regions and cities have larger fiscal autonomy, as measured by fiscal decentralization. Investors will profit from such overinvestment in infrastructure and increase their investment, potentially explaining the positive effect of fiscal decentralization. This argument is also in line with the findings on the differential effect of expenditure and revenue decentralization, since it essentially relies on expenditure decentralization. Given the nature of this infrastructure competition, it is less likely in this case that fiscal decentralization is to the benefit of the country.

Finally, we should also point out that our results regarding tiers are derived on a cross-sectional base only and are therefore sensitive to unobserved country differences that could be correlated with CBAs and tiers. This is a common problem of research addressing the effects of government architecture, as variation over time is negligible compared to cross-sectional differences, and we do not have any *a priori* evidence for why such a correlation should exist, but this caveat needs to be mentioned. This caveat also holds with respect to our findings for fiscal decentralization. Nevertheless, we see our results as a useful first step uncovering the effects of the various facets of decentralization on FDI and more detailed analysis should be very welcome. This is particularly true with respect to quantifying the potential effects, as our results showed

them to be sensitive to the set of controls, the specification regarding the decentralization variables themselves, and the sample of countries included.

5. POLICY IMPLICATIONS

Important policy lessons can be learned from our results on the impact of decentralization on FDI. Both in the developed and developing world policy reforms towards
decentralization are high on the policy agenda. Frequently, it is argued that decentralization is beneficial for improving the investment climate. In particular, the competition between regional governments could result in improved investment conditions
for private investors and reduced possibilities for local governments to appropriate
parts of the investment's return through taxation after an investor has invested in a
particular location. This competition effect is caused by the *horizontal dimension* of
decentralization, the breaking up of one state in many jurisdictions.

Policy makers who want to attract FDI, however, need to be aware of the pitfalls of
decentralization. The horizontal dimension of decentralization need not resolve the hold-
up problem in FDI, since this problem is rooted in the *ex post* irreversibility of investment.
And the *vertical dimension* of decentralization, implied by the inevitable multiplicity of
government levels that are created in the process of decentralization, has potentially
negative effects for FDI. These theoretical arguments find strong support in the data, and
suggest that decentralization programmes can be detrimental to growth and efficiency.

To avoid these negative consequences, policies and constitutional set-ups should be
designed in a way as to minimize the negative potential arising from vertical disintegration. Our theoretical perspective leads to a number of important considerations.
First, the number of government layers should not be overly expanded. In fact, the
number of government levels should be reduced wherever possible. Second, as a
certain amount of vertical disintegration will be unavoidable, policies and constitutional
set-ups need to minimize the negative effects originating from this vertical dimension.
The overlap regarding tax bases, regulatory authority, and other policies that impinge
on investors should be reduced as far as possible. Thus a clear delineation of responsibilities is a pivotal aspect of the proper functioning of federal systems. But since
some overlap will be unavoidable, coordination devices need to be installed that
coordinate the actions of the different government levels. Such coordination has the
potential to resolve the free-riding and common pool incentives outlined in Section 2.

There is also good news for proponents of decentralization. Fiscal decentralization
may improve the investment climate, such that, from an investment policy perspective,
expenditure and revenue decentralization can have positive effects for FDI. Further,
the results on the differential effect of expenditure and revenue decentralization point
at the importance of expenditure decentralization for improving the investment
climate for foreign investors. As can be seen from Table 2, there is large variation in
fiscal decentralization among countries, such that there is scope for many countries
to engage in fiscal decentralization. Of course, the measures of fiscal decentralization

are rather crude measures and do not say much about the actual autonomy, nor do they tell us something about the kind of taxes and expenditures that are more effective in improving the investment climate. As can be conjectured from the results regarding the differential effect of expenditure and revenue decentralization, interesting results are to be expected from more detailed analyses of the structure of fiscal decentralization if the appropriate data was available. Going deeper into the structure of actual fiscal powers regarding different taxing rights and expenditure responsibilities would also allow much better targeted policy advice than what can be offered currently.[18]

Decentralization is often proposed as a means to improve the governance within a country. While we have treated governance as exogenously given in our empirical analysis, our findings nevertheless shed some light on the potential of decentralization to improve governance. It appears that the vertical dimension impinges negatively on the quality of governance. Fiscal expenditure decentralization appears to have positive effects. Of course, this evidence is rather indirect, but seems to point towards the same direction as our above arguments. If the problems of the vertical dimension cannot be sufficiently controlled, decentralization might not appear very suitable to improve governance. But if the vertical dimension can be controlled, decentralization in the form of fiscal decentralization has potential to improve governance.

Our results may also provide a further argument in favour of special economic zones. Such zones with special conditions regarding taxes and tariffs have been set up in many developing countries for foreign investors. From our perspective, one of the main advantages of such zones may be that several local or regional government actors, which would play a role elsewhere in the country, are locked out in such zones and the investor will typically have to deal with one government authority only.

Finally, it should again be stressed that for a sound formulation of decentralization policies two considerations are central. On the one hand, one has to consider what level of decentralization is most appropriate for the government to perform its tasks in the most efficient way. On the other hand, it is also important to consider the interaction of various government players at various levels in the government hierarchy. Our results point towards the intrinsic tension between these objectives.

Discussion

Allan Drazen
University of Maryland

Any comprehensive discussion of the determinants of foreign direct investment (FDI) in a country needs to consider the effect of government policy choices on FDI.

---

[18] The recent contribution by Stegarescu (2006) can be regarded as a first important step in that direction.

This includes not only actual policy decisions, but also the decision-making mechanism itself, since this will be a key determinant of the investment environment. The decision of foreigners on whether or not to invest in a country will in turn depend on their expectations of the policy environment.

This paper by Kessing, Konrad and Kotsogiannis makes a crucial contribution to this question. It has long been realized that decentralization of government decision making across levels of government may have a significant effect on FDI. Along the horizontal dimension, that is, with competing jurisdictions at a given level of government with some autonomy in decision making, decentralization may have a positive effect on FDI. Local governments may be more able to tailor fiscal programmes to the needs of the local constituency, and this increases accountability. More importantly for FDI, potential competition and benchmarking between regions may help attract FDI, among other things because it is argued to reduce the risk that governments will expropriate wealth.

What has been less appreciated, and is the focus of this paper, is the potential *negative* effect along the vertical dimension, that is, at different levels of government, for example: local, regional, state (in a federal system), and national. More specifically, less than total vertical decentralization, so that there is overlapping authority on investment decisions may have a strong negative effect. This is the 'dark side' of decentralization. When investors are subject to jurisdiction of several tiers of government, there may be significant problems of coordination failures, free-riding, common pool problems, and 'enforcement' of implicit contracts between government and private investors.

The authors have done an extremely good job not only of highlighting this issue, but also of investigating it. Moreover, since many of my concerns about earlier drafts were admirably addressed, this discussion will be short.

Several types of arguments are presented on why less-than-complete vertical 'disintegration' may have a negative effect on FDI. These problems are most easily understood by comparing, as the paper does, two hypothetical countries, identical in all respects, except that in country U there is a unitary government, while in country F there is a federal system with multiple tiers of government (for simplicity, say two tiers) that have overlapping fiscal authority. Kessing, Konrad and Kotsogiannis assume that in both countries 'property rights are weak' in the sense that government cannot credibly commit to not extracting revenue from the investors' projects *ex post*, that is once the investment is sunk and cannot be relocated. Moreover, investors are aware of government incentives to expropriate one investment is irreversibly in place. (I return to a discussion of the hold-up problem below, and, following the organization of the paper, begin by assuming both types of countries share equally weak property rights.)

First, there is the common pool problem. If government maximizes tax revenue that can be extracted from a foreign direct investor, U will choose the tax rate that maximizes overall tax revenue. In F if the two levels of government that can both tax the foreign investor choose tax rates non-cooperatively, the overall tax rate on the investor will be higher, and both investment (which is chosen anticipating this problem) and tax revenue will be lower. (Similar considerations apply when governments give subsidies to attract foreign investment – the free-rider problem is simply another inter-government externality.)

This is certainly true, but governments can foresee this common pool problem as well as investors. Hence, to the extent that the common pool problem has the potential to significantly lower investment, one might expect a federal system to try to alleviate it, for example, by defining property rights to tax bases. (In many US states, for example, certain types of taxes are constitutionally reserved for the state government, others reserved for local governments.) Kessing, Konrad and Kotsogiannis are aware of this when they write that 'the common pool problem could be avoided if the ability to expropriate revenues from the foreign direct investor could be attributed to one of the government tiers'. They argue, however, that in practice such effective assignment is hard to do. But, this is an empirical question: do we in fact see such mechanisms in place in some countries, but not others? It would not be easy, but nonetheless useful, to see empirical evidence on the success or failure of federal systems to assign such property rights to taxes across government tiers. Their tests suggest that countries don't fully solve the problem, but it would be nice to see more direct evidence.

It also seems that there is no reason to believe that all government tiers in a given country actually have fiscal jurisdiction over FDI and certainly not equal jurisdiction. Of course, any 'weighting' scheme for tiers would depend on country specifics and hence could not be applied across the sample, even if it could even be discovered. Hence, this is not a criticism of construction of the variable itself, but more a question of what are the limitations of this sort of cross-country empirical analysis.

The severity of the *ex post* 'hold-up' problem depends on the extent that governments try to commit themselves successfully not to expropriate sunk investment. An inability of government to make it convincing that *ex post* expropriation will not take place is listed by investors as a major disincentive to investment. However, country governments clearly differ significantly in the extent they can credibly commit not to expropriate. Hence, though in theory the hold-up problem certainly exists, its seriousness in practice is also an empirical question of effective government pre-commitment mechanisms.

A key question then becomes whether countries having a federal structure where different tiers have overlapping authority are less likely to develop institutions which address the hold-up problem than countries with a unitary government. As Kessing, Konrad and Kotsogiannis point out, since the hold-up problem in FDI may be more severe in a federal system due to the common pool problem, F countries have more to gain than U countries from developing mechanisms or institutions that address it, and hence, they may in fact have more incentive to do so.

To suggest why this may not happen, Kessing, Konrad and Kotsogiannis consider repeated interaction between governments and investors as an important mechanism in the case of FDI. Will reputational effects in the 'implicit contract' inherent in repeated interactions help constrain governments, and, more importantly, is the implicit contract weaker in federal systems? Based on oligopoly theory concerning collusion among firms, they argue that the enforcement of good behaviour in the 'implicit contract' will be weaker in F than in U countries. With repeated interaction, agents – government levels and an investor – can adopt strategies that depend on behavior in previous interactions. Good behaviour is enforced by the threat of punishing a 'player' that deviates from the collusive (that is, lower-tax) equilibrium. However, as with an increase in the number of firms in oligopoly, the ability to punish a deviating government may be reduced with an increase in the number of governments. The benefit from cooperation is lower as the number of governments increase, while the net benefit from deviating may be higher.

This argument makes sense, but governments are not exactly like firms in this analogy. Government is defined as having (or supposed to have) monopoly on the use of certain powers. Hence, higher levels may have far greater powers than firms in enforcing cooperation by lower tiers (and the number of tiers is often small). The analogy of governments colluding among themselves in this repeated interaction game (induced by the existence of a dominant player on the government side) may be more realistic.

To summarize, I think Kessing, Konrad and Kotsogiannis have pointed out a number of reasons why the problems of government interaction and overlap in a federal system may depress FDI when investment has an irreversible component and investors are forward-looking. By the same token, overlapping governments that care about attracting FDI should be forward-looking as well. Hence, their attempts to address these problems may mitigate the effects. More generally, simple stylized models of government behaviour focusing on institutional differences can be very misleading. Modelling is necessarily simple and stylized, but in fact, governments facing problems due to institutional features (multiple tiers, allocation of powers, etc.) have incentives to get around them. Predictions of what can happen due to these features may be in error if it fails to take this into account.

Hence, theory alone cannot answer the question of how strong an effect the problems of incomplete vertical decentralization will have on FDI. Moreover, since even in theory, horizontal decentralization may have strong positive effects, the overall empirical effect could certainly go in either direction. I think the authors are wise therefore to focus on investigating the empirical relation between government tiers and FDI.

At the same time, I think one should be careful about interpreting the results. My point is a standard one. When countries are so different in institutional features which we cannot easily measure or control for (such as institutions to address the dark side of decentralization or even comparability of government tiers across countries), cross-country studies like this are suggestive, but far from definitive. I think that in the final analysis, some sort of country studies may also be needed to shed more light on the effect of tiers on FDI. Not to replace the analysis here, but to supplement it. The question is too important and the paper too interesting not to take this next step.

Manuel Arellano
CEMFI and CEPR

This paper reports empirical evidence on the effects of various aspects of decentralization on FDI. This is an interesting question. The paper provides a detailed background discussion of the literature and potential effects according to theory. The central part of the paper develops an empirical strategy:

- The FDI annual flow from a source country to a host country is proxied by the number or the value of firms acquired by firms from the source country in the host country.
- In this way it is possible to use data from up to 74 source countries and 177 host countries for 7 years.
- The basic empirical equation is a knowledge-capital regression model to which decentralization variables are added as extra regressors.

The main decentralization variable is the number of government tiers. Its estimated effect on FDI is negative, and this is the 'dark side' of decentralization.

Assessment

This is a welcome contribution to the empirical assessment of decentralization. The paper contains much useful discussion and empirical results on an issue of policy relevance. It is nicely written and I enjoyed reading it.

The contribution of the paper is empirical: the finding of a negative association between the number of government layers and FDI after controlling for country differences. Since FDI itself is positively associated with growth, the policy implication is that the number of government levels should be reduced 'wherever possible'.

Most of the limitations of this exercise are related to problems with data that hamper credibility of the estimates as causal effects. Moreover, the causal effect of decentralization on FDI is likely to be heterogeneous across countries. Understanding this heterogeneity and being able to relate it to observables is important for policy. In the remainder, I review some data limitations and provide some suggestions for future work.

Data issues

Lack of data on FDI flows.   As the authors note, the choice of dependent variable is problematic. One problem is that CBA is only a part of FDI (firm creation is excluded) and we do not know how the CBAs' share of FDI depends on decentralization and other variables. Thus, the reported estimates compound the effects of decentralization on FDI and the effects of decentralization on the CBA/FDI ratio.

The other problem is the focus on counts of CBAs due to severe under-reporting of the value of the investments. Aside from necessity, there are no good reasons for using counts of CBAs as a measure of FDI.

However, from the perspective of evaluating decentralization, CBA counts could be regarded as an outcome of interest in its own right. After all, it is also associated with growth. One can also take some comfort in the fact that count and value based estimates tend to be similar to each other, at least as far as the signs of effects and their significance is concerned.

Lack of variation in policy regimes.   Results are based on cross-sectional comparisons: differences in FDI associated with differences in number of tiers. So it is the effect of 'being in a situation with so many government levels' that we are looking at, as opposed to the before-after effect of undergoing decentralization. The latter is a closer notion to the policy effect of interest. The fact that results are cross-sectional (together with lack of instrumental variables) diminishes their causal credibility, because they are sensitive to unobserved country differences that cause both FDI and number of tiers.

The policy effect of decentralization

The number of tiers has a statistically significant negative effect on FDI, but how large is this effect? Is it economically plausible? Given the exponential specification of the model for counts of CBAs, an estimated coefficient on tiers of −0.4 implies that the average number of CBAs becomes 50% larger when one government tier is removed, which is a very large effect. Probably too large. The estimated effect is even larger in some of the specifications excluding countries with extreme values of tiers.

One explanation for such large effects would be the potential endogeneity of the number of tiers. Since this variable does not vary with time, we would expect a larger scope for endogeneity if the error term also contains a substantial component which does not vary with time. In this regard, it would be nice to do an analysis of variance of the residuals in order to ascertain the importance of time-invariant country-pair effects.

Heterogeneity

Large variations in the size of the estimated effect for different subsamples suggests that heterogeneity may be important. I consider some possible dimensions.

Different effects at different margins.   In the baseline model, the FDI effects of going from, say, 6 to 5 tiers or from 2 to 1 tier are constrained to be the same. The authors find evidence of non-linearities, but the lack of stability of the non-linear pattern across subsamples suggests that non-linear responses are not a major reason for heterogeneity in responses.

Cross-country dependence.   The theoretical predictions implicitly hold the amount of decentralization in other countries constant. Empirically, this creates the possibility that decentralization in one potential host country affects FDI in another. Also, spacial clustering in number of tiers suggests that the effects of *TIERS* may differ depending on the neighbours' situation. One way of addressing this issue would be to divide the world in broad regions and include an interaction of *TIERS* with average *TIERS* in the region.

Other interactions and optimal decentralization.   The effect of *TIERS* on FDI may vary with country size, political culture, diversity, or with the nature of decentralization. It may also vary with characteristics of the source country. Regarding country size, interaction terms are as theoretically plausible as additive controls.

As for the nature of decentralization, the effect may be different, for example, depending on whether decentralization goes alongside with fiscal decentralization or not. In fact, the policy discussion in the paper suggests an interest in the effects of the nature of decentralization as much as in decentralization itself. Taken *prima facie*, the paper estimates suggest that the less decentralization the better. A different policy perspective is to presume an optimal degree of decentralization and seek its empirical characterization (searching for 'U shapes').

The analysis of heterogeneity in the impact of *TIERS* is important because an estimated effect that is an average of very different country effects is not so useful for policy (i.e. what is good for some may be bad for others). Unfortunately, we do not seem to have enough data variability to capture well determined interaction effects.

Econometric remarks

There are nearly 7500 country pairs and more than 22 000 data points in the panel. The error terms of a given host country are likely to be correlated, and so are the errors for a given pair over time. Standard errors that treat these errors as independent may be overoptimistic. Standard errors reported in the paper are clustered by country-pair. So it is potentially important to allow for clustering in these dimensions, as done in the paper for country pairs.

Over-dispersion may be a problem for Poisson probabilities but not for estimates of the conditional mean, which are robust to distributional misspecification. In fact, they are more robust than estimates from the negative binomial model.

The Tobit model is a restrictive specification for values in that it presumes that the same equation that determines total values when investments are positive, also determines the probability of zeros.

Conclusion

This paper is an honest and thorough investigation of the relationship between FDI and government decentralization, which has uncovered an interestingly dark empirical regularity. It makes a policy relevant contribution and, no doubt, it will be a rich source for further research.

Panel discussion

Wendy Carlin wondered about the welfare implications of the paper's analysis: there may or may not be good reasons to focus on incentives to attract FDI, and the relevant institutions and policies certainly have other roles. Gilles Duranton noted that perhaps the same countries that can afford the high bureaucratic costs of multi-tiered governments are also inclined to let their local governments engage in wasteful policies meant to attract FDI. Several panellists wondered whether the paper's empirical results are robust to examination of subsamples and to correlation between the number of government tiers and other relevant factors, such as corruption and the availability of natural resources, and encouraged the authors to perform the robustness checks now reported in the published version of the paper. Pierre Pestiau noted that different mechanisms may be at work in very heterogeneous countries. Decentralization may be more or less democratically chosen, and while it is often motivated by concern for efficiency, it may also lead to inefficient conflicts between layers of government. Hans-Werner Sinn and Gilles Duranton emphasized the important role of hierarchical power in layered government structures. In federal countries, such as Germany and Canada, decentralization of fiscal powers is not as extensive as it may appear, as higher levels of government can react to the behaviour of lower levels by adjusting transfers of resources.

APPENDIX 1: ECONOMETRIC SPECIFICATION

For our study of the determinants of the number of CBA between source and host countries we use standard methods for the econometric analysis of count data. The theory of count data analysis is well summarized by Cameron and Trivedi (1998), see Cameron and Trivedi (1999) for a comprehensive introduction. The structure of the econometric model we estimate can be described by the expected number of cross-border acquisitions, conditional on the vector of controls, $CONTROLS$, the decentralization variables DEC, β, the parameter vector to be estimated and a shift variable d_{ij}:

$$E\,[CBA_{ijt}\,|\,x_{ijt}, d_{ijt}] = \exp(CONTROLS'_{ijt}\beta_1 + DEC'_{ijt}\beta_2 + d_{ijt}). \tag{1}$$

In their simplest form, count data models assume that the counts, that is in our case the number of CBA from source country i to host country j in year t, denoted by CBA_{ijt} follow a Poisson distribution with parameter λ_{ijt}. Thus,

$$f(CBA_{ijt}\,|\,x_{ijt}) = \frac{e^{-\lambda_{ijt}}\lambda_{ijt}}{CBA_{ijt}!}, \tag{2}$$

where

$$\lambda_{ijt} = \exp(x'_{ijt}\beta), \tag{3}$$

with x_{ijt} the vector of covariates, and β the parameter vector to be estimated. However, given the assumption of the Poisson distribution, this model assumes equality of mean and variance. This property is termed equi-dispersion. However, in most applications the analysed data displays over-dispersion, that is, a larger variance larger than the mean. Also in our case, standard tests clearly reject equi-dispersion. This problem can be resolved, if one assumes that the Poisson parameter λ_{ijt} is also affected by an additional shift parameter d_{ijt} that is:

$$\tilde{\lambda}_{ijt} = \exp(x'_{ijt}\beta + d_{ijt}) = \exp(x'_{ijt}\beta)\exp(d_{ijt}). \tag{4}$$

In this case, the Poisson parameter λ_{ijt} becomes itself a random variable with realization $\tilde{\lambda}_{ijt}$. Further, we assume that $\alpha_{ijt} = \ln d_{ijt}$ is gamma distributed with precision parameter θ, so that $E[\alpha_{ijt}] = 1$ and $V[\alpha_{ijt}] = 1/\theta$. In this case, the marginal distribution of CBA_{ijt}, given the covariates, can be shown to follow a negative binomial distribution, and the parameter vector β can be estimated via maximum likelihood estimation.

APPENDIX 2

Table A1. Description of covariates used in the analysis and their sources

Variable	Units	Description	Source
Number of cross border acquisitions	Count	Number of international merger and acquisition deals between source and host countries.	Compiled from Thomson Financial by Herger et al. (2005).
Value of cross border acquisitions	US$ millions	Value of international merger and acquisition deals between source and host countries.	Compiled from Thomson Financial by Herger et al. (2005).
ΣGDP	US$ billions	Real Gross Domestic Product in US$ with base year 1995 cumulated over source and host country.	Compiled from World Development Indicators (WDI).
ΔGDP	US$ billions	Real Gross Domestic Product in US$ with base year 1995 in terms of difference between source and host country.	Compiled from WDI.
POPULATION	Count (in millions)	Total population in host country.	Compiled from WDI.
AREA	Thousand square km	Area of host country.	Compiled from WDI.
$\Delta SKILL$	US$ thousands	Wage difference between source and host country measured by the corresponding difference in real GDP per capita with base year 1995.	Compiled from WDI.

Table A1. *Continued*

Variable	Units	Description	Source
DISTANCE	Thousand km	Great circular distance between capital cities of source and host country.	Compiled.
COMMON LANGUAGE	Indicator	Indicator variable identifying a common official language between host and source country.	Compiled from CIA World Factbook.
COMMON BORDER	Indicator	Indicator variable identifying a common border between host and source country.	Compiled from CEPII, available online at http://www.cepii.fr/anglaisgraph/bdd/distances.htm.
DOMESTIC MARKET CAPITALIZATION	Percent	Average market capitalization as a percentage of GDP in source country calculated by dividing the value of traded stocks in percent of GDP through the turnover ratio.	Compiled from WDI.
REAL EXCHANGE RATE	Ratio	Real exchange rate in terms of price conversion factor multiplied with the nominal exchange rate.	WDI.
CUSTOMS UNION	Indicator	Indicator variable identifying a customs union between source and host country.	Compiled from WTO.
FREE TRADE AGREEMENT	Indicator	Indicator variable identifying a free trade agreement between source and host country.	Compiled from WTO, provided by Herger *et al.* (2005).
SERVICE AGREEMENT	Indicator	Indicator variable identifying a service agreement between source and host country.	Compiled from WTO, provided by Herger *et al.* (2005).
DURATION	# of days	# of days it takes to start a business in host country.	Djankov *et al.* (2002).
PROCEDURES	Count	# of procedures to be completed before starting a business.	Djankov *et al.* (2002).
SET-UP COSTS	Percent	Cost of starting business expressed as % of host country GDP per capita.	Djankov *et al.* (2002).
TIERS	Count	Number of government tiers.	Provided by Daniel Treisman.
SUB-NATIONAL EXPENDITURE SHARE	Percent	Ratio of sub-national government expenditure to total government expenditures, 1980–1995 average.	Provided by Nils Herger, based on IMF government finance statistics.

Table A1. *Continued*

Variable	Units	Description	Source
SUB-NATIONAL REVENUE SHARE	Percent	Ratio of sub-national government tax revenues to total government tax revenues, 1980–1995 average.	Provided by Nils Herger, based on IMF government finance statistics.
PROPERTY RIGHTS PROTECTION	Index Score	Rating of property rights in host country. Original values have been reversed on a scale from 1 to 5 with higher values indicating more secure property rights.	Heritage Foundation.
VOICE AND ACCOUNTABILITY	Index Score	Rating of voice and accountability in host country. Ranges from −2.5 to 2.5 with higher values indicating higher accountability.	Kaufman *et al.* (2005).
CORRUPTION	Index Score	Rating of the control of corruption in host country. −2.5 to 2.5 with higher values indicating a better control of corruption.	Kaufman *et al.* (2005).
RULE OF LAW	Index Score	Rating of the rule of law in host country. −2.5 to 2.5 with higher values indicating a stronger rule of law.	Kaufman *et al.* (2005).
GOVERNMENT EFFECTIVENESS	Index Score	Rating of government effectiveness in host country. −2.5 to 2.5 with higher values indicating higher effectiveness.	Kaufman *et al.* (2005).
CORPORATE TAX RATE	Percent	Statutory corporate tax rate.	Provided by Margarita Kalamova, compiled from Ernst & Young (2002).

REFERENCES

Bardhan, P. and D. Mookherjee (2000). 'Capture and governance at local and national levels', *American Economic Review, Papers and Proceedings*, 90(2), 135–39.

— (2005). 'Decentralizing antipoverty program delivery in developing countries', *Journal of Public Economics*, Special Issue ISPE, 89(4), 675–704.

Besley, T. and M. Smart (2003). 'Fiscal restraints and voter welfare', London School of Economics, *mimeo*.

Blonigen, B.A., R.B. Davies and K. Head (2003). 'Estimating the knowledge-capital model of the multinational enterprise: Comment', *American Economic Review*, 93, 980–94.

Boadway, R., M. Marchand and M. Vigneault (1998). 'The consequences of overlapping tax bases for redistribution and public spending in a federation', *Journal of Public Economics*, 68, 453–78.

Brennan, G. and J.M. Buchanan (1977). 'Towards a tax constitution for Leviathan', *Journal of Public Economics*, 8, 255–73.

— (1980). *The Power to Tax: Analytical Foundations of a Fiscal Constitution*, Cambridge University Press, Cambridge.

Buch, C.M., J. Kleinert, A. Lipponer and F. Toubal (2005). 'Determinants and effects of foreign direct investment: Evidence from German firm-level data', *Economic Policy*, 20(41), 52–110.

Cai, H. and D. Treisman (2005). 'Does competition for capital discipline governments? Decentralization, globalization, and public policy', *American Economic Review*, 95(3), 817–30.

Cameron, A.C. and P.K. Trivedi (1998). *Regression Analysis of Count Data*, Cambridge University Press, Cambridge.

— (1999). 'Essentials of count data regression', *mimeo*.

Carr, D.L., J.R. Markusen and K.E. Maskus (2001). 'Estimating the knowledge-capital model of the multinational enterprise', *American Economic Review*, 91(3), 693–708.

— (2003). 'Estimating the knowledge-capital model of the multinational enterprise: Reply', *American Economic Review*, 93(3), 995–1001.

Charlton, A. (2003). *Incentives for Foreign Direct Investment*, MPhil thesis, St John's College, Oxford University.

Dahlby, B. (1996). 'Fiscal externalities and the design of intergovernmental grants', *International Tax and Public Finance*, 3, 397–412.

De Mooij, R.A. and S. Ederveen (2003). 'Taxation and foreign direct investment: A synthesis of empirical research', *International Tax and Public Finance*, 10(6), 673–93.

Di Giovanni, J. (2005). 'What drives capital flows? The case of cross-border M&A activity and financial deepening', *Journal of International Economics*, 65(1), 127–49.

Djankov, S., R. La Porta, F. López-de-Silanes and A. Shleifer (2002). 'The regulation of entry', *Quarterly Journal of Economics*, 117, 1–37.

Dreher, A. (2006). 'Power to the people? The impact of decentralization on governance', KOF Working Paper No. 121.

Eaton, J. and M. Gersovitz (1983). 'Country risk: Economic aspects', in R.J. Herring (ed.), *Managing International Risk*, Cambridge University Press, Cambridge, 75–108.

Ernst & Young (2002). 'Worldwide corporate tax guide', Ernst & Young.

Fisman, R., and R. Gatti (2002). 'Decentralization and corruption: Evidence across countries', *Journal of Public Economics*, 83, 325–45.

Hayek, F.A. (1939/1960). *The Constitution of Liberty*, University of Chicago Press, Chicago.

Herger, N., C. Kotsogiannis and S. McCorriston (2005). 'Cross border acquisitions and institutional quality', *mimeo*, University of Exeter.

Hindriks, J. and B. Lockwood (2005). 'Fiscal centralization and electoral accountability', University of Warwick, *mimeo*.

Janeba, E. (2000). 'Tax competition when governments lack commitment: Excess capacity as a countervailing threat', *American Economic Review*, 90(5), 1508–19.

Johnson, W.R. (1988). 'Income redistribution in a federal system', *American Economic Review*, 78(3), 570–73.

Kaufman, D., A. Kraay and M. Mastruzzi (2005). *Governance Matters IV: Governance Indicators for 1996–2004*, World Bank, Washington.

Keen, M.J. (1998). 'Vertical tax externalities in the theory of fiscal federalism', *IMF Staff Papers*, 45, 454–85.

Keen, M.J. and C. Kotsogiannis (2002). 'Does federalism lead to excessively high taxes?', *American Economic Review*, 92(1), 363–70.

— (2003). 'Leviathan and capital tax competition in federations', *Journal of Public Economic Theory*, 5, 177–99.

— (2004). 'Tax competition in federations and the welfare consequences of decentralization', *Journal of Urban Economics*, 56, 397–407.

Keen, M.J. and M. Marchand (1997). 'Fiscal competition and the pattern of public spending', *Journal of Public Economics*, 66(1), 33–53.

Kehoe, P.J. (1989). 'Policy cooperation among benevolent governments may be undesirable', *Review of Economic Studies*, 56, 289–96.

Kessing, S.G., K.A. Konrad and C. Kotsogiannis (2006a). 'Federalism, weak institutions and the competition for foreign direct investment', Social Science Research Centre, Berlin, *mimeo*.

— (2006b). 'Federal tax autonomy and the limit of cooperation', *Journal of Urban Economics*, 59, 317–29.

Kessler, A., C. Lülfesmann and G. Myers (2005). 'Federations, constitutions and bargaining', *mimeo*.

Konrad, K.A. and K.E. Lommerud (2001). 'Foreign direct investment, intra-firm trade and ownership structure', *European Economic Review*, 45(3), 475–94.

Kydland, F.E. and E.C. Prescott (1980). 'Dynamic optimal taxation, rational expectations and optimal control', *Journal of Economic Dynamics and Control*, 2(1), 79–91.

Markusen, J.R. (1997). 'Trade versus investment liberalization', National Bureau of Economic Research Working Paper 6231, Cambridge, MA.

Markusen, J.R., A.J. Venables, D.E. Kohan and K.H. Zhang (1996). 'A unified treatment of horizontal direct investment, vertical direct investment, and the pattern of trade in goods and services', National Bureau of Economic Research Working Paper 5696, Cambridge, MA.

Markusen, J.R. and K.E. Maskus (2002). 'Discriminating among alternative theories of the multinational enterprise', *Review of International Economics*, 10, 694–707.

North, D.C. and B.R. Weingast (1989). 'Constitutions and commitment: The evolution of institutional governing public choice in seventeenths-century England', *Journal of Economic History*, 49, 803–32.

Oates, W.E. (1972). *Fiscal Federalism*, Harcourt-Brace, New York.

— (1999). 'An essay on fiscal federalism', *Journal of Economic Literature*, 37, 1120–49.

OECD (2002). *Fiscal Decentralization in EU Applicant States and Selected EU Member States*, Paris.

Qian, Y. and B.R. Weingast (1997). 'Federalism as a commitment to preserving market incentives', *Journal of Economic Perspectives*, 11, 83–92.

Riker, W.H. (1964). *Federalism: Origin, Operation and Significance*, Little, Brown and Company, Boston.

Rossi, S. and P. Volpin (2004). 'Cross-country determinants of mergers and acquisitions', *Journal of Financial Economics*, 74(2), 277–304.

Schnitzer, M. (1999). 'Expropriation and control rights: A dynamic model of foreign direct investment', *International Journal of Industrial Organization*, 17, 1113–37.

Seabright, P. (1996). 'Accountability and decentralisation in government: An incomplete contracts model', *European Economic Review*, 40, 61–89.

Shleifer, A. and R. Vishny (1993). 'Corruption', *Quarterly Journal of Economics*, 108(3), 599–617.

Stegarescu, D. (2006). *Decentralised Government in an Integrating World*, Physica-Verlag, Heidelberg.

Thomas, J. and T. Worrall (1994). 'Foreign direct investment and the risk of expropriation', *Review of Economic Studies*, 61, 81–108.

Tiebout, C.M. (1956). 'A pure theory of local expenditures', *Journal of Political Economy*, 64, 416–24.

Treisman, D. (1999a). 'Russia's tax crisis: explaining falling revenues in a transitional economy', *Economics and Politics*, 11, 145–69.

— (1999b). 'Political decentralization and economic reform: A game-theoretic analysis', *American Journal of Political Science*, 43, 488–517.

— (2000a). 'Decentralization and the quality of government', UCLA *mimeo*.

— (2000b). 'The causes of corruption: a cross-national study', *Journal of Public Economics*, 76, 399–457.

— (2003). 'Rotten boroughs', UCLA, *mimeo*.

UNCTAD (2001) *World Investment Report 2000*. United Nations Conference on Trade and Development, Geneva.

Wei, S.-J. (2000). 'How taxing is corruption on international investors?', *Review of Economics and Statistics*, 82(1), 1–11.

Weingast, B.R. (1995). 'The economic role of political institutions: Market-preserving federalism and economic development', *Journal of Law, Economics and Organization*, 11, 1–31.

Wildasin, D.E. (1989). 'Interjurisdictional capital mobility: Fiscal externality and a corrective subsidy', *Journal of Urban Economics*, 25, 193–212.

World Bank (2004). 'A better investment climate for everyone', *World Development Report 2005*, World Bank and Oxford University Press.

Wrede, M. (1996). 'Vertical and horizontal tax competition: Will uncoordinated *Leviathans* end up on the wrong side of the Laffer curve?', *FinanzArchiv*, 53, 461–79.

— (1997). 'Tax competition and federalism: The underprovision of local public goods', *FinanzArchiv*, 54, 494–515.

— (2000). 'Shared tax sources and public expenditures', *International Tax and Public Finance*, 7, 163–75.

Wage inequality, investment and skills

SUMMARY

In flexible labour markets, capital increases the productivity of skilled workers more than that of unskilled workers, and in the US faster investment is associated with wider wage inequality. But labour market institutions that keep unskilled workers' wages high also imply that firms may find it profitable to invest so as to boost those workers' productivity. Our empirical analysis based on industry-level data confirms that a higher capital intensity in Germany is associated with smaller wage differentials and with a larger share of unskilled workers in the labour costs. Changes in capital–labour ratios during the 1980s reduced wage differentials by 5–8% in German industries, while in the US capital deepening in such industries as machinery and retail was accompanied by an increase of wage differentials larger than 7%.

— *Winfried Koeniger and Marco Leonardi*

Capital deepening and wage differentials: Germany versus US

Winfried Koeniger and Marco Leonardi

IZA and University of Bonn; University of Milan and IZA

1. INTRODUCTION

European labour markets are different not only in terms of unemployment (see Blanchard, 2006), but also in terms of wage inequality. The two aspects are related, in that distributional concerns may make it difficult to employ low-skilled people at low wages. In Germany, for example, a generous welfare system and powerful unions induce wage floors which prevent wages of unskilled workers from falling, and while unemployment is very much a problem there is substantial political support for such statements as 'A person who does a good job must earn enough to support a family' or 'It is shameful for a civilized society if human beings are put off with 3.50 euro per hour for decent work.'[1] In the US, where unemployment is much less of a problem, low wages are only mildly

For very helpful comments we thank Lans Bovenberg, Gilles Duranton, Omer Moav, Hans-Werner Sinn, Gianluca Violante, anonymous referees, participants of the *Economic Policy* panel in Vienna and the IZA workshop on 'Structural Change and Labor Markets'. Bertrand Koebel, Plutarchos Sakellaris, Focco Vijselaar, Gianluca Violante and Daniel Wilson kindly provided some of the data we use in our analysis. Financial support of DAAD-Vigoni is gratefully acknowledged.

The Managing Editor in charge of this paper was Giuseppe Bertola.

[1] The citations are from the recent German debate on minimum wages, published in the magazine *Stern*. Franz Müntefering (Minister for Labor and Social Affairs): 'Wer seinen Job richtig macht, muss auch so viel Geld bekommen, dass er seine Familie davon ernähren kann.' Michael Sommer (head of the German unions, DGB): 'Dass Menschen für anständige Arbeit mit 3.50 Euro pro Stunde abgespeist werden, ist beschämend für eine zivilisierte Gesellschaft' (*Stern*, 9.2.2006).

Economic Policy January 2007 pp. 71–116 Printed in Great Britain
© CEPR, CES, MSH, 2007.

constrained by the federal minimum wage ($5.15 per hour), unemployment benefits are short-lived, and union membership rates average half the German ones over the 1970–90 period, and have declined much more sharply.

1.1. Two theories and the facts

These institutional differences are related to the differences in the evolution of unemployment and wage inequality in these and other countries (see for example, Blau and Kahn, 1996; Abraham and Houseman, 1995; and further references in Koeniger *et al.*, 2006). The wage differential between skilled and unskilled workers has remained remarkably stable in Germany but has increased substantially in the US in the last decades (see Tables A1 and A2 in the Appendix, which we will discuss further below). Krugman (1994, p. 37) argued that 'the growth of earnings inequality in the United States – and quite possibly therefore much of the rise in structural unemployment in Europe – has been the result of technological changes that just happen to work against unskilled workers'. Indeed, different labour market institutions may have implied different responses in the European and US labour markets in the aftermath of a common positive shock to the relative demand for skilled labour. In countries like the US where wages are flexible, the positive relative demand shock for skills increases the skill-wage differential. In countries like Germany with wage floors, the relative unemployment among the unskilled increases.

This 'Krugman hypothesis' of a well-defined trade-off between wage inequality and employment is at the core of the debate on labour market policy. But is the choice facing developed countries so simple? In this paper, we bring to bear on the relevant issues another interesting and less well-known cross-country difference: the capital–labour ratio has increased more in Germany than in the US in the period 1975–91, especially in the unskilled labour intensive sectors.

A larger increase of the capital–labour ratio in Germany than in the US may appear consistent with the standard 'Krugman hypothesis': after an adverse relative demand shift, institutions that prevent unskilled wages from falling might well induce substitution not only between unskilled and skilled workers, but also between labour and capital (Blanchard, 1997; Caballero and Hammour, 1998). As we discuss below, however, this cannot explain the fact that unskilled employment and value added have behaved very similarly in both countries and across sectors with different skill intensities. It is also difficult for the 'Krugman hypothesis' to explain other aspects of the evidence, such as the fact that the stronger German increase of the capital/labour ratio in unskilled labour intensive sectors was driven by faster capital accumulation rather than by a decline of (unskilled) employment levels.[2]

---

[2] Some empirical features related to those we document have already been noted in the literature. Krueger and Pischke (1998) show that employment trends are similar across skill groups in Germany (and not worse for the unskilled as the 'Krugman hypothesis' implies). Nickell and Bell (1996) have argued that the evolution of the relative unemployment of unskilled workers in Germany is much the same as in the US in the 1980s and early 1990s while wage inequality is stable in Germany but rising in the US.

Since it is difficult for the 'Krugman hypothesis' to explain the different joint evolution of capital, employment, and wage inequality in Germany and the US, what alternative mechanisms might have been at work? We confront the evidence with an alternative hypothesis, according to which wage floors reduce the skill premium by encouraging more investment in capital equipment complementary to unskilled workers (in Germany). This perspective blends institutions and skill-biased investment as an explanation for the different evolution of wage differentials in the US and Germany, and views changes in the relative price of capital equipment as a key common driving process. Cheaper capital implies higher capital intensity and, as in Krusell et al. (2000), can explain some of the increase in the skill-wage differential in the US since the 1970s (see also Caselli, 1999; Moaz and Moav, 2004; Hornstein et al., 2005; and Leonardi, 2006). We point out that the same change in the relative price of capital has very different implications if investment is also influenced by institutional wage floors, and labour market frictions do not allow firms to easily substitute expensive unskilled workers with cheaper capital. When replacing a worker would require costly 'search and matching' activities, workers can appropriate, through higher wages, a portion of their employers' investments in their job's productivity, and this 'hold-up' problem reduces employers' incentives to invest. This is mitigated when wages are rigid, and unresponsive to productivity. Hence, wage rigidity increases employers' incentives to train their workers or invest in capital complementary to their skills (Acemoglu and Pischke, 1999). To the extent that wage floors lead to increases in the productivity of low-wage workers, rather than to their substitution with other factors, smaller skill-wage differentials are accompanied by more intense investment directed to unskilled workers.

1.2. Empirical evidence

Some previous literature has looked into the relationship between minimum wages and training finding inconclusive or quantitatively small effects (see Neumark and Wascher, 2001; Acemoglu and Pischke, 2003, for evidence within US states and Pischke, 2005, for a comparison across OECD countries).[3] We focus on capital investment and we investigate whether firms invest in different types of capital goods in Germany compared with the US because of institutional constraints on wages of unskilled workers. For example, firms might invest in a conveyor belt which is complementary to unskilled labour due to wage floors in Germany whereas in the US with flexible wages firms invest more in high-tech machines for a chemical laboratory which are complementary to skilled labour. Since we do not have data which allow

---

[3] Nickell and Bell (1996), in a model without capital, argue that unskilled workers have enjoyed higher wages and low unemployment rates in Germany (relatively to the US at least until 1991) because the German schooling system induces a stronger performance of the bottom half of the ability range thanks to the comprehensive system of vocational training. We investigate this hypothesis further below when we check the robustness of our results defining the skill premium according to different skill groups.

us to link explicitly workers by skill type to capital equipment, our empirical strategy is to use information on factor prices and quantities to test whether capital equipment is more complementary to unskilled workers in Germany than in the US.

We provide descriptive evidence at the industry level on the association between capital–labour ratios and wage differentials in the US and Germany. Following Acemoglu and Pischke (1999) and Acemoglu (2003), we investigate how institutions affect wage differentials and also firm investment. We find evidence consistent with the view that German institutions distort investment towards unskilled workers and thus compress wage differentials relative to the US. Our estimates imply that capital deepening in Germany in the 1980s is associated with a reduction in the skill-wage differential of about 5–8% in most industries. In the US instead, capital deepening is associated with an increase of the wage differential between 7 and 8% in important industries like machinery and retail. Similarly, capital deepening in the 1980s is associated with a 3–5% lower share of unskilled labour in the wage bill in the US in sectors like machinery and retail whereas there is no significant association in Germany. This suggests that differences in firm investment are an important part of the overall effect of institutions on wage inequality and on the unskilled labour share.[4]

1.3. Policy relevance

Our empirical results indicate that the implications of institutions for equality and efficiency interact with investment patterns, as well as with structural shocks, in important and policy relevant ways. Through their influence on productivity-enhancing investments, the effect of labour market institutions on inequality may well be stronger than would be implied by their commonly considered direct effects on wages and employment. But of course investments that foster unskilled workers' productivity are no free lunch. The investment that is induced by wage rigidities in equilibrium reduces employers' profits and job-creation incentives. Thus, our theoretical perspective and empirical findings can explain patterns of industry development. As industries with low skill intensity invest relatively more, and in low-skill-complementary capital, there will be slower growth of high-skill intensive sectors like banking and insurance, and business, personal or health services. This may explain the slow pace of structural change in Germany, where manufacturing industries are still strong, and its negative implications for employment growth (which in other countries mostly takes place in the service sector), as well as for efficiency and income growth. While our results may tempt governments to subsidize investment complementary to unskilled labour, in

---

[4] These results relate to previous work of Beaudry and Green (2003) who show that the wage differential between skilled and unskilled workers would have been smaller in the US if the capital accumulation in the US had matched the German pattern. Whereas they analyse interactions between different accumulation patterns and changes in technology, this paper proposes institutions as one possible explanation for why countries use different capital intensities (see also Pischke, 2005).

order to alleviate the employment and profit impacts of institutions that constrain wages of unskilled workers, that goal is addressed more directly and efficiently by policies that improve the human capital of workers at the bottom of the skill distribution.

2. THEORETICAL BACKGROUND AND EMPIRICAL PREDICTIONS

In this section we first present the predictions of a simple neoclassical model and confront these predictions with some facts. These facts then motivate an alternative explanation based on costly locating and hiring of workers.

2.1. A neoclassical view

Neoclassical theory predicts that a binding minimum wage for unskilled workers induces substitution by either capital, skilled labour or both where the quantitative importance of this cost-induced substitution depends on the chosen production function. We focus on substitution between capital and unskilled labour since the facts we present below show striking differences in capital investment between the US and Germany in the *unskilled labour intensive* sectors.

Consider a sector in which capital is combined with unskilled labour and the rental price of capital is determined in the global capital market (see Web Appendix I.A for formal derivations). Capital and unskilled labour are imperfectly substitutable and each factor has decreasing returns to scale (but both of them together have constant returns to scale). With such a standard production function, a binding wage floor induces substitution of unskilled labour by capital as unskilled labour becomes more costly. This is illustrated in Figure 1 which plots the marginal product of capital as a function of the capital–labour ratio. In a flexible economy like the US, the equilibrium ratio $(K/L)_{\text{flex}}$ equates the marginal product to the global rental price of capital. In a rigid economy like Germany instead the employment level of unskilled labour will be lower so that that the marginal product of *unskilled labour* equals the binding minimum wage. Lower employment also implies a higher capital–labour ratio $(K/L)_{\text{rigid}}$, which is not sustainable, however, since the marginal product of capital is below the rental price of capital on global capital markets. The only way that the unskilled labour intensive sector can remain in business in Germany is that production falls and unskilled workers become unemployed until the final good is sufficiently scarce and its price increases (Krugman, 1995). The final-good price goes up until the marginal product of both capital and unskilled labour are high enough to equal the global rental price of capital and the minimum wage, respectively. In the figure, the increase of the final-good price shifts the marginal-product of capital up and the capital–labour ratio $(K/L)_{\text{rigid}}$ to the left (the dashed lines in the figure). The new capital–labour ratio is $(K/L)^*$.

Thus, this simple neo-classical framework predicts that in the unskilled labour intensive sector of a rigid economy like Germany,

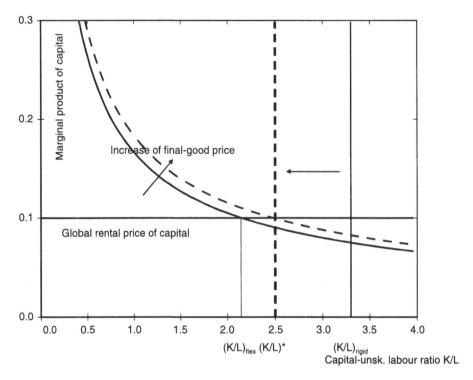

Figure 1. The minimum wage and capital–labour substitution in the neoclassical model

Source: Authors' calculation.

- the capital–labour ratio is higher because unskilled employment is lower,
- the output of the unskilled labour intensive sector is lower than in the flexible economy.

An adverse shock to the relative demand of unskilled labour (as analysed by Krugman, 1995) increases the bite of the minimum wage and also the difference between the rigid and flexible economy in terms of these two predictions.

2.2. Some facts

In order to assess the relevance of this theoretical perspective, let us first consider the evolution of the capital–labour ratio and the skill-wage differential in the US and Germany for two important industries in our sample period: the machinery industry as a representative industry for the manufacturing sector and the retail industry for the service sector. To facilitate comparisons, we normalize all variables to one in 1975.

Figure 2 displays three-year averages on the evolution of wage differentials by education (which we also call skill premium, that is, the logarithm of the ratio of wages of workers with some college education over the wages of workers with no

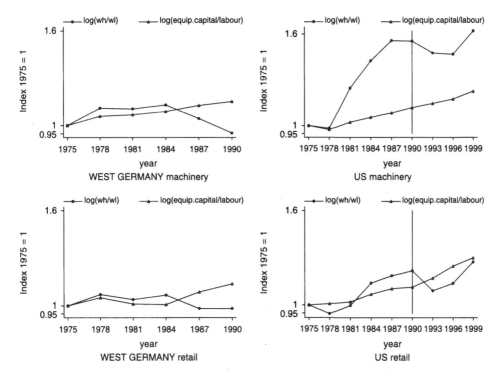

Figure 2. Wage differentials by skill and capital equipment per worker in the machinery and retail industry in the US and West Germany, 1970s–1990s, three-year averages

Source: Authors' calculations based on CPS, IAB, and national accounts data.

college education) and the capital-equipment per worker in the US and Germany. Wage differentials increased substantially in the US especially in the 1980s whereas they remained relatively stable in West Germany. On the contrary, the capital–labour ratio increased more in West Germany than in the US. In Germany, the capital–labour ratio increased by 15% in the machinery sector and by 13% in the retail sector from 1975 to 1990. In the same sectors and in the same period in the US, the increase was only 11% until 1990 (the vertical line in the right panels of Figure 2).

The descriptive graphs could be explained by simple capital–labour substitution. We now provide further evidence, however, which casts doubt on the simple explanation of factor substitution. In Table 1 we take a closer look at the predictions of the neoclassical framework in the previous subsection concerning value added, capital equipment and *employment*. Capital–labour substitution, due to wage floors induced by generous unemployment insurance, of course also implies *unemployment*. This might be considered a more problematic measure, however, since it depends on the generosity of benefit payments as well as on other policy details which matter for labour market participation, for example whether these benefits are paid conditional on active job search.

Table 1. Average three-year percentage changes of production factors and value added in the 1980s

	Capital equipment/ Value added		Low-skilled employment/ Value added		Capital equipment/ Low-skilled employment		Skilled/Low-skilled employment		Value added	
	US (1)	Germany (2)	US (3)	Germany (4)	US (5)	Germany (6)	US (7)	Germany (8)	US (9)	Germany (10)
Low-skill-intensive industries	−0.029 (0.082)	0.043 (0.048)	−0.037 (0.077)	−0.054 (0.035)	0.008 (0.098)	0.098 (0.051)	0.072 (0.038)	0.115 (0.039)	0.037 (0.051)	0.046 (0.046)
Skill-intensive industries	0.101 (0.085)	0.076 (0.065)	−0.026 (0.046)	−0.049 (0.037)	0.127 (0.084)	0.125 (0.077)	0.098 (0.022)	0.158 (0.052)	0.085 (0.035)	0.099 (0.040)

Notes: The averages for the low-skill and skill-intensive industries are weighted by real value added. The ten low-skill-intensive industries (in increasing order in the US in year 1975) are Textiles, Plastic and Leather, Wood, Stone and Clay, Food and Tobacco, Construction, Primary Metals, Transport Equipment, Agriculture and Mining, Electrical Machinery. The ten skill-intensive industries are Transport and Communication, Machinery, Utilities, Paper and Printing, Professional Goods, Wholesale and Retail, Business and Personal Services, Chemicals and Petroleum, Health Services, Banking and Insurance. The correlation with the skill intensity ranking in Germany is 0.76. Standard deviations are in parentheses. See the Web Data Appendix for further details.

Source: Authors' calculations.

In Table 1 we display average three-year percentage changes of factor inputs and value added for the ten sectors with the highest skill ratios in the US in 1975, and compare them with changes in the ten sectors that, on the same basis, appear least skill-intensive. We find the following patterns:

- Capital equipment (columns (1) and (2)): changes in capital equipment per unit of value added are quite evenly spread across all industries in Germany. In the US instead, they are concentrated in the skill intensive industries.
- Unskilled employment (columns (3) and (4)): unskilled employment per value added falls more in Germany than in the US. The difference, however, is larger in the skill-intensive industries.
- Capital-unskilled labour ratio (columns (5) and (6)): consequently, the capital–labour ratio increases in Germany across all industries, but only in the skill-intensive industries in the US.
- Skill intensity (columns (7) and (8)): the skill intensity increases in all industries both in the US and Germany.
- Value added (columns (9) and (10)): value added grows at similar rates in the US and Germany but more in the skill-intensive industries in both countries.

These patterns are robust to using the different capital or skill measures which we introduce in our robustness checks below. The most striking fact of Table 1 is the larger increase of the capital–unskilled labour ratio in the low-skill-intensive sectors in Germany compared with the US which is accompanied by faster labour productivity growth in Germany (the inverse of the statistics reported in Table 1, columns (3) and (4)).[5]

The patterns documented in Table 1 are not in line with the two predictions of the simple neoclassical framework in the previous subsection. The stronger increase of the capital–unskilled labour ratio in the low-skill intensive sectors is due to a larger increase in capital equipment (the numerator) rather than a stronger decrease of unskilled employment (the denominator). Moreover, the difference in the employment trend of unskilled workers between Germany and the US is larger, if anything, in the skill-intensive industries. In a neoclassical model with some factor complementarity, one would expect more capital–unskilled labour substitution in the low-skill intensive sector and a relative decrease in the output of that sector. Furthermore, this fall in output should be larger in Germany. Empirically, however, value added grows at a similar rate in the low-skilled industries in the US and Germany.

2.3. A search-and-matching view

Confronting comparative evidence with the neoclassical model's predictions, we have found that simple cost-induced substitution mechanisms do not suffice to explain the

---

[5] The differences in capital investment across developed countries have been already noted by Pischke (2005). He finds that investment growth is more positively correlated with the skill intensity across sectors in Anglo-Saxon countries than in continental European countries where labour market institutions compress wages.

differences in capital investment in the unskilled labour intensive sectors. Substituting expensive unskilled workers with capital, in fact, need not be as easy in reality as in that model. If workers and employers meet in a random, costly process, some investment decisions have to be taken *after* a worker (of a given skill level) has been located and hired: and since replacing that worker would be costly, the worker can in general try and bargain for higher wages if investment increases the job's productivity. The employer is 'held up' by the worker which lowers the employer's incentive to invest.

In models with such frictions in the labour market, rent sharing and binding minimum-wage constraints, different mechanics are at work (see Web Appendix I.B for formal derivations) and can explain some key aspects of the evidence in Table 1. To see how the interaction between investment and wage floors may be very different from that outlined in Section 2.1, imagine a US firm that produces shirts. The firm posts a vacancy for a worker who produces such shirts where we suppose that the wage of the worker is half of his output. There are two ways to produce the shirt, either by using a sewing machine or by hand. The firm decides whether to buy a sewing machine only after the vacancy is matched with a worker. Once the vacancy has been matched, it is costly to search for another worker to perform the same task so that the firm employs either an unskilled or a skilled worker depending on whom it meets first. After the match, the firm decides whether to increase the productivity of the worker by pur-chasing a sewing machine. Here it is important to note that the firm only appropriates half of the output increase if the sewing machine is bought since the worker's bargained wage increases in output. Thus, if workers have low skills and are not productive enough, firms do not find it optimal to invest. Firms only purchase the sewing machine if the vacancy is matched with a more productive skilled worker: this worker knows better how to operate the sewing machine so that the output increase, which is shared between the worker and firm, is larger to begin with. In this case, the hold-up problem implies purchases of the sewing machine only for matches with skilled workers.

Imagine the same firm in Germany where wage floors are binding for low-skilled workers. It is now easy to see how the presence of wage floors will change the purchase decision for German firms that employ low-skilled workers (these workers are still hired when located since it is costly to search for a more skilled worker). Although a binding minimum wage implies a higher wage *level*, it also implies no *change* of the wage if the firm buys the sewing machine. Hence, the minimum wage mitigates the hold-up problem and results in firms buying the sewing machine also for unskilled workers. In general, this is true also if investment in the sewing machine increases the worker productivity above the minimum wage. In this case unskilled workers appropriate part of the productivity increase in the form of a higher wage and the skill premium is reduced further. Given that the minimum wage is binding *before* the firm's investment, the change of the wage after the investment is still smaller compared with a US firm so that the hold-up problem continues to be mitigated.

Now consider how a fall in the price of the sewing machine affects the investment incentives in Germany and the US. As a starting point, consider a price of the sewing machine that is so high that neither German nor US firms purchase sewing machines. The interesting case is now if the price of the sewing machine falls so that US firms buy a sewing machine for the skilled but not for the unskilled workers (if the price is very low, US firms also invest in unskilled workers). German firms buy a machine for both skilled *and* unskilled workers even if the price falls to a level at which US firms do not find it optimal to invest in unskilled workers. The reason is, as explained above, that firms in Germany appropriate more of the job's productivity increase since binding minimum wages make wages of unskilled workers less responsive to output changes. Because investment of firms is less skill-biased in Germany, the skill premium remains more compressed than in the US.

This simple example is meant to illustrate the important differences in investment incentives in the US and Germany. The interaction of the well-documented fall in the price of capital (Krusell *et al.*, 2000) with labour market institutions in this modelling environment can explain the stronger investment in the unskilled labour intensive sector in Germany than in the US which we observed in Table 1. Notice that a fall in the price of capital does not help to fully reconcile the qualitative predictions of the neoclassical model with the empirical evidence. Cheaper capital helps neoclassical firms to sustain the minimum wage so that output of the final good needs to fall less and fewer unskilled workers become unemployed. In terms of Figure 1, the loci of the marginal product of capital and $(K/L)_{\text{rigid}}$ would shift less so that the new capital–labour ratio $(K/L)^*$ is higher at the new *lower* global rental price of capital. The problem remains, however, that in contrast to the facts in Table 1 the higher capital–labour ratio in the unskilled labour intensive sector in Germany compared with the US should be borne out in differences in employment rather than investment. Finally, if the price of capital falls so much that the minimum wage is no longer binding, there should be no differences in employment and the use of capital equipment between the US and Germany. In Figure 1, the minimum wage stops to bind if the global rental price is below the intersection point of $(K/L)_{\text{rigid}}$ and the schedule of the marginal product of capital.

Let us briefly discuss the main differences between the neoclassical framework and the search-and-matching environment which is used for the argument in this subsection. Costly search for vacancies by workers and costly filling of these vacancies by employers imply that each job match earns rents after such a match is formed between a worker and employer. These rents are split so that, compared with the neoclassical framework, employers can afford to pay a minimum wage above the neoclassical flexible market wage. Employers anticipate this higher labour cost and will post fewer vacancies so that job creation is lower. As a consequence equilibrium unemployment is higher, like in the neoclassical model, unless the minimum wage helps to alleviate the search congestion externality: firms do not take into account that their posting of vacancies congests the market and in the aggregate reduces the probability of filling a vacancy for each individual employer.

The fact that workers and firms split rents is especially important since wages are bargained after the firm sinks the full cost of the investment and the worker appropriates part of the gains of that investment. Knowing this, firms invest less. The key in this subsection is that labour market institutions may alleviate this hold-up problem and increase investment (Acemoglu, 2003). In the example given above, unskilled workers receive the binding minimum wage before and after the investment so that they do not appropriate part of the rents of the *additional* investment and firms are more willing to invest in them. We have chosen minimum wages as a simple way to explain this mechanism. In reality, in countries like Germany, other institutions like benefit replacement ratios or unions do not only matter for the wage floor but also for the share of rents which the worker appropriates in the bargain. Hence, the hold-up problem is not necessarily fully solved by these institutions as in the simple example presented in this subsection. Such complications are less important, however, if the level of bargaining is not at the level of the individual worker-firm pair but at the level of a centralized union. In this case, the union sets wages at the aggregate level and individual employers take them as exogenous when deciding about investment. Therefore, the hold-up problem does not arise.

It is important to emphasize that investment in unskilled workers in Germany is a second-best response by firms to distorted wages. Firms would not boost low-skilled workers' productivity in the absence of the minimum wage floor, and their costly investments in the presence of the distortion reduce job creation so that overall efficiency is lower than in the flexible economy.

We have assumed for our argument that matches are found at random. If firms could 'direct' their search more towards a specific pool of workers, it would be towards the more productive skilled workers, especially if the minimum wage is binding. A fall in the price of capital then would imply a different employment trend for skilled and unskilled workers in Germany compared with the US which is not supported empirically in our sample period 1975–91.

Importantly for the empirical application, costly search and matching implies interindustry wage differentials. The same worker can earn a different wage depending on the firm and industry. Search frictions imply imperfect labour mobility and impede factor-price equalization across industries. These more realistic implications of the model come at the cost of simplifications concerning the missing distinction between jobs and firms or an explicit modelling of sector-specific labour supply.

3. EMPIRICAL SPECIFICATION AND DATA

The theory and simple evidence reviewed in the previous section indicate that, in frictional labour markets, cheaper capital prices can induce a smaller increase of the wage differential in Germany than in the US if institutions (which induce wage floors) encourage employers to invest in equipment that is complementary to unskilled labour.

In this section, we proceed to seek more formal and detailed support for this prediction using industry-level data on skill-wage differentials and capital–labour ratios for the US and Germany. We estimate the different degree of complementarity between capital and unskilled labour in the two *countries*, exploiting data variation across *industries* and *time*. Variation across time is essential since our hypothesis is that the interaction of a time change (the fall of the price in capital) and country differences (labour market institutions that induce a wage floor) cause the different degree of complementarity between capital equipment and worker skill types. Industry variation is useful because the effect of labour market institutions and the fall of the price of capital can be expected to differ across them.

The ideal data would allow us to combine information on the skills and type of equipment capital of a worker. Unfortunately it is impossible to tell which (skilled or unskilled) workers use each piece of equipment in each industry. Under the maintained hypothesis, however, that technology is the same (for each industry) in the two countries, and to the extent that wages contain information on workers' productivity, standard production-function relationships between factor quantities and prices allow to infer whether changes in capital intensity influence the productivity of skilled and unskilled workers differently in the two countries.

In our specifications, we control for unobserved time-invariant differences across industries and countries as well as industry-specific linear time trends. These trends control for time changes of omitted variables like biased changes in technology within industries (as is suggested by the more formal expressions for the specifications in Box 1). Since these trends may pick up a lot more than technology, such as changes in demand conditions or price and cost shocks, we will report results using R&D as an alternative observable measure of technology (see Table 4 in Section 4 below).

Box 1. Econometric specifications

Specification 1. The first specification approximates the relationship between the skill premium, skill intensity and capital equipment which is implied by a nested CES production function (Acemoglu, 2002, and Krusell *et al.*, 2000). Assume that the production function uses capital K, skilled labour H and unskilled labour L so that:

$$F(K, H, L) = \left[\lambda \left[\mu (A_k K)^\rho + (1 - \mu)(A_h H)^\rho \right]^{\frac{\sigma}{\rho}} + (1 - \lambda)(A_l L)^\sigma \right]^{\frac{1}{\sigma}}$$

The skill premium is then:

$$\frac{w_h}{w_l} = \frac{\lambda (1 - \mu)(A_h H)^{\rho-1} \left[\mu (A_k K)^\rho + (1 - \mu)(A_h H)^\rho \right]^{\frac{\sigma-\rho}{\rho}}}{(1 - \lambda)(A_l L)^{\sigma-1}}$$

Since the elasticity between unskilled labour and capital is $1/(1 - \sigma)$ and the elasticity between skilled labour and capital is $1/(1 - \rho)$, capital is more complementary to skilled than unskilled labour if $\sigma > \rho$. In this case, the skill premium increases if firms employ more capital as:

$$\partial\left(\frac{w_h}{w_l}\right)/\partial K > 0 \ \text{ if } \ \sigma > \rho$$

If we assume that the same production function applies in each industry i in country c, we can approximate the skill premium at time t as a function of capital and the skill intensity:

$$\ln\left(\frac{w_h}{w_l}\right)^c_{it} = a^c_i + \gamma^c_1 \ln\left(\frac{H}{L}\right)^c_{it} + \gamma^c_2 \ln(K)^c_{it} + \gamma^c_3 \ln\left(\frac{A_h}{A_l}\right)^c_{it}$$

The coefficient of interest is γ^c_2, which indicates the degree of complementarity between capital and skilled labour. Under the assumption that the US and Germany have the same technology for each industry, our hypothesis that capital is more complementary to unskilled labour in Germany than in the US corresponds to $\gamma^{US}_2 > \gamma^{GER}_2$.

This specification implies permanent differences a^c_i across industries. This assumption is difficult to defend in a neoclassical model but can be more easily motivated by a search and matching framework in which costly search frictions prevent factor-price equalization across industries (see Section 2.3).

Several concerns arise in estimating the specification above, which we discuss further in the paper. The first concern is the measurement of the technology changes $(A_h/A_l)^c_{it}$. We proxy these by using industry-specific linear trends in all specifications and in Table 4 we report results using R&D as an alternative observable measure of technology. The second concern is the measurement of skills and capital so that we provide robustness checks using different measures in Section 4. See also the description of the measures in the data section, Section 3.1. The third concern is the endogeneity of the skill intensity and capital–labour ratio which we discuss further in Section 4 when we present the results.

Specification 2. The second specification is based on a trans-log cost function C with two variable factors, skilled labour H and unskilled labour L for industry i in country c and year t:

$$C\left[\log(w_h)^c_{it}, \log(w_l)^c_{it}, \log(K)^c_{it}, \log(y)^c_{it}, A^c_{it}\right]$$

where w_h, w_l are the wages of the skilled and unskilled, and y denotes value added. Capital intensity K and technology A are quasi-fixed factors. From Sheppard's lemma it follows that the cost share of unskilled labour in the wage bill is:

$$\left(\frac{w_l L}{w_h H + w_l L}\right)^c_{it} = \alpha^c_i + \beta^c_1 \ln\left(\frac{w_h}{w_l}\right)^c_{it} + \beta^c_2 \ln(K)^c_{it} + \beta^c_3 \ln(y)^c_{it} + \beta^c_4 A^c_{it}$$

> The equation for the share of H is redundant because the cost shares sum to unity. If $\beta_2^c > 0$, capital and unskilled labour are complementary. The hypothesis that wage-compressing labour market institutions in Germany induce investment in capital equipment which is more complementary to unskilled labour than in the US is a test of $\beta_2^{GER} > \beta_2^{US}$.
>
> As in specification 1 we include industry fixed effects to control for time-invariant unobserved differences across industries and countries, and industry-specific linear trends to proxy changes in technology. The same estimation issues of endogeneity and measurement arise (as for specification 1) which will be discussed further in Section 4 and in the data section, Section 3.1.

The differences in the degree of capital–skill complementarity in the US and Germany are thus estimated by using time variation that remains after controlling for linear time trends within industries. We argue that the different estimates of capital–skill complementarity for the US and Germany are due to interactions between (rather persistent) differences in labour market institutions and cheaper capital. As we discuss further in Section 5, however, we will not be able to rule out completely that the estimates are affected by changes of other country-specific factors. As an attempt to check the importance of labour market institutions for our results, we use available measures of institutions that vary over time (but not across industries) in each country. If the differences in the estimates of capital–skill complementarity are due to changes in labour market institutions in the US and Germany, we expect that the difference in the estimates becomes less significant if we include measures for institutions in our specifications. We have also tried to add interactions of these measures with the (price of) capital equipment to gauge the importance of the interaction directly. The limited sample size and variation, however, prevented us from estimating these interactions with enough precision.

We estimate two specifications that relate employment, capital, and wages (see also Box 1). The first specification can be derived from standard profit-maximizing behaviour of neoclassical firms, as in Section 2.1, and focuses on the relationship between skill premia and capital equipment (for US evidence based on aggregate data see Krusell *et al.*, 2000; Acemoglu, 2002). Estimating this specification with industry-level data is consistent with a search-and-matching model in which skill premia may differ across industries because of costly frictions. The second specification is based on cost mini-mization and relates labour shares (compounding wages and employment) to capital equipment (for example, Machin and van Reenen, 1998). In both specifications, the coefficient estimate of capital equipment allows us to infer the degree of capital–skill complementarity in each of the two countries.

In the first specification, a positive coefficient of the capital–labour ratio indicates complementarity between capital equipment and skilled labour. The prediction that capital is more complementary to unskilled labour in Germany than in the US corresponds to the test that the coefficient of the capital–labour ratio is *smaller* in Germany than in the US.

The second specification links the share in labour costs of *unskilled* workers to the capital–labour ratio. In this case a positive coefficient of the capital–labour ratio indicates complementarity between capital equipment and *unskilled* labour. The prediction that capital is more complementary to unskilled labour in Germany than in the US corresponds to the test that the coefficient of the capital–labour ratio is *larger* in Germany than in the US.

3.1. Data

In this subsection we mention how we construct the data used for the analysis and briefly describe some of the variables before we provide the results of the estimations in the next section.

3.1.1. Equipment capital.
We use data on capital equipment from the national accounts (Bureau of Economic Analysis and Statistisches Bundesamt, respectively). We construct the stock of capital equipment for Germany using the series on gross capital equipment formation and applying the perpetual inventory method. Capital equipment in both countries is deflated with the chain-price indices provided by the respective statistical office. Since these price deflators have been criticized for their accuracy, we check the robustness of our results below using an alternative deflator provided by Cummins and Violante (2002). As adjustment of capital equipment takes time and we are interested in the medium and low-frequency variation of the data, we use three-year averages and check robustness of the results for five-year averages. This also helps us to reduce problems of measurement error in the data for higher frequencies.

3.1.2. Wages and employment by skill type.
Wages and employment by skill and industry are constructed using CPS data (May surveys and Outgoing Rotation Group) for the US and the dataset on the social-security records from the Institut für Arbeits- und Berufsforschung (IAB) for Germany. For both countries our sample includes employees in full-time employment, age 20–60 with potential labour market experience up to 39 years. In the German IAB dataset we only use the information on West Germany and drop all East German observations after 1990. We prefer to omit later years in our estimations since disentangling East and West German data is not straightforward for all variables. Thus, in the estimations the sample period is 1975–91. Note further that the CPS is a representative sample of all employees whereas the IAB dataset is a 1% random sample of employees with a social-security record.

We define skilled workers as those with at least some college in the US and at least *Abitur* (high-school degree) in Germany. This educational skill measure achieves some comparability (if imperfect) across the two countries because 13 years of schooling imply a high-school degree in Germany and some college in the US. All those with less education in the respective country are classified as unskilled. Although Fitzenberger *et al.* (2005) find evidence of under-reporting for higher education degrees in the IAB data, they show that these measurement issues are not important when they estimate the college premium, controlling for other worker characteristics like gender and experience in Mincer-type wage regressions. We find that our results are robust when we use the college premium obtained from such regressions which control for some observable worker heterogeneity (see Table 3 in Section 4 below).

One major issue is to compare skills across countries. Our skill measure implies that the skill *ratio* (H/L) is much smaller in Germany, with an average of 0.05 across industries, than in the US, with an average of 0.5 (see also the industry averages in Tables A1 and A2). The main reason is that the education system in the US and Germany is very different. The German education system is a two-tier system in which vocational training is important to enter many occupations. Only those who intend to go to college obtain a formal high school degree (*Abitur*). Thus, a high school degree is not as prevalent in Germany as in the US and approximately 60% of the working population in Germany between 1975 and 1991 had only a vocational degree. Hence, we also construct two alternative skill measures for Germany. One can be considered an upper bound and includes all employees with a vocational degree in the skilled group. In this case the sample average of the skill ratio is 2.43 (see Table A2, third column). Since this skill ratio is substantially higher than in the US, we also construct an alternative measure where we only include in the skilled group those workers with a vocational degree who are in a white-collar position (*Angestellter*). These vocational degrees should be most comparable to college education in the US. With this skill measure the resulting average skill-ratio for Germany is 0.68 and more similar to the US (see Table A2, fourth column). However, the skill ratio is still quite high in Germany in some industries. For example, the skill ratio is 3.91 in the banking and insurance sector which has a lot of white-collar workers. Because of these measurement problems we will check the robustness of our results for all of the three measures.

We prefer the education-based measure of skills since it measures the level of general human capital. The other measures contain more firm-specific skills acquired through vocational training, and are more likely to be endogenous in our application: a firm can make a worker more productive with equipment capital or firm-specific training. Of course, as Acemoglu and Pischke (1999) point out, the same applies to general training if minimum wages are binding but we suspect the endogeneity problem to be less severe for a measure of general skills. We suspect that few (if any) workers are classified as having a high-school degree or some college in Germany just because firms have subsidized their general education due to wage compression.

3.1.3. R&D intensity.   We proxy changes in technology by industry-specific linear trends in our econometric specification. As an alternative observable measure for technology we also use the R&D intensity in Section 4. The R&D intensity is defined as R&D expenditure divided by value added. Value added is taken from the 60-Industry Database available online at the Groningen Growth and Development Centre. The data on R&D expenditure are from the Stan-Anberd database provided by the OECD. An obvious criticism of the OECD measure is that it need not be related to technology improvements in the same industry and country. As an alternative, we construct a measure of technology change embodied in one important input, capital equipment. This variable is based on data by Wilson (2002) who combines data on R&D expenditure for capital equipment goods with data on capital equipment inputs by industry.

3.1.4. Descriptive statistics.

Tables A1 and A2 display the averages of the main variables of interest: the wage differential, skill intensity and capital equipment per worker. Besides reporting the averages for each industry in the 1970s, we compute the three-year average percentage changes in the sample period. Tables A1 and A2 show that while the skill intensity has increased in all industries in both countries, the skill premium has increased in the US but has remained stable in Germany. Equipment capital per worker has increased in all industries but one in Germany and eight in the US. In most industries capital equipment per worker has increased at a higher rate in Germany than in the US.

4. RESULTS

Table 2, panel A, presents the results of the first specification that relates the skill premium to the capital–labour ratio. Panel B presents the results of the regression of the share of unskilled labour in the wage bill on the capital–labour ratio. The coefficients are estimated on the full sample of 20 industries in the US and West Germany in the period 1975–91. All specifications include industry fixed effects to control for unobservable heterogeneity and industry-specific trends to proxy for changes in technology. All observations in the regressions are weighted by industry employment.

The robust finding in panel A is that capital equipment and the skill premium are less positively associated in West Germany than in the US. Consistently with our hypothesis we find that capital is more complementary to unskilled labour in Germany, that is, the point estimate of capital equipment for Germany is smaller.

One concern in our estimations is the endogeneity of the skill intensity. This endogeneity could arise if the supply of skills responds to the skill premium. Endogeneity is a concern for us only if it biases the coefficient estimate of capital equipment which is our main interest. To assess the sensitivity of our results we estimate specifications with and without skill intensity. We exclude the skill intensity in columns (1a) and (2a). The results show that a 1% increase in capital equipment per worker is associated with an increase of the skill premium of 9 basis points in the US and with a statistically insignificant decrease of the skill premium in Germany. These results

Table 2. Estimation results for the skill premium and unskilled-labour share as a function of capital equipment per worker

Panel A: Dependent variable is the log-skill premium

Independent variables	Benchmark specification without skill intensity		Benchmark specification		Benchmark specification with institutions	
	US (1a)	Germany (2a)	US (3a)	Germany (4a)	US (5a)	Germany (6a)
log(equipment capital per worker)	0.087 (0.039)**	−0.039 (0.025)	0.091 (0.042)**	−0.032 (0.025)	0.046 (0.044)	−0.028 (0.023)
log(skill intensity)			−0.019 (0.070)	−0.108 (0.063)*	0.026 (0.065)	−0.101 (0.058)*
union density					0.313 (0.589)	1.814 (0.454)***
minimum wage					−0.474 (0.152)***	
Adjusted R-squared	0.9614	0.9341	0.9610	0.9356	0.9676	0.9460

Panel B: Dependent variable is the share of unskilled labour in the wage bill

Independent variables	Benchmark specification without skill premium		Benchmark specification		Benchmark specification with institutions	
	US (1b)	Germany (2b)	US (3b)	Germany (4b)	US (5b)	Germany (6b)
log(equipment capital per worker)	−0.073 (0.019)***	−0.001 (0.005)	−0.057 (0.017)***	−0.004 (0.005)	−0.058 (0.019)***	−0.002 (0.005)
log(value added)	−0.005 (0.018)	−0.003 (0.013)	−0.009 (0.016)	0.002 (0.013)	−0.020 (0.018)	−0.014 (0.013)
log(skill premium)			−0.204 (0.044)***	−0.057 (0.019)***	−0.233 (0.050)***	−0.081 (0.020)***
union density					−0.129 (0.267)	0.291 (0.098)***
minimum wage					−0.037 (0.068)	
Adjusted R-squared	0.9929	0.9957	0.9944	0.9961	0.9944	0.9965

Notes: Estimated with ordinary least squares using 120 observations for 20 industries based on three-year averages 1970–91 in both countries. All regressions include industry dummies and industry-specific time trends for each country. Observations are weighted by employment in each industry. Standard errors in parentheses. See the notes of Table 1 and the Web Data Appendix for further details. * 10%; ** 5%; *** 1% significance level.

Source: Authors' calculations.

are confirmed in our benchmark specification which includes the skill intensity in columns (3a) and (4a), suggesting that the possible endogeneity of the skill intensity does not bias the coefficient estimate of capital. Consistently with a downward sloping relative demand for skilled labour, the coefficient of the skill intensity is negative in both countries.

The theory we want to test implies that the differences in the degree of capital–skill complementarity across countries are due to labour market institutions. When laying out the econometric specification in Section 3, we have discussed one imperfect but informative way to assess the importance of changes in labour market institutions. Controlling directly for measures of labour market institutions which vary across time (but not across industries), we assess the importance of institutions for our results by checking whether the differences in the coefficient estimates of capital become less significant for both countries when we insert these measures in our specifications.

In columns (5a) and (6a) we include the OECD measures of the federal minimum wage and union density for the US and union density for Germany (Germany has no economy-wide minimum wage, minimum wages have only been introduced in some industries in the 1990s). The coefficient of the minimum wage in the US is negative and significant as expected. The coefficient of the union density in Germany, however, is positive and significant. This result is not necessarily opposite to the expected wage-compressing effect of more powerful unions across industries since the positive coefficient is estimated using only aggregate time variation in union density. More interestingly, the results show that the coefficient of capital becomes insignificant in the US once we control for institutions. This suggests that the coefficient in the benchmark specification (which excludes institutional measures) reflects the effect of time-varying institutions on the skill premium through capital investment. Getting more directly at the effect of the interaction of *persistent* differences of labour market institutions across countries and the change in the price of capital is more challenging and the limited variation in our data has not allowed us to estimate interaction terms with enough precision.

Although the coefficient estimates are not estimated precisely enough in some specifications to allow us to formally reject the hypothesis that the coefficients are the same in the US and Germany at standard significance levels, our evidence suggests that capital equipment is more complementary to unskilled workers in Germany than in the US. This result remains robust if we use capital equipment per worker *hour* to control for differences in hours worked across countries, time and industries.

The insignificance of the coefficient of capital in Germany may pose a concern about our interpretation of the coefficient on capital as a measure of complementarity between capital and skills. It could be that we find an insignificant coefficient because relative wages in Germany do not reflect relative productivities (for example because of institutional constraints) rather than because capital is more complementary to unskilled labour. This cannot explain, however, the *significantly* negative coefficient of capital equipment for Germany when we use alternative measures for skills (Table 3 below). Moreover, this concern should apply less to our specification with the unskilled labour share which we discuss next because this dependent variable combines wage and employment effects.

One remaining concern is that the capital–labour ratio is endogenous. Even after controlling for unobserved time-invariant differences across industries and linear industry-specific time trends, firms within an industry may change their capital in response to a change in the skill premium. Without a suitable source of exogenous variation that would allow us to instrument the capital–labour ratio, we cannot interpret the coefficients as causal. Endogeneity is more of a problem in this specification than in the next specification which *assumes* that capital is a quasi-fixed factor so that it is predetermined when firms decide about employment of skilled and unskilled labour. Obviously this assumption may be violated and the estimates below also have to be interpreted with care.

Panel B reports the results of the regression of the unskilled labour share on the capital intensity. These results provide even stronger evidence that equipment capital is more complementary to unskilled labour in Germany than in the US. Consistently with our hypothesis we find that the point estimate of capital equipment for Germany is larger in this specification. This is good news if one believes the assumption that capital is a quasi-fixed factor so that endogeneity is less of a concern.

Similar to Panel A we approach the issue of the possible endogeneity of the skill premium comparing the results including or excluding the skill premium from the estimated equation. The issue of endogeneity arises because changes in wages affect both the skill premium (the regressor) and the share of workers in the wage bill (the dependent variable). If we exclude the skill premium from the regression, the coefficients on capital intensity in columns (1b) and (2b) show that a 1% increase in capital intensity is associated with a reduction of the share of the unskilled in the wage bill of 7 basis points in the US. The association is insignificantly different from zero in Germany. These results indicate that unskilled labour and capital are substitutes in the US but much less so in Germany. The implied elasticity of substitution evaluated at the mean of the unskilled labour share is -0.104 in the US and -0.005 in Germany. These results are qualitatively robust to the inclusion of the skill premium (columns (3b) and (4b)) and suggest that endogeneity of the skill premium is not a serious issue for the estimation of the coefficient of capital.

Compared with the results of panel A, adding the measures of labour market institutions to the specification leaves the difference between the coefficients for the US and Germany nearly unchanged (columns (5b) and (6b)). In this case, time-variation of institutions does not matter for the different degree of capital–skill complementarity in the two countries. This does not exclude that interactions between (persistent differences in) labour market institutions and exogenous shocks (like the fall in the price of capital) matter for the different degree of capital–skill complementarity.

Concerning the control variables, value added is never significant in any of the regressions whereas the skill premium has the expected negative sign. The institutional variables are not significant for the US but the union density in Germany is positively related to the unskilled workers' share in the wage bill. This is more in line with the expected effect of more powerful unions compared with the results of panel A.

As a further robustness check for the results of both specifications in panels A and B, we dropped one industry at a time from our sample. We found that for both specifications the difference in the coefficients of capital equipment does not depend on a specific industry. Moreover, the results are robust to restricting the sample to the manufacturing sector and to using five-year averages (not reported). Finally, the adjusted R-squared statistic shows that our specifications explain most of the variation in the data.

Quantitative implications   To gauge the quantitative size of the association between capital equipment and the skill premium in West Germany, we use the predicted skill premium obtained from the benchmark regression specification in Table 2, column (4a). We compare these values with the predicted values obtained holding capital equipment per worker constant at the initial level in 1975. Taking the difference of these two measures of predicted skill premia at the end of the sample (1991), we find that the skill premium would have been about 5–8% higher in most industries in Germany had capital per worker remained unchanged at its value in 1975.

The industries where the accumulation of capital equipment per worker had the smallest effect on the wage differential are primary metals, utilities, business and personal services, and health services. The biggest effect of capital equipment per worker is in the banking sector where the wage differential would have been 33% higher had the capital–labour ratio stayed at the same level as of 1975.

Doing the same exercise for the US (on the basis of the coefficients in Table 2, column (3a)), we find that, had the capital–labour ratio not grown beyond its 1975 level, the skill premium would have been between 7 and 8% lower in important industries like machinery and retail than what was observed in 1991. Weighting the industry-specific results by valued added, we find an aggregate average change of 3%. This number is below the estimates presented in Krusell *et al.* (2000) who, in a similar exercise, use aggregate time-series data for the US and a different estimation method. One of the main differences is that we control for (industry-specific) time trends in our specification. Time trends are likely to be correlated with capital deepening at the industry level so that their inclusion in the regression changes the estimate of the capital coefficient. A linear time trend, for example, wipes out the significant effect of capital on the skill premium for aggregate data in the US (Acemoglu, 2002).[6] Hence, it is not surprising to find a smaller association of capital deepening and skill premia than Krusell *et al.* (2000) in our regressions which include linear industry-specific trends. Moreover, the differences in the degree of capital–skill complementarity between Germany and the US are robust to the inclusion of trends in our estimations.

[6] Acemoglu (2002), Table 2, finds that a 1% fall of the relative price of capital equipment is associated with a 0.323% increase of the college premium in a regression without a time trend. With a time trend this number falls to 0.051%.

Doing the same counterfactual exercise for the share of unskilled labour in the wage bill (on the basis of the coefficients in Table 2, columns (3b) and (4b)), we find that changes in capital equipment per worker have a negligible effect on the share of unskilled labour in Germany. In the US instead, the unskilled labour share would have been between 3 and 5% higher in the machinery and retail industries had capital equipment stayed at its level in 1975.

4.1. Robustness

We probe the robustness of the results across two dimensions. Regarding the definition of the skill premium and the unskilled labour share, we check robustness using two alternative measures for skills for Germany. Concerning the measurement of capital and technology, we construct two alternative measures for the capital stock and a measure for embodied R&D as proxy for process innovations.

4.1.1. Robustness of wage measures. The first two columns of Table 3, panels A and B, display the results for two alternative skill measures in Germany. As mentioned in the data section, Section 3.1.2, skill intensities are much lower in Germany than in the US if we define skilled workers as those workers with some college education. A common concern is that this is because workers without a high-school degree are of higher quality in Germany than in the US due to the important vocational training system (Nickell and Bell, 1996). Hence, we construct a first measure (columns (1a) and (1b)) which includes all employees with a vocational degree in the skilled group and can be considered an upper bound. The second skill measure (columns (2a) and (2b)) only includes those workers with a vocational degree in the skilled group who are in a white-collar position.

We find that in both specifications these alternative skill measures deliver even stronger support for the hypothesis of more complementarity of capital and unskilled labour in Germany. Equipment capital in Germany is negatively associated with the skill premium and positively associated with the share of the unskilled in the wage bill. In both specifications the coefficients are significant at least at the 5% level. These two alternative education-based skill measures have the drawback that the extent of vocational training may be itself endogenous to the institutional environment. Hence, we prefer the skill measure which we use in our benchmark specification.

Worker heterogeneity   As a further robustness check, we improve our measure of the wage differential exploiting the information in the CPS and IAB micro data sets to control for differences in worker characteristics such as gender and experience across industries. The wage differential is obtained by regressing log wages on a dummy for education (at least some college in the US and *Abitur* or more in Germany) controlling for experience, experience squared, gender and their interactions. The regression is run for each industry and year in the CPS and IAB data, respectively. We then keep the

Table 3. Robustness for different measures of the wage differential
Panel A: Dependent variable is the log-skill premium

Independent variables	Include vocationally trained in skilled group for Germany (two alternative measures)		College premium of Mincer-type wage regression	
	Germany (1a)	Germany (2a)	US (3a)	Germany (4a)
log(equipment capital per worker)	−0.022 (0.009)**	−0.030 (0.013)**	0.079 (0.035)**	−0.037 (0.023)
log(skill intensity)	−0.113 (0.027)***	−0.096 (0.034)***	0.018 (0.059)	−0.060 (0.057)
Adjusted R-squared	0.9898	0.9857	0.9344	0.9148

Panel B: Dependent variable is the share of unskilled labour in the wage bill

Independent variables	Include vocationally trained in skilled group for Germany (two alternative measures)		College premium of Mincer-type wage regression	
	Germany (1b)	Germany (2b)	US (3b)	Germany (4b)
log(equipment capital per worker)	0.018 (0.007)**	0.030 (0.009)***	−0.053 (0.012)***	−0.001 (0.002)
log(value added)	−0.006 (0.018)	−0.044 (0.023)*	−0.001 (0.011)	−0.002 (0.005)
log(skill premium)	0.067 (0.074)	−0.079 (0.067)	−0.428 (0.035)***	−0.063 (0.008)***
Adjusted R-squared	0.9960	0.9990	0.9955	0.9951

Notes: Standard errors in parentheses. * 10%; ** 5%; *** 1% significance level. The Mincer-type wage regressions in columns (3) and (4) are run for each industry and year in the CPS and IAB, respectively. The regressors are education and experience, experience squared, gender and their interactions. The coefficients of the education dummy are a measure of the education wage differential after controlling for the other variables. We use the inverse of the standard errors to weigh each obtained estimate. See the notes to Table 1 and the Web Data Appendix for further details.

Source: Authors' calculations.

coefficients of the education dummy as a measure of the college premium. We use the inverse of the standard errors to weigh each obtained estimate.

The results of both specifications in columns (3) and (4) in Table 3 indicate that controlling for observed worker heterogeneity leaves the results nearly unchanged with respect to the benchmark specification in Table 2, columns (3) and (4).

Overall the difference in the coefficients of capital equipment in Germany compared with the US is robust across regressions which are based on quite different skill measures. This gives us some confidence that the difficulties in comparing education-based skill measures between the US and Germany are not driving the results. We now investigate whether measurement of capital is important for our results.

4.1.2. Robustness of capital measures and embodied R&D.   Table 4 displays
the results for different measures of capital and embodied R&D. Since an appropriate
deflator of capital is notoriously hard to build, we first check the robustness of the
benchmark specification in Table 2, columns (3) and (4), by applying the capital–price
deflator provided by Cummins and Violante (2002). This deflator controls better for
quality adjustments and updates the price deflator for capital equipment in the US
constructed by Gordon (1990). Compared with the deflator of Cummins and Violante,
the deflator of the Bureau of Economic Analysis underestimates quality improvements and thus results in a slower decline of relative prices for capital equipment. We
apply the deflator of Cummins and Violante, available for 1975–99, to our measure
of capital in the US and Germany. The estimation results in Table 4, columns (1a)
and (2a), show that the capital equipment is no longer significantly positively associated with the skill premium in the US[7] but is still larger than the coefficient for
Germany which remains negative and is now significant at the 10% level. The results
for the share of unskilled labour in the wage bill are more robust for the US (see
columns (1b) and (2b)): capital equipment is negatively associated with the share of
unskilled labour in the wage bill in the US but not in Germany.

The RAS procedure   The construction of internationally comparable capital stocks requires
particular attention with respect to the use of comparable price deflators when
constructing capital from investment series and comparable depreciation rates and
lifetime periods for different equipment types.

We further investigate whether the different results for Germany are driven by composi-
tional effects in terms of different equipment types. We use information from the German
statistical office on capital formation for different equipment types to construct a time series
for capital equipment by investment good and industry, applying the so-called RAS procedure
(see the Web Data Appendix for a detailed description). This procedure allows us to apply
separate depreciation rates and price deflators for five different categories of equipment
goods, before we aggregate the series at the industry level. This way of constructing
the stock of capital equipment implies a growth rate in the stock of capital equipment
that is more than twice as high (see Sakellaris and Vijselaar, 2005, for similar results).

Using the new measure, the coefficient of capital equipment per worker turns
positive for Germany (see Table 4, column (3a)). The result is not robust, however,
if we use the capital equipment for communication technology in Germany (see
column (4a) where we lose some observations due to data availability). In this case
the coefficient returns to be negative and is significant at the 5% level.[8] Moreover,

[7] The lack of positive significance is not inconsistent with Krusell *et al.* (2000) since we have time trends in our specifications
which are correlated with capital deepening.

[8] Using the series for the other types of equipment, we do not find significant results. We also used the series on office machinery
and computers for Germany constructed by Falk and Koebel (2004): the coefficient of capital equipment per worker and the
corresponding standard error changes to −0.0254 (0.013) which is significant at the 10% level. This coefficient is less negative
than the coefficient of capital equipment in the benchmark specification of Table 2, column (4a).

Table 4. Robustness for different measures of capital and embodied R&D

Panel A: Dependent variable is the log-skill premium

Independent variables	Capital deflated with Violante and Cummins deflator		Capital calculated with RAS	Software capital calculated with RAS	Benchmark with embodied R&D instead of trends	
	US (1a)	Germany (2a)	Germany (3a)	Germany (4a)	US (5a)	Germany (6a)
log(equipment capital per worker)	-0.002 (0.044)	-0.040 (0.023)*	0.045 (0.013)***	-0.017 (0.008)**	0.032 (0.029)	-0.012 (0.030)
log(skill intensity)	0.037 (0.071)	-0.110 (0.062)**	-0.136 (0.059)**	-0.085 (0.063)	0.076 (0.045)	-0.024 (0.027)
log(embodied R&D)					0.058 (0.016)***	-0.002 (0.009)
Number of observations	120	120	120	106	72	72
Adjusted R-squared	0.9586	0.9368	0.9429	0.9581	0.9126	0.8782

Panel B: Dependent variable is the share of unskilled labour in the wage bill

Independent variables	Capital deflated with Violante and Cummins deflator		Capital calculated with RAS	Software capital calculated with RAS	Benchmark with embodied R&D instead of trends	
	US (1b)	Germany (2b)	Germany (3b)	Germany (4b)	US (5b)	Germany (6b)
log(equipment capital per worker)	-0.050 (0.017)***	-0.004 (0.004)	0.006 (0.003)*	0.0003 (0.002)	-0.042 (0.015)***	-0.0004 (0.011)
log(value added)	-0.005 (0.016)	-0.0004 (0.012)	-0.018 (0.013)	-0.007 (0.012)	-0.061 (0.010)***	-0.076 (0.010)***
log(skill premium)	-0.239 (0.044)***	-0.057 (0.019)***	-0.069 (0.020)***	-0.069 (0.025)***	-0.331 (0.068)***	0.062 (0.052)
log(embodied R&D)					-0.029 (0.008)***	0.008 (0.004)**
Number of observations	120	120	120	106	72	72
Adjusted R-squared	0.9942	0.9961	0.9963	0.9965	0.9786	0.9691

Notes: Standard errors in parentheses. * 10%; ** 5%; *** 1% significance level. Regressions in columns (1)–(4) include industry dummies and industry-specific trends. Regressions in columns (5) and (6) only include industry dummies. See the notes of Table 1 and the Web Data Appendix for further details.

Source: Authors' calculations.

the new measure is positively associated with the share of unskilled labour in the wage bill in Germany at a significance level of 10% (see column (3b)). If we use only capital equipment for communication technology, the coefficient remains positive but is no longer significant. Thus, whereas the association of the new measure with the skill premium gives mixed results, the coefficients on the association with the share of unskilled labour in the wage bill are more supportive for the hypothesis that capital equipment is more complementary to unskilled labour in Germany than in the US.

Embodied R&D   As mentioned when we discussed the econometric issues, approximating technology change with (industry-specific) time trends leaves much to be desired since it is unclear what the time trends really capture. In this section we use R&D as a more direct measure for technology change instead of the industry-specific time trends. The measure of R&D expenditure provided in the OECD STAN database captures expenses for all inputs (such as capital and labour) used for product as well as process innovations. These measures turn out not to be significant if added to the specifications (not reported). An obvious criticism of the OECD measure is that this R&D expenditure need not be related to technology improvements in the same industry and country. As an alternative measure we construct technology change embodied in one important input, capital equipment, for the manufacturing industries.

Wilson (2002) combines data on R&D expenditure for capital equipment goods provided by the National Science Foundation with data on capital equipment inputs by industry from the Bureau of Economic Analysis for the years 1973–97. This allows us to compute a measure of R&D embodied in the capital equipment per value added in each industry which is more likely to capture process innovations. Assuming that the R&D contained in capital goods is the same in the US and Germany, we use the different investment into capital equipment by good type and industry to construct the corresponding series for Germany. Columns (5a) and (6a) show that the coefficient for R&D embodied in capital equipment is positively and highly significantly associated with the skill premium for the US, reducing the size of the coefficient of capital equipment so that it is no longer significant. The coefficient of embodied R&D for Germany is negative but not significant. Moreover, R&D intensity embodied in capital equipment is negatively and significantly associated with the share of unskilled labour in the wage bill in the US but positively in Germany (see columns (5b) and (6b)).

Overall the results for alternative measures of capital equipment and embodied R&D in capital equipment suggest that the difference in the association with the skill premium and unskilled labour share in the US and Germany is very robust. The differences seem to stem from different types of capital investment in the US and Germany and thus also different technology improvements embodied in capital goods.

5. DISCUSSION

The empirical evidence presented above is consistent with our hypothesis that wage-compressing labour market institutions might have induced changes in capital equipment or embodied R&D which in turn have reduced the skill premium and increased the share of unskilled labour in Germany compared with the US in the period 1975–91.

Of course, the available data do not allow us to interpret the different coefficient estimates as causal. Since the US and Germany differ across many dimensions, one main concern is that the correlations reflect changes of other omitted variables which might cause both changes in the skill premium and capital equipment or R&D. For example, governments that regulate the labour market do also tend to regulate the product market or financial market. Then the estimated results could capture the effects of product or financial market institutions rather than of labour market institutions. In this case controlling for time-invariant differences across countries and industries would help little to distinguish the effect of different types of institutions. Institutions in product markets and financial markets, however, have become more similar in Germany and the US as both markets have been deregulated since the 1970s (see, for example, Alesina *et al.*, 2005). Labour markets instead have remained much more regulated in Germany. This is why we consider it more likely that the differences in the estimated coefficients on capital in the two countries (which remain after controlling for industry dummies and industry-specific time trends) capture the persistent differences of labour market institutions rather than the withering differences in product and financial market institutions (which are more likely to be accounted for by industry trends).

5.1. Employment trends versus investment patterns

We have argued that the different association between the skill premium and the capital–labour ratio in the US and Germany is due to different investment patterns in these countries (that is, we stress differences in the numerator rather than the denominator of the capital–labour ratio). We now try to distinguish the quantitative importance of changes in capital from changes in employment. While there is no strong evidence for different trends in the *composition* of employment across skills in the US and Germany in our sample period (see Table 1 and Beaudry and Green, 2003), *total* employment growth has been higher in the US than in Germany.

As a first rough assessment of whether these different employment trends are important, we do a simple statistical decomposition exercise. We apply the US employment growth rates to the German employment levels in 1975 for each industry. We then use this employment series to compute the counterfactual capital–labour ratio had Germany experienced the same employment performance as the US. Since the US has had a stronger employment performance than Germany, the counterfactual capital–labour ratio is smaller. Recall that the predicted values for the skill premium with the actual German capital–labour ratios imply a decrease of the wage differential of about 5–8% in most manufacturing industries (see Section 4 above). The predicted values for the skill premium using the *counterfactual* capital–labour ratio (holding the estimated coefficient constant), still imply a fall in the skill premium in Germany for 15 industries out of 20. The negative association between the capital–labour ratio and the skill premium does not vanish if we correct for the worse employment performance in Germany, suggesting that the differences in capital investment between the US and Germany are important. This relates to results of Beaudry and Green (2003) who find in a similar exercise that wages of the low educated workers would have been 17% lower had Germany experienced the US employment miracle, and 40% lower if Germany had also had the US capital accumulation.

5.2. Alternative explanations

In principle, all changes of omitted variables, which are correlated with capital investment and factor prices and are not captured by the linear trends, challenge our interpretation of the results. For example, differences in technology change that are not captured by the linear trends might explain our findings. Such differences across countries could arise, for example, because skills of workers in Germany are more specific than in the US. Krueger and Kumar (2004) have argued that growth differences between the US and Europe are explained by the higher degree of skill specificity in Europe.[9] In their model, more vocational training hampers technology adoption and, if technology change is skill-biased, this implies that the skill premium increases less in Europe than in the US. Slower technology adoption *per se*, however, cannot explain a negative correlation between the skill premium and capital equipment or embodied R&D in Germany which we find in most specifications. Moreover, the amount of vocational training might be related to wage compressing institutions, as firms can make workers more productive by giving them equipment and/or training them. To distinguish these two hypotheses further, one would need detailed data with a time series dimension and information on capital equipment and worker training.

Another view is that wage differentials in Germany are compressed because labour market institutions imply not only wage floors but also wage ceilings. In the latter case, however, the skilled would be paid below their marginal product and firms would appropriate all productivity increases. Therefore capital investment and technology change should be directed more towards skilled workers in Germany. As we have seen in Table 1, however, the striking difference in capital investment patterns between Germany and the US occurs in the unskilled labour intensive sectors. Moreover, wages of the very unskilled workers have fallen in the US since the 1970s (Acemoglu, 2002) whereas this has not been the case in Germany. Since both economies

---

[9] See also Gould *et al.* (2001) for a model with endogenous specific versus general skill accumulation to explain changes in wage inequality in the US.

are exposed to similar exogenous changes, this suggests that wage floors have prevented the wages of German unskilled workers from falling to levels that are as low as in the US.

Instead of the fall in the price of capital, an alternative exogenous driving force is more openness to trade, which occurred both in Germany and the US since the 1970s. Interactions of more openness with different labour market institutions can also explain the observed differences in the evolution of skill premia or labour shares and capital equipment. The consensus is that the direct effect of trade on skill premia, in flexible economies like the US, and employment, in more rigid countries like Germany, has been quantitatively small in our sample period 1975–91, although this debate is not completely settled. Interactions of openness and labour market institutions, however, are a plausible alternative explanation. A fall of the relative price of the unskilled labour intensive good caused by more openness to trade (especially with less developed countries) makes the minimum wage binding for firms producing that good, generating similar results as the fall in the price of capital discussed in this paper (Koeniger, 2006). Distinguishing these alternative explanations is challenging and requires much better data than we currently have, especially if one takes seriously the interactions between exogenous changes in prices (due to changes in technology or market structure), institutions and investment.

Finally, the larger increase of the capital–labour ratio in Germany compared with the US documented in Figure 2 could be explained by Germany converging towards the same balanced growth path as the US. This cannot easily explain, however, why at the same time the skill premia diverge in both countries and the larger increase of the capital–labour ratio occurs mostly in the (unskilled labour intensive) manufacturing industries which are already strong in Germany compared with the US.

6. CONCLUSIONS AND POLICY IMPLICATIONS

We have argued that capital deepening affects the evolution of the wage differential between skilled and unskilled workers differently in countries with different labour market institutions. If labour market institutions raise the wage of unskilled workers in Germany and frictions in the labour market make locating and hiring of workers costly, a fall in the price of capital can induce investment of firms into capital equipment that is more complementary to unskilled workers. Instead in the US, where wage floors are lower, firms invest more in high-skilled workers.

We have provided evidence consistent with this view based on an industry panel for West Germany and the US between the 1970s and 1990s. We have shown that capital equipment per worker is less positively associated with the skill premium in West Germany than in the US. Furthermore, capital investment tends to increase the share of unskilled labour in the labour cost in Germany but decreases it in the US. This descriptive evidence is robust to using alternative measures of capital and skills. Our descriptive evidence is not conclusive: more detailed firm-level data is needed to shed further light on the mechanism of how and why firms invest in unskilled workers in countries with stronger wage-compressing institutions. This would also allow to control further for changes in the composition of firms and workers over time.

Moreover, it would be interesting to extend the analysis to later years. Germany experienced a large increase in unemployment of unskilled workers in the 1990s which suggests that unskilled labour substitution has become more important. It would be interesting to investigate whether one can still detect more complementarity of capital and unskilled labour in Germany than in the US notwithstanding the big increase in unskilled unemployment after German reunification.

Our evidence has important policy implications. The debate on the role of institutions needs to consider the indirect effect of institutions on wage inequality due to distorted investment incentives. Our estimates imply that capital deepening in Germany in the 1980s is associated with a reduction in the skill premium of about 5–8% in most industries. In the US instead, capital deepening is associated with an increase of the wage differential between 7 and 8% in important industries like machinery and retail. Similarly, capital deepening in the 1980s is associated with a 3–5% lower share of unskilled labour in the wage bill in the US in the same sectors but there is no significant association in Germany. If we consider that at least some of this effect of capital is due to institutions, we have to reconsider the importance of institutions in the classic efficiency-equality trade-off. Institutions might have stronger effects on wage inequality than commonly perceived (if both the standard direct effect *and* the indirect effect through investment matter) and they distort investment decisions in favour of the unskilled. The investment distortions which boost the productivity of unskilled workers are no free lunch, however, and also imply lower employment. Hence, our findings also bear on the observed differences in the speed of structural change across developed countries (Rogerson, 2005). Since industries with low skill intensity in Germany invest relatively more and some of the service sectors like banking and insurance, business, personal or health services are skill intensive, the distorted incentives for capital investment in Germany may slow down the structural change from manufacturing industries towards services. Since most of the employment growth occurs in the service sector, these distortions may reduce employment growth, efficiency and income growth.

Since our results suggest that institutions induce higher investment complementary to unskilled labour in Germany, governments may be tempted to subsidize this investment in order to reduce the fall of firms' profits and the implied lower job creation. Policies that directly try to improve human capital at the bottom of the skill distribution, however, are more promising to reduce inequality in economic outcomes since they avoid the allocation and incentive distortions implied by subsidies in a second-best environment. An alternative would be to deregulate markets to reduce rents and mitigate the hold-up problem. More efficient financial markets would also allow workers to improve their productivity by paying for training out of their own pockets. However, more competitive markets at the same time make it more difficult to achieve distributional goals by institutional wage floors as labour and product demand become more elastic.

Discussion

Lans Bovenberg
Tilburg University, CentER, Netspar and CEPR

This paper combines two views on what lies behind the development of the skill premium. The literature has debated extensively whether institutional or technological factors are responsible for changes in wage inequality over time. This paper argues that institutions and technologies interact in determining the wage premium. The institutional setting affects the direction of technology and the nature of the capital–skill complementarity. In particular, institutions that compress wages result in less complementarity between capital investment and skill so that capital investment decreases rather than increases the skill premium. One thus cannot look at technology and institutions in isolation, but should explore the interaction between them.

This research also sheds a different light on the wage-compressing institutions in Europe. It is often argued that these institutions create more low-skilled unemployment and inactivity by pricing the low skilled out of the labour market. This paper argues instead that these institutions also encourage societies to invest more in low-skilled workers, thereby raising their productivity. Hence, wage-compressing institutions do not price low-skilled labour out of the labour market, but rather encourage employers to invest more in low-skilled workers. This is an important hypothesis, and if true, would have major consequences for how we should appreciate various European labour-market institutions that keep the wages of unskilled labour at high levels.

While I find the hypothesis intriguing, I am not yet convinced by the evidence in this paper that wage-compressing institutions would indeed invest low-skilled workers into the labour market rather than pricing these workers out of the labour market.

Do unskilled workers appropriate returns in the presence of wage floors?

Let me explain why, beginning with the analytical framework. The paper argues that minimum wages alleviate the hold-up problem associated with investments in physical capital. In the absence of minimum wages, workers tax away part of the benefits from investment. They do so by raising wage demands after firms have sunk their investments, thereby raising quasi rents from the employer-employee relationship. In the presence of binding minimum wages, in contrast, the model in the paper assumes that the benefits from investments accrue mainly to shareholders. The reason is that the wage remains at the binding wage and is thus not increased after investment has been sunk.

The presumption that employers enjoy all the benefits of investment in the presence of minimum wages relies on the strong assumption that the minimum wages do not affect the wage negotiations themselves. An alternative, more natural, assumption would be that the minimum wages affect the outside option of the workers. Indeed, wage floors in Germany are not the result of a legal minimum wage, which in fact does not exist, but rather of welfare benefits, which provide an outside option for workers. With welfare benefits determining the outside option for German workers, employers and employees negotiate over the quasi rents over and above the outside option of workers. Hence, workers are able to appropriate a share of the benefits of an investment – also in the presence of minimum wages. In fact, the empirical results show that investment in Germany does indeed raise unskilled wages. This shows that unskilled workers do indeed appropriate part of the benefits from investment. In fact, the empirical results suggest that German unskilled workers are more successful than US unskilled workers in appropriating the benefits from investment. Hence, the empirical results falsify the theoretical presumption that German labour-market institutions (including minimum wages) induce unskilled workers to expropriate a smaller part of the benefits of capital investments.

Substitution or complementarity?

The key policy question is whether higher wages for unskilled labour result in less low-skilled employment (as employers get rid of unskilled workers) or whether high labour costs induce firms to invest more in unskilled labour. The paper argues that German investment does not substitute for unskilled labour but rather augments the productivity of the unskilled.

In order to resolve the important issue whether high prices for unskilled labour cause less unskilled employment or upgrading of the productivity of the low skilled, I would encourage the authors to examine in their future work the volume of sectoral employment and output over time. Looking only at sectoral investment and wages is not enough to resolve whether capital investment is a substitute or complement to unskilled employment. For example, one would want to know whether the volume of employment of workers with little initial schooling is rising in sectors with high levels of capital investment. Indeed, it may well be that capital investments correlate with higher low-skilled wages because both investment and low-skilled wages are increased by early retirement schemes and active labour-market programmes that reduce the supply of low-skilled labour to a particular sector.

Indeed, in many European countries the unskilled workers in certain sectors were taken out of the labour market through disability or early retirement schemes in the period considered; many unskilled workers who were the victims of industrial restructuring were simply put in soft-landing schemes such as social insurance or early retirement schemes (i.e. hidden unemployment). In Germany, unemployment schemes have in fact acted as early retirement schemes, especially after the surge in unskilled unemployment following unification. Unfortunately, the study does not include the period since 1991, during which unskilled unemployment in Germany increased and the nature of capital investment changed as a result of the ICT revolution. This reduces the relevance of the study for modern economies in which ICT has not only fundamentally changed the nature of capital investment but has also weakened the position of older, low-skilled workers.

Another way through which governments try to depress the supply of unskilled labour is through training schemes and active labour-market policies. Indeed, an interesting hypothesis is whether wage-compressing institutions induce governments to invest more in education. Thus, whereas the paper argues that wage-compressing institutions induce firms to invest more in unskilled workers, I would expect that such institutions induce governments to do so. In this connection, it is of interest to note that the aggregate skill intensity of production rises more quickly in Germany than in the US (see the seventh and eighth column of Table 1 in the paper). Germany seems to be more successful in increasing the skill-intensity of production, both by training its workforce better and by taking unskilled workers out of the workforce through early retirement schemes and other soft-landing schemes.

Hold-up: labour-market institutions . . .

The theoretical model underlying the paper implies that minimum wages are the key determinant of the seriousness of the hold-up problem. Other labour-market institutions, however, are much more relevant in this context. For example, corporatist institutions that allow workers to delegate wage negotiations to unions alleviate the hold-up problem (see, e.g., Teulings and Hartog, 1998). Indeed, negotiations between long-lived unions and firms can help address contract incompleteness by making reputation considerations more important. This may explain why union density has in fact the wrong sign in the estimated equations for the skill premium.

Various other contractual arrangements (e.g. the length of employment and wage contracts) can also help address the hold-up problem. Whereas European economies rely on long-term implicit contracts to address the hold-up problem, the US relies more on competition and labour market mobility and flexibility to contain the search and transaction costs that give rise to hold up. By pointing mostly to binding minimum wages as the solution for the hold-up problem, the authors overstate the differences in efficacy in which Europe and the US address hold-up problems.

. . . and empirical proxies for them . . .

One of the basic problems of the empirical analysis in the paper is that it argues that labour-market institutions drive the different correlations between investment and wage inequality in Germany and the US, but that these labour-market institutions remain largely implicit in the paper. Put differently, the paper lacks institutional instruments for the endogenous capital–labour ratio at the right-hand side of regression. Indeed, one would need much more variation in labour-market institutions to test the hypothesis put forward in the paper. To illustrate, one would like to look at the variation of unionization, the nature of collective bargaining, employment protection and especially the replacement rates across sectors and time and explore whether capital–skill complementarity varies with these institutional variables. Also the nature of human capital is relevant in this context – particularly whether it is general or specific (i.e. whether labour is mobile across sectors or not).

If data on variation in sectoral institutions are not available, one might alternatively want to rely more on cross-country variation in institutions. The current paper does not exploit data on intersectoral variations in institutions and thus, in effect, relies on only two observations on institutions: Germany and the US. Indeed, in the current study, sectoral variation does not seem to help to identify the separate effects of capital–skill complementarity and skill-biased technological change: the difference in the coefficients for investment in the wage equations between the two countries is never statistically significant. The paper thus does not contain enough information to test its main hypothesis. What is needed in order to identify the effects the paper is after is either more detailed information on sectoral institutions or more cross-country variation.

... and capital-market institutions

Another important variable one would like to control for is the nature of capital and goods markets. Whereas the authors argue that product markets and financial markets have become similar during the period 1973–91, major differences remain during this period. In Germany, capital markets operate less efficiently, so that firms must rely mainly on internal and bank finance. Moreover, goods markets are less competitive in Germany, especially in non-traded sectors. Hence, high sectoral investment in Germany is likely to be correlated with high sectoral rents in less competitive sectors. These rents not only boost sectoral investment but also unskilled wages. In the US, in contrast, capital markets are likely to operate better, while goods market are more competitive. Hence, more investment occurs in new, innovative sectors employing more skilled labour. In this context, some more information on the types of investment in the two countries would be welcome. In any case, also here, one would like the authors to explore not only sectoral wages and investment but also other things such as the financial structure of the firms, the competitiveness of the markets these sectors operate on, and output in the various sectors. Indeed, one would like to have institutional variables as instruments for endogenous capital investment. These institutional instruments may work better than instruments for the labour market because exclusion restrictions are more likely to be met.

Empirical exercise: how to compare skills internationally?

One of the challenges facing the authors is to compare skills across countries. The authors employ initial education as a measure for skills. However, a possible response of employers to wage-compressing institutions is that they invest in training and raise the skills of workers, because wage costs do not rise much with skill.

Indeed, when workers with low skills are overpaid and workers with substantial skills are underpaid, employers face incentives to raise the skills of their workers. At the same time, they select those workers who can be trained. In view of these incentives to train and select employees, German unskilled workers who are employed are likely to be more skilled than the workers in the US who are classified as unskilled. It also suggests that initial training may not be a good indicator for skill, but that skill is endogenous. In any case, more attention to investment in human capital rather than physical investment is called for, although the separate impacts of these two types of investment may be difficult to identify if human capital and physical capital are complementary.

Another problem with the skill classification is that for the classification the authors prefer, only a very small portion of the German workforce of less than 10% is skilled, while in the US this percentage is 50%. This suggests that the unskilled in Germany are in fact on average more skilled than the American unskilled. Thus, the unskilled in the US seem to be a rather different category than the unskilled in Germany. Moreover, for the very large group of German unskilled, minimum wages seem to be relevant only for a small subgroup. When exploring the impact of minimum wages on unskilled employment, it would seem better to define the unskilled more narrowly, for example by confining attention to the lowest 20% of the skill distribution in both countries. My presumption would be that many of these individuals are in soft-landing schemes in Germany (disability, welfare, early retirement, unemployment without an obligation to apply for jobs), but in marginal employment in the US.

Conclusion

I like the idea that high minimum wages encourage societies to invest more in the unskilled so that their productivity matches at least the minimum wage. Whereas I believe there is certainly something in this hypothesis on a society-wide level, I am more sceptical about whether high minimum wages induce profit-seeking firms to invest more in low-skilled labour.

In any case, the empirical exercise in this paper does not have enough power to distinguish between the two main competing hypotheses about the impact of wage-compressing institutions – the one hypothesis being that these institutions price low-skilled workers out of the labour market and the alternative hypothesis being that these institutions induce employers to invest low-skilled workers into the labour market (by training workers, investing in complementary capital equipment or direct-ing technological change so as to make low-skilled workers more productive). We need more information on sectoral and especially cross-country employment and training performances and labour-market institutions to identify the causal relation-ship between, on the one hand, labour-market institutions and, on the other hand, the complementarity between capital and skill and the labour-market position of the unskilled.

Gilles Duranton
University of Toronto

Over the last 15 years, very few topics in the economic literature have received more attention than the rise in wage inequalities. Despite this, we are still very far from a consensus about what has really happened. This fine paper by Koeniger and Leonardi gives us some clues about why. It is also part of a new generation of work in the literature indicating what the road ahead for research on this topic may be made of.

To be more precise about wage inequalities, think of the following production function for 'aggregation unit' (sector, country, or both) i and year t:

$$y_{i,t} = Q_{i,t} F_{i,t} \left(A_{i,t}^k k_{i,t}, A_{i,t}^l l_{i,t}, A_{i,t}^h h_{i,t} \right) \tag{1}$$

where Q is the price of the final output, k is capital, l is unskilled labour, h is skilled labour and the As are technology shifters.

The first generation of work about wage inequalities in the early 1990s (e.g., Katz and Murphy, 1992) mainly provided a careful descriptive account of what happened during the 1970s and 1980s. Following this, the second generation of work during most of the 1990s carefully scrutinized four major possible explanations. At a time of increased trade openness with developing countries (and particularly China), factor price equalization was a strong candidate driver behind the widening wage gap. Unfortunately, the action on Q turned out to be too small to be more than an accessory part in the main plot. Changes on the supply side were also problematic. It is true that the supply of unskilled labour may have increased more in the US than in Continental Europe. However, the supply of skills probably increased together with their price in many developed countries. No simple theory about changes in the supply of k, l and h is able to replicate convincingly the evolution of wage inequalities in the US, let alone the diverging evolution between English-speaking countries and Continental Europe.

The last two contenders, institutions and technology, seemed more promising. The 1980s was a decade of considerable institutional turmoil particularly in the labour markets of the US and the UK (two countries were wage inequalities rose markedly). However, changes in the way the price of skilled and unskilled labour form also turned out to be a problematic explanation. Most of the action on the institutional front seems to be associated with the minimum wage. This raises two issues. First, the minimum wage is possibly only a channel through which some deeper forces percolate rather than a true driver of wage inequalities. Depending on the institutional setting, these deeper forces may lead to rising wage inequalities or rising unemployment. This was captured by Krugman's famous aphorism: 'Europe jobless, America penniless'. Second, institutional change could be endogenous. After all, these changes were accepted by the electorate in many countries.

In the era of massive computerization of the economy, skill-biased technological change (i.e., changes in the shifters A^k, A^l and A^l) quickly became the favourite explanation of many. Intuitively, changes at the workplace seemed big enough to explain the profound divergence between skilled and unskilled wages. Again, although there was some support in the data for skill-biased technological change, it was far from overwhelming. Since technology is not observable directly, skill-biased technological change might be invoked to explain *any* evolution. If the differential evolution of the technology shifters is not enough, one can always add changes in the degree of substitutability or complementarity between factors (i.e., changes in the coefficients of $F(.)$ or even a change of specification). One way to circumvent this last criticism is to argue that technology itself evolves endogenously. Making technology endogenous puts some bounds on its possible evolutions and limits the scope for *ad-hoc* explanations. Following the lead of Daron Acemoglu, an abundant theoretical literature was developed to look at how technology could evolve endogenously (Acemoglu, 2002).

The empirical consensus at the turn of the century was that all four families of explanations probably mattered. The strategy then became to try to quantify the relative importance of these explanations by pitching them against each other in the same empirical framework. Unfortunately, this type of exercise does not seem to lead to any consensus about the relative importance of the four main explanations. At the same time, the theoretical literature about endogenous technological evolutions started to make the case that technology could interact with the supply of factors, for instance, through the development of innovations that benefit particular factors depending on their relative supply. Technology may also interact with trade or institutions. Hence, the rising wage gap may not be about technology *versus* institutions but instead technology *and* institutions.

The paper by Koeniger and Leonardi is at the forefront of the empirical work that takes this suggestion seriously. Since no simple mono-causal approach appears to explain the bulk of the rising wage gap, it is only natural to consider more complex explanations relying instead on two factors. Koeniger and Leonardi consider what might be the simplest relevant model of institutions and biased technological change. For a worker of skill level h, the general production function (1) is simplified into

$$y_{i,t} = A(1 + g(k_{i,t}))h_{i,t}$$

where $g(k_{i,t}) = \alpha$ if $k_{i,t} \geq 1$ and zero otherwise. In this framework investment is obviously skill-biased because it multiplies the skills of the workers (by α). The maintained assumption is that the price of investment, P^k, declines over time – an empirically plausible case. Imagine now that this production function is embedded into a standard random search framework in which successful labour market matches lead to a split of the production surplus between the worker and the firm. In an economy like the US, a firm wants to invest when its share of the surplus exceeds the cost of investment, that is, when: $(1 - \beta)\alpha Ah \geq P^k$ where β is the share of the surplus that accrues to the worker. In this case, there is a time when firms in that country start investing to increase the productivity of their skilled workers but not that of their unskilled workers. This implies that the wage ratio (the wage of skilled workers divided by that of unskilled workers) increases by a factor of $1 + \alpha$. Consider now an economy like Germany with a minimum wage. When the minimum wage is not binding, the decision rule of firms is the same as in the US. When the minimum is binding, firms act as residual claimants for the entire surplus and invest when $\alpha Ah \geq P^k$. A straightforward comparison between the two investment rules shows that the skill threshold above which firms invest is lower when the minimum wage is binding.

This simple framework is consistent with a number of the facts presented by the authors about the relative evolutions of the wage gap in Germany and the US. Unfortunately, the framework also delivers some predictions for which the *prima facie* evidence is much weaker. First, with the continuing decline of the price of investment all workers should eventually benefit and the prediction is thus of a decline in wage inequalities in the US. Nobody really expects this any time soon. Furthermore, the possibility of making profitable investment to improve low skill productivity in Germany should imply that low-skill jobs should become relatively more profitable for firms. In turn, with the matching framework used here, this should have led to more unskilled job openings. Thus, the rate of unskilled unemployment in Germany should have declined relative to the US. Is it really the case? Finally, more investment in Germany should also imply a higher productivity growth than in the US. Did we really observe this?

It would be harsh to blame the authors for these counterfactual predictions. The reason is that several ingredients are required to replicate the facts. In turn, having more ingredients generates more predictions than the more economical models of the previous generation. Then, with a large number of predictions, it is always easy to find some that fail. Put differently, with rising wage inequalities, no simple explanation will do and more sophisticated stories inevitably runs into counterfactual predictions. It is unclear to me how this major problem will be solved.

Turning to the empirics of the paper, a strict reading of the model indicates that a lower cost of investing and institutions determine both investments and wages. Hence, full consistency with theory requires regressing wages and investment on the price of investment, the institutional setting, and some interactions between the two. This is not what the authors do. There are very good reasons for that. Regressing wages and investment on the price of investment and institutions looks like a hopeless task. Investment per worker is impossible to get in the data. Besides, the two explanatory variables are extremely hard to measure and may be simultaneously determined with the outcomes.

In their empirical work, the authors use a slightly different framework which relates the shares of skilled and unskilled labour in the wage bill, the wage ratio, productivity, output, and the capital stock. This type of specification raises insurmountable simultaneity problems so that the authors finally end up regressing wages on the capital per worker, the skill intensity, and some measures of institutions across sectors for both Germany and the US. Put differently, they look for differences in the coefficient on capital across Germany and the US. This is arguably rather far from the initial theoretical specification (which assumes that technology is the same everywhere). Again, it would be harsh to hold this too much against the authors. The general issue behind this is that looking at institutions or technology was already hard enough when each was considered in isolation. Looking at the interactions between institutions and technology raises very serious empirical difficulties that we may not be able to solve.

The findings of Koeniger and Leonardi are suggestive that something may be happening at the interface between technology and institutions. This is an important conclusion. The case that institutions and technology matter 'together' is very useful to rationalize crucial stylized facts relating to the evolution of the wage gap across countries. On the other hand, the analysis of Koeniger and Leonardi is also suggestive that the technology–institutions interaction may not be the main driving force behind the evolution of US wage inequalities. This may be due to the specification chosen by the authors and measurement problems in the data. Better specification and better data may give better results. Alternatively, the technology and institution nexus may only be yet another small part of the overall story. The complete version of the wage inequality evolution may also require thinking about trade and supply changes as well. Allowing for all those things to interact with one another is a nice suggestion. Nonetheless, the interaction between technology and institutions is already at the limit of what we can deal with (or even beyond this limit). Allowing for more sophisticated frameworks may not be manageable. This suggests a very though road ahead. Some creative ideas will be needed to make progress.

Panel discussion

The panel had mixed views on the general idea that binding minimum wages would induce training and investment. Rudolf Winter-Ebmer mentioned that microeconomic evidence does support the notion that binding minimum wages induce more training and more careful selection of workers, but Hans Werner-Sinn pointed out that in standard models higher wages decrease demand for complementary equipment, and that in Germany expensive unskilled labour does appear to be rather frequently unemployed at the same time as investment lags behind other OECD countries. The authors replied that while capital–labour substitution does play a role, empirically it may be outweighed by the non-standard mechanisms put forward by recent theoretical contributions. In the Germany–US empirical comparison, employment trends are rather similar across skill, at least in the available sample, and Germany does feature strong investment trends.

Several panelists thought that other data, if available, could be usefully analysed from the paper's perspective. Wendy Carlin suggested that the results of numeracy and literacy tests could provide alternative benchmarks to define skilled and unskilled labour. In particular, she cited a large difference in the ratios of the 95th and 5th percentile of test scores in Germany (1.7 : 1) than in the USA (2.7 : 1). Francesco Daveri mentioned that he would be interested to see analysis for Germany including the post-reunification period, which would cover changes in capital intensity associated with the IT revolution, and Hélène Rey wondered whether differential outsourcing of jobs could play a role over the more recent period.

APPENDIX

Table A1. Summary statistics for the US 1975–1991

Sector name	H/L in 1975–1991	3-year average %-change in (H/L)	wh/wl in 1975–1991	3-year average %-change in (wh/wl)	Equipment capital per worker in 1975–1991	3-year average percentage change in (equipment per worker)
Agriculture and Mining	0.505	0.063	1.329	0.026	191.421	−0.001
Construction	0.334	0.062	1.165	0.022	60.740	−0.142
Wood	0.234	0.052	1.425	0.009	15.056	−0.068
Stone, Clay etc.	0.263	0.094	1.453	0.007	22.474	−0.040
Primary Metals	0.350	0.052	1.253	0.030	76.185	0.009
Machinery	0.536	0.115	1.365	0.034	35.801	0.076
Electrical Machinery	0.515	0.125	1.553	0.036	24.623	0.126
Transport Equipment	0.459	0.121	1.289	0.032	43.186	0.005
Professional Goods	0.558	0.130	1.778	−0.006	8.217	0.237
Food and Tobacco	0.333	0.053	1.331	0.031	41.134	0.046
Textiles	0.138	0.119	1.811	0.0003	24.181	−0.018
Paper and Printing	0.549	0.086	1.326	0.009	52.057	0.021
Chemicals and Petroleum	0.818	0.089	1.505	0.013	86.439	0.002
Plastic and Leather	0.221	0.123	1.467	0.030	26.959	−0.060
Transport and Communication	0.523	0.113	1.147	0.018	326.717	−0.077
Utilities	0.538	0.118	1.226	0.016	132.994	0.014
Wholesale and Retail	0.570	0.052	1.377	0.014	109.663	0.062
Banking and Insurance	1.143	0.073	1.628	0.004	110.845	0.109
Business and Personal Services	0.581	0.091	1.515	0.019	168.297	−0.080
Health Services	0.913	0.118	1.708	0.013	21.380	0.076
Total	0.504	0.092	1.433	0.018	78.918	0.015

Notes: Authors' calculations based on the data described in the Web Data Appendix. The total is the arithmetic mean across industries.

Table A2. Summary statistics for West Germany 1975–1991

Sector name	H/L in 1975–1991	3-year average %-change in (H/L)	H/L (vocational) in 1975–1991	H/L (vocational, white-collar) in 1975–1991	wh/wl in the 1975–1991	3-year average %-change in (wh/wl)	Equipment capital per worker in 1975–1991	3-year average percentage change in (equipment per worker)
Agriculture and Mining	0.027	0.114	1.268	0.145	1.413	−0.017	124.211	0.075
Construction	0.024	0.082	3.526	0.141	1.372	−0.005	61.504	0.068
Wood	0.014	0.153	1.683	0.176	1.341	−0.007	8.817	0.079
Stone, Clay etc.	0.030	0.105	1.095	0.210	1.366	−0.006	25.666	0.143
Primary Metals	0.040	0.077	1.366	0.262	1.361	0.001	102.068	0.014
Machinery	0.054	0.128	3.597	0.411	1.287	−0.002	51.917	0.114
Electrical Machinery	0.092	0.153	1.478	0.444	1.439	−0.003	72.145	0.119
Transport Equipment	0.044	0.127	2.516	0.294	1.294	0.005	56.596	0.159
Professional Goods	0.039	0.177	1.658	0.320	1.424	−0.001	13.013	0.099
Food and Tobacco	0.018	0.135	2.010	0.431	1.458	0.002	65.275	0.083
Textiles	0.017	0.142	0.924	0.204	1.572	−0.014	21.314	0.137
Paper and Printing	0.027	0.165	1.547	0.256	1.310	−0.006	38.192	0.142
Chemicals and Petroleum	0.082	0.127	1.604	0.486	1.316	−0.006	101.087	0.045
Plastic and Leather	0.018	0.225	0.838	0.218	1.576	−0.018	17.607	0.154
Transport and Communication	0.027	0.157	2.166	0.346	1.223	0.002	169.799	0.068
Utilities	0.081	0.096	5.058	0.595	1.229	−0.006	126.320	−0.042
Wholesale and Retail	0.038	0.123	4.309	1.575	1.350	−0.001	104.728	0.091
Banking and Insurance	0.087	0.219	5.264	3.906	1.205	−0.022	131.310	0.182
Business and Personal Services	0.164	0.092	3.570	1.210	1.509	0.001	60.920	0.037
Health Services	0.090	0.107	3.185	1.939	1.444	0.004	68.748	0.025
Total	0.051	0.135	2.433	0.678	1.374	−0.005	71.062	0.090

Notes: Authors' calculations based on the data described in the Web Data Appendix. The total is the arithmetic mean across industries.

WEB APPENDIX

Available at http://www.economic-policy.org

REFERENCES

Abraham, K. and S. Houseman (1995). 'Earnings inequality in Germany', in R.B. Freeman and L.F. Katz (eds.), *Differences and Changes in Wage Structures*, University of Chicago Press, Chicago.

Acemoglu, D. (2002). 'Technical change, inequality, and the labor market', *Journal of Economic Literature*, 40, 7–72.

— (2003). 'Cross-country inequality trends', *Economic Journal*, 113, F121–49.

Acemoglu, D. and J.-S. Pischke (1999). 'The structure of wages and investment in general training', *Journal of Political Economy*, 107, 539–72.

Acemoglu, D. and J.-S. Pischke (2003). 'Minimum wages and on-the-job training', in S.W. Polachek (ed.), *Research in Labor Economics*, 22, 159–202.

Alesina, A., S. Ardagna, G. Nicoletti and F. Schiantarelli (2005). 'Regulation and investment', *Journal of the European Economic Association*, 3, 791–825.

Beaudry, P. and D.A. Green (2003). 'Wages and employment in the United States and Germany: What explains the difference', *American Economic Review*, 93, 573–602.

Blanchard, O. (1997). 'The medium run', *Brookings Papers of Economic Activity*, 2, 89–157.

— (2006). 'European unemployment: the evolution of facts and ideas', *Economic Policy*, 21, 5–59.

Blau, F.D. and L.M. Kahn (1996). 'International differences in male wage inequality: Institutions versus market forces', *Journal of Political Economy*, 104, 791–837.

Caballero, R.J. and M.L. Hammour (1998). 'The macroeconomics of specificity', *Journal of Political Economy*, 106, 724–67.

Caselli, F. (1999): 'Technological revolutions', *American Economic Review*, 89, 78–102.

Cummins, J. and G.L. Violante (2002). 'Investment-specific technical change in the United States (1947–2000): Measurement and macroeconomic consequences', *Review of Economic Dynamics*, 5, 243–84.

Falk, M. and B. Koebel (2004). 'The impact of office machinery, and computer capital on the demand for heterogeneous labour', *Labour Economics*, 11, 99–117.

Fitzenberger, B., A. Osikominu and R. Völter (2005). 'Imputation rules to improve the education variable in the IAB employment subsample', ZEW Discussion Paper. No. 05-10.

Gordon, R. (1990). *The Measurement of Durable Good Prices*, University of Chicago Press, Chicago.

Gould, E., O. Moav and B.A. Weinberg (2001). 'Precautionary demand for education, inequality, and technological progress', *Journal of Economic Growth*, 6, 285–315.

Hornstein, A., P. Krusell and G.L. Violante (2005): 'The effects of technical change on labor market inequalities', in P. Aghion and S.N. Durlauf (eds.), *Handbook of Economic Growth*. Vol. 2, ch. 20, North-Holland, Amsterdam.

Katz, L.F. and K.M. Murphy (1992). 'Changes in relative wages, 1963–87: Supply and demand factors', *Quarterly Journal of Economics*, 107 (February), 35–78.

Koeniger, W. (2006). 'Openness, wage floors and technology change', *Berkeley Electronic Press, Contributions to Macroeconomics*, forthcoming.

Koeniger, W., M. Leonardi and L. Nunziata (2006). 'Labor market institutions and wage inequality', *Industrial and Labor Relations Review*, forthcoming.

Krugman, P. (1994). 'Past and prospective causes of high unemployment', *Economic Review*, Federal Reserve Bank of Kansas City, 4, 23–43.

— (1995). 'Growing world trade: Causes and consequences', *Brookings Papers on Economic Activity*, 1, 327–77.

Krueger, A.B. and J.-S. Pischke (1998). 'Observations and conjectures on the U.S. employment miracle', in *Public GAAC Symposium: Labor Markets in the USA and Germany*, German-American Academic Council, Bonn, 99–126.

Krueger, D. and K.B. Kumar (2004). 'Skill-specific rather than general education: A reason for US-Europe growth differences', *Journal of Economic Growth*, 9, 167–207.

Krusell, P., L.E. Ohanian, J.-V. Rios-Rull and G.L. Violante (2000). 'Capital-skill complementarity and inequality: A macroeconomic analysis', *Econometrica*, 68, 1029–53.

Leonardi, M. (2006). 'Firm heterogeneity in capital-labor ratios and wage inequality', *Economic Journal*, forthcoming.

Machin, S. and J. van Reenen (1998). 'Technology and changes in skill structure: Evidence from seven OECD countries', *Quarterly Journal of Economics*, 113, 1215–44.

Moaz, Y.D. and O. Moav (2004). 'Social stratification, capital-skill complementarity, and the non-monotonic evolution of the education premium', *Macroeconomic Dynamics*, 8, 295–309.

Neumark, D. and W. Wascher (2001). 'Minimum wages and training revisited', *Journal of Labor Economics*, 19, 563–95.

Nickell, S. and B. Bell (1996). 'Changes in the distribution of wages and unemployment in OECD countries', *American Economic Review, Papers and Proceedings*, 86, 302–308.

Pischke, J.-S. (2005). 'Labor market institutions, wages and investment: Review and implications', *CESifo Economic Studies*, 51, 47–75.

Rogerson, R. (2005). 'Structural transformation and the deterioration of European labor market outcomes', Arizona State University, *mimeo*.

Sakellaris, P. and F. Vijselaar (2005). 'Capital quality improvement and the sources of economic growth in the Euro area', *Economic Policy*, 20, 267–306.

Teulings, C.N. and J. Hartog (1998) *Corporatism or Competition? Labour Contracts, Institutions and Wage Structures in International Comparison*, Cambridge University Press, Cambridge.

Wilson, D.J. (2002). 'Is embodied technology the result of upstream R&D? Industry-level evidence', *Review of Economic Dynamics*, 5, 285–317.

Age, seniority and labour costs

SUMMARY

The bad labour market performance of the workforce over 50 indicates that an aged workforce is often a burden for firms. Our paper seeks to investigate whether and why this is the case by providing evidence on the relation between age, seniority and experience, on the one hand, and the main components of labour costs, namely productivity and wages, on the other, for a sample of plants in three manufacturing industries ('forest', 'industrial machinery' and 'electronics') in Finland during the IT revolution in the 1990s. In 'average' industries – those not undergoing major technological shocks – productivity and wages keep rising almost indefinitely with the accumulation of either seniority (in the forest industry) or experience (in the industry producing industrial machinery). In these industries, the skill depreciation often associated with higher seniority beyond a certain threshold does not seemingly raise labour costs. In electronics, instead, the seniority-productivity profile shows a positive relation first and then becomes negative as one looks at plants with higher average seniority. This body of evidence is consistent with the idea that fast technical change brings about accelerated skill depreciation of senior workers. We cannot rule out, however, that our correlations are also simultaneously produced by worker movements across plants. The seniority-earnings profile in electronics is instead rather similar to that observed for the other industries – a likely symptom of the prevailing Finnish wage bargaining institutions which tend to make seniority one essential element of wage determination. In the end, seniority matters for labour costs, not age as such. But only in high-tech industries, not in the economy at large. This is well tuned with previous research on gross flows of workers and jobs in the US and other OECD countries which unveiled the productivity-driving role of resource reallocation (or lack thereof) between plants. To improve the employability of the elderly at times of fast technical change, public policy should thus divert resources away from preserving existing jobs and lend more attention to the retraining of old workers to ease their reallocation away from less productive plants (or plants where they have become less productive) into new jobs.

— *Francesco Daveri and Mika Maliranta*

Economic Policy January 2007 Printed in Great Britain
© CEPR, CES, MSH, 2007.

Age, seniority and labour costs: lessons from the Finnish IT revolution

Francesco Daveri and Mika Maliranta

Università di Parma and IGIER; ETLA, Helsinki

1. INTRODUCTION

Workers over 50 participate less in the labour market than their younger counterparts and, when unemployed, they remain longer on the dole.[1] These are clear symptoms that companies are more reluctant to hire the elderly and that, ultimately, an aged workforce is a burden for most firms. Whether and why this is the case is not obvious, however.

We are very grateful to our discussants Wendy Carlin and Rudolf Winter-Ebmer, two referees and other panel participants for their comments on a previous draft. Previous drafts of this paper previously circulated as IGIER Working Paper 309 and ETLA Discussion Paper 1010 under the title 'Age, Technology and Labour Costs' and benefited from the comments of seminar participants at the Government Institute of Economic Research (Helsinki), Bocconi (Milan), Humboldt (Berlin), Parma, the 5th 'Economics of ICT Conference' in Mannheim, the 2005 ONS Conference on the 'Analysis of Enterprise Micro-Data' in Cardiff. Gilbert Cette, Pekka Ilmakunnas, Olmo Silva and Alexandra Spitz provided useful comments on previous drafts. Maliranta gratefully acknowledges financial support provided by Tekes within the Research Programme for Advanced Technology Policy (ProAct). We are grateful to the Research Laboratory of Statistics Finland for providing access to these data and especially to Satu Nurmi, the Head of the Laboratory, for constructing these data.

The Managing Editor in charge of this paper was Paul Seabright.

[1] While labour market participation (the ratio between the labour force and the total population in working age) ranges between 90% and 95% in all OECD countries, the same ratio was instead substantially lower for older workers (from a high of some 80% in Sweden to a low of about 45% in Italy). The OECD data on labour market transitions (see OECD, 2006) document that the hiring rate of older workers is much lower (between one-third and one-half) than for younger workers; very few of the older unemployed find a job and very few of those who left the labour force come back to work; older workers are more likely to quit their jobs than younger workers; finally, the old no longer working rarely move into unemployment, while more than half retire early and a significant proportion does not work because of reported disability.

Economic Policy January 2007 pp. 117–175 Printed in Great Britain
© CEPR, CES, MSH, 2007.

1.1. The controversy

Workforce ageing is known to entail skill deterioration and lessened ability to adapt and learn new things. The studies of psychologists and medical scientists have in fact often shown that cognitive abilities tend to deteriorate with age. Although this decline is not uniform across abilities, after a certain age threshold, further advancements in age are seemingly associated with lower productivity at work. Beyond that threshold, further increases of experience add little or nothing to the working ability of a given worker.[2]

This skill depreciation effect is possibly more pronounced, though, for a worker who stays within the same company for a long time. A senior worker is more likely to have exhausted her learning potential on the particular job or work environment she is attached to, while a worker of the same age but new to the firm and to the job may have not. This begs the question of whether seniority, rather than age, is behind the bad labour market performance of the elderly that we see in the data.

The importance of distinguishing the effects of age from those of seniority manifests itself in a related aspect too. Declining productivity is in fact not enough to make an old (or senior) worker a burden for her firm, as long as the additional year of age (or seniority) goes hand in hand with a parallel flattening of the individual earnings profile. Unfortunately, this is rarely the case. In many OECD countries, labour market institutions associated with the presence of collective agreements make the seniority-related part of the wage a particularly large fraction of workers' wages, thereby preventing companies from keeping wages aligned to the declining productivity of senior workers. And a seniority wage may also be the result of the internal dynamics of the firm. Workers with a high degree of seniority have usually reached top positions in their company, which often enable them to extract a rent over and above their productivity contribution to the company. Or employees and employers may have entered an implicit contract implying a deferred compensation scheme, so that the young are underpaid and the old overpaid with respect to their productivity. In all these cases, the stop or outright reversal in the process of skill accumulation becomes more pronounced right at a time when firms find it particularly hard to detach seniority from earnings. Note, however, that it is seniority, not age as such, that is the most likely cause of rising labour costs.

The productivity-wage race during the individual career paths and its counterpart for company costs is in turn crucially affected by the pace of technical change. Fast technical change, usually embodied in new machines and methods of work, accelerates

---

[2] It should not be forgotten that workforce ageing is not necessarily a burden, and may actually be a blessing for the firm. An older labour force is more experienced, and therefore potentially more productive. Moreover, having had more time to hang around and search the labour market, an old worker has potentially good chances of finding herself in a better job. Finally, thanks to the secular improvements in healthcare, ageing has the potential to raise workers' productivity by enhancing ability and attitude to work, also increasing and lengthening labour force participation. The balance between the good and the bad sides of ageing is duly discussed in the paper.

the depreciation of existing skills naturally occurring with age or seniority and thus makes it more likely that senior workers become a burden for the firm. As a result, the adverse effects of seniority on labour costs may be particularly striking in high-tech industries and, more generally, in firms where incessant changes in the methods of production and the set of goods and services offered to the public are crucial ingredients of the maintained competitive ability of the company.

1.2. Policy relevance

Policy-makers are increasingly worried about the labour market consequences of workforce ageing. In the last few years, the rapid diffusion of outright new and 'globalized' methods of production and work in those countries and industries most heavily affected by the IT revolution have possibly made the skill deterioration of older workers faster and hence contributed to the worsening of their labour market position. The shape of the relation between seniority and labour costs is seemingly well known to Wal-Mart managers, as exemplified by the following quote:

> 'Over the past 4 years, the average Associate tenure [at Wal-Mart] has increased by 0.2 months per calendar year. As a result, more Associates qualify for participation in benefits programs . . . and for more paid time off. An even more important factor is wages, which increase in lock-step with tenure and directly drive the cost of many benefits. Given the impact of tenure on wages and benefits, the cost of an Associate with 7 years of tenure is almost 55 per cent more than the cost of an Associate with 1 year of tenure, yet there is no difference in his or her productivity'. (Internal memorandum to the Board of Directors, Wal-Mart, March 2006)

But not too dissimilar preoccupations also probably underlie the recent move by Ericsson, the Swedish telecoms equipment maker, which, in April 2006, offered a voluntary redundancy package to up to 1000 of its Sweden-based employees between the ages of 35 and 50. Interviewed by the *Financial Times*, Carl-Henric Svanberg, Ericsson's CEO, justified his move as follows: 'the company's age structure and low staff turnover – about 1 per cent in a year – is storing up problems for the future and has to be addressed'. Accordingly, Mr Svanberg has set the minimum target for staff turnover at 3% per year.

The anecdotes on such almost quintessentially global companies as Wal-Mart and Ericsson may be representative of the problems that an enlarging set of companies will have to deal with in the future. If companies take action to stop the rise in labour costs due to declining or stagnating ability above a certain age or seniority threshold and higher wages than ever in career, this may further worsen the labour market position of the elderly. Yet the seniority of their employees seems to be the problem for Wal-Mart and Ericsson managers, not their age as such.

Whether the envisaged mechanism of wage-productivity misalignments potentially at the roots of the weak labour market position of the elderly is due to age or seniority also has far-reaching implications for the type of policy correction to undertake. If

ageing as such is behind the worse labour market outcomes of the elderly, this calls
for age-specific active labour market and educational policies to counteract depreci-
ating skills, improve the employability and eventually facilitate the re-entry of old
workers into the labour force. If instead seniority is really the problem, then no age-
biased active labour market policy is warranted. Labour market policy should instead
be mainly aimed at easing worker reallocation across jobs and firms, for instance by
reducing firing and hiring costs.

1.3. Our contribution

Our paper seeks to illuminate the debate on the implications of workforce ageing for
companies by contrasting age, seniority and general experience profiles with productivity and earnings for a sample of plants in three manufacturing industries ('forest',
'industrial machinery' and 'electronics') in Finland.

Finland is an appropriate laboratory to study our issues of interest in two respects.
First, it was hit by the IT revolution in the 1990s, which affected firms in the various
industries in different ways. Second, it has good data to study the problem. So not
only does Finland provide the scope, but also the means for properly analysing the
relation between seniority, experience, productivity and wages at the plant level.

To evaluate whether such relations differ across industries, we pick a subset of three
industries that include the most traditional Finnish industry one can think of (the forest
industry) and two industries producing capital goods, one (production of electronics
equipment) playing a crucial role and another one (production of machinery and
equipment) less involved in the IT revolution. We can thus study the relation between
age, seniority and experience on the one hand and labour cost variables (productivity
and earnings) in 'treated' industries (electronics) and 'control' industries (the other two industries),
one of which is technologically dissimilar but representative of the average Finnish
industry and another not too dissimilar from electronics. Altogether, our statistical analysis
provides a reasonably coherent picture of the empirical relation between age-related
variables, plant productivity and wages in Finland in the years of the IT revolution.

Our empirical exercise is implemented in two steps. First, we compute an overall
productivity index for each plant from labour productivity data. Then, we analyse
the statistical relation between the plant productivity index and age-related variables
(age first but also, and crucially, seniority and potential experience) in each of the
three industries separately. Clearly, within each industry, plant productivity may vary
for many reasons in addition to changes in seniority or experience of workers. Some
of these determinants – workers' education, vintage, foreign ownership, size of the
plant – are observed. Some others (such as managerial ability) are not, but there are
statistical methods to implicitly account for their effect. We investigate the significance of the same set of variables for earnings as well.

At first sight, our results seem to support the view that workforce ageing as such
has adverse effects on labour costs. Age is essentially unrelated with productivity while

it is positively correlated with wages. Upon a closer scrutiny, though, when we duly distinguish the effects of seniority on productivity and wages from those of general experience, we find that the picture sharply differs across industries.

In 'average' industries – those not undergoing major technological shocks – productivity and wages keep rising almost indefinitely with the accumulation of either seniority (in the forest industry) or experience (in the industry producing industrial machinery). In these industries, skill depreciation does not seemingly raise labour costs. Instead, the responses of plant productivity and wages to seniority are very different from each other in electronics – the industry where people are exposed to rapid technological and managerial changes. In electronics, the seniority-productivity profile shows a positive relation first and then becomes negative as one looks at plants with higher average seniority. This holds for plants with similar education, plant age and size and other conditions and is thus not related to plant differences in these other respects. The inverted-U-shaped correlation between plant seniority and productivity in electronics is most precisely measured when data are averaged over time, that is, when purged of the potential noise arising from year-to-year fluctuations, but a weaker correlation is still there when the time series variation of the data is considered.

This body of evidence is consistent with the idea that fast technical change brings about accelerated skill depreciation of senior workers. We cannot rule out, however, that our correlations are also simultaneously produced by worker movements across plants. The negative correlation between seniority and productivity may in fact also reflect the reallocation away of younger (and more productive) workers who leave behind older plants attracted by the career prospects offered in newly born high-productivity firms and plants. While we cannot precisely quantify the relative importance of the two effects in our statistical analysis, we conclude that both skill depreciation and worker reallocation affect the relation between seniority and productivity in the Finnish high-tech industry.

The change of sign (first positive, then negative) in the seniority-productivity profiles is not there for plant wages. The seniority-earnings profile in electronics is rather similar to that observed for the other industries – a likely symptom of the prevailing Finnish wage bargaining institutions which tend to make seniority one essential element of wage determination.

These latter findings indicate that the looming rise in labour costs coming about from seniority-based wages is particularly significant in high-tech industries (the most dynamic industries of the economy). This is well tuned with previous research on gross flows of workers and jobs in the US and other OECD countries which unveiled the productivity-driving role of resource reallocation (or lack thereof) between plants. The adverse link between seniority and productivity and the discrepancy between productivity and earnings profiles are instead less apparent for firms in other industries. In the end, seniority matters mostly for labour costs, not age as such. But in high-tech industries only, and not in the economy at large.

1.4. Organization of the paper

The structure of this paper is as follows. In Section 2 we discuss the main ideas that economists bring to bear when thinking about the relation between ageing, seniority, experience, productivity and wages. In Section 3 we present data explaining why Finland is an interesting case in point and how our variables of interest correlate to each other in the data set employed in our statistical analysis. In Section 4 we present and discuss our empirical strategy and main results. Section 5 concludes. This paper also includes an appendix, where we give a more detailed description of our data.

2. AGE, SENIORITY, EXPERIENCE, PRODUCTIVITY AND WAGES: THEORIES AND EMPIRICAL PREDICTIONS

Various theories of the functioning of the labour market bear distinct empirical predictions and help think about the relation between age, seniority, experience and the main components of labour costs, productivity and earnings. We briefly survey the various theories below before contrasting them with the data.

2.1. Age, productivity and wages: theories

The most straightforward way of tackling the question whether ageing is associated to higher labour costs for the firm is to look at whether workforce ageing drives a negative wedge between the worker's productivity and its wage.

But answering this question is not enough. Ageing usually manifests itself in two main guises: seniority and overall experience. Plainly, an older worker has very often spent more time in the labour market – and has thus a bigger general experience – than a younger worker. Instead, an old worker need not be a senior worker in a particular firm. Distinguishing the two facets of ageing in the labour market – as the various theories do – is particularly important for policy purposes, as ageing is essentially exogenous to the individual worker, while potential experience and, to an even greater extent, seniority are not.

2.1.1. The human capital hypothesis. The most obvious benchmark for our discussion on ageing and labour costs is Becker's human capital hypothesis (1962, p. 119), according to which an older labour force is more experienced and therefore more productive.

First of all, ageing often – not always – comes about with higher seniority of the worker within a given firm. As long as some learning and training is undertaken on the job early on in a career, higher seniority should be associated to higher worker's productivity. Moreover, the human capital hypothesis posits that ageing should be associated with the acquisition of generic experience in the labour market over and above the increased seniority within a given firm. If generic experience buys enhanced flexibility and adaptability to the worker, this is again likely associated to higher productivity and market wages. Yet such productivity and wage enhancements are not the counterpart of higher seniority.

In turn, the extent to which higher productivity results in higher wages depends on whether training is general or firm-specific as well as on incentive considerations. If training is general, the worker fully appropriates the productivity increase enabled by training at a later stage in his/her career. If instead training is firm-specific, worker and firm will share the quasi-rents generated by training. In other words, with at least partially firm-specific human capital, one should expect the seniority-productivity profile to be steeper than the seniority-wage profile so that the productivity of senior workers eventually exceeds their earnings, while the opposite applies at early career stages.

Altogether, ageing affects productivity and wages both through seniority and general experience. Their effects, however, need not coincide empirically.

Finally, the theory of human capital also suggests that the returns from seniority and experience alone (i.e. without further educational or training inputs) do not stay constant over the worker's lifetime. As emphasized in the psychometric studies undertaken by medical scientists (see Skirbekk, 2003), cognitive abilities tend to deteriorate with age, so that, after a certain age threshold, growing older is seemingly associated to lower, not higher, productivity. (See Box 1 for a discussion of the main issues.)

Box 1. Age and individual productivity

The productivity of individual workers depends on a host of characteristics, such as education and skills, experience, motivation, intellectual and physical abilities. Some of these worker characteristics – notably the productive value of skills – may deteriorate with age.

Verhaegen and Salthouse (1997) present a meta-analysis of 91 studies on how mental abilities develop over the individual life span. Based on these studies, they conclude that the cognitive abilities (reasoning, speed and episodic memory) decline significantly before 50 years of age and more thereafter. Maximum levels are instead achieved in the 20s and the 30s. This is a universal phenomenon, independent of country and sex (this same phenomenon appears to hold even among non-human species – from fruit flies to primates). Kanazawa (2003) shows that age-genius curve of scientists bends down around between 20 and 30 years. Similar curves are also found for jazz musicians and painters. Given that the decline seems to apply mainly to married men, Kanazawa ventures the idea that changed levels of testosterone provide the psychological micro-foundation for this productivity decline.

In putting together our pieces of evidence, we will leave aside a few important aspects, which are likely to make the picture more complicated than this. First, a distinction must be drawn between fluid abilities and crystallized abilities. Fluid abilities concern the performance and speed of solving tasks related to new material, and they include perceptual speed and reasoning. They are strongly reduced at older ages. Crystallized abilities, such as verbal meaning and word fluency, even improve with accumulated knowledge and remain at a high functional level until a late age in life. The distinction between fluid and crystallized abilities is supported by empirical findings, where the psychometric test results of young and old men are analysed. It is found that verbal abilities remain virtually unchanged, while reasoning and speed abilities decline with age. Hence, one should not expect to see the declining part of the age-productivity profile to set in equally for all tasks and jobs.

Second, the relative demand for work tasks that involve certain cognitive abilities may have shifted asymmetrically over recent decades. As argued and empirically documented by Autor *et al.* (2003), the demand for interactive skills (hence for abilities that stay relatively stable over the life cycle) has likely increased more than the demand for mathematical aptitude (which instead declines substantially with age). This suggests that older workers may become relatively more productive in value terms over time. Whether such countervailing factors are relevant for Finland remains to be seen, being presumably particularly important for IT users rather than for the workers involved in the production of IT goods. The micro data employed by Maliranta and Rouvinen (2004) indicate that the use of ICT has had a particularly significant effect on productivity in ICT producing and using manufacturing industries. That study also provided evidence that the use of ICT has a stronger positive effect on productivity in younger organizations.

Our plant-level data set does not give us much leeway to exploit such additional interesting implications, and we leave them aside.

Particularly relevant for the topic of this paper, the deterioration of individual ability may be a more serious shortcoming at times of – and in companies and industries subject to – fast technological change. The misalignment of plant productivity and earnings was apparent in the Wal-Mart and Ericsson examples in Section 1. This has also possibly been the case in the Finnish economy since the early 1990s, when information technology started radically changing modes of production and work over a relatively short period of time. If these rapid changes had an impact, one would expect to observe an age-productivity (or seniority-productivity) profile with an earlier turnaround point and/or a steeper decline in high-tech industries (such as those today producing electronic equipment) than in traditional, technologically mature, industries (such as forest) as well as relatively less IT-intensive but still capital-good-producing industries (such as machinery and equipment).

To sum up, based on the human capital hypothesis, accumulation of skills, within and outside the firm, is an important, but not unceasing, productivity driver. Individual productivity profiles are expected to have an upward sloping part possibly changing its slope into negative beyond a certain threshold. Under the same hypothesis, wages are instead supposed to follow a flatter time profile than productivity.

A major problem for the research on the connections between age and productivity at the micro level has been the difficulty of measuring the marginal productivity of individuals, although their earnings can be measured with a reasonable degree of precision (see Box 2).

Box 2. Measures of individual productivity

To gauge indirect information about individual productivity, three main approaches have been followed: supervisors' ratings, piece-rate samples and the study of age-earnings data within matched employer-employee data sets.

Studies based on supervisors' ratings tend not to find any clear systematic relation between the employee's age and his/her productivity. At most, a slightly negative relation is found, albeit small. A problem with these studies is that managers often wish to reward loyalty rather than productivity. Hence supervisory evaluations may be inflated and results biased. Bosses are often senior workers and many older workers have been familiar to them for a long time. This may be positively reflected in the wage levels of older workers.

Work-samples provide evidence from task-quality/speed tests. Here, a negative relation between age and productivity is typically found. The slope of the decline is not steep for blue-collar workers and leads to cumulative declines of around 15–20% compared to peak levels, while the productivity decline of older workers in creative jobs is probably more pronounced.

Employer-employee linked data sets, such as the one we are using in this paper, are less prone to subjectivity issues than the studies based on supervisors' ratings and to selectivity issues than work-samples. The problem here is to isolate the genuine contribution of the age of the marginal worker to the company's value added from other intervening factors. How to deal with these issues is discussed in the main text.

One way out is to use data on wages. If wages were directly related to productivity, the age-earnings profile would also measure the productivity profile. Indeed, as reported by the OECD (2006, p. 66), earnings profiles are often hump-shaped, especially for men, which may reflect results from the decline of individual productivity.

2.1.2. The deferred compensation hypothesis. The human capital hypothesis offers one explanation and a few testable predictions on the relation between age, seniority, experience, productivity and earnings. It is not the only game in town, however. Its predictions on the wage-productivity race throughout the working career have been challenged by Lazear's deferred compensation hypothesis.

Seniority-based wages are indeed commonplace in many countries. This often comes in parallel with mandatory retirement.[3] In general, earnings appear to continue to grow well beyond the moment when the age-productivity profile would be predicted to flatten or change its sign into negative according to the human capital approach.

These pieces of evidence are at odds with one of the main implications of the human capital hypothesis, namely that the wage profile is flatter than the productivity profile. But they also raise the question of why firms should accept to grant workers pay raises in excess of their productivity performance. One possibility (see Lazear, 1981) is that firms are willing to pay high wages to motivate workers whose performance is hard to monitor to exert their work effort until late in career. Deferred compensation schemes would, however, distort workers' decisions to retire. Hence, deferred compensation schemes come together with mandatory retirement – an effective way to eventually put old workers out of the labour force and resolve the eventual unsustainability of the underlying pay systems.

The seniority-based wage systems observed in Korea and Japan are broadly consistent with the deferred compensation hypothesis. A complementary possibility – plausibly relevant for European countries – is the presence of collective agreements or social norms that often make seniority a firmly embedded feature of the wage setting process.

2.1.3. Sorting and matching models. Another problem with the human capital approach is its assumption that worker seniority and experience are essentially exogenous to the firm. Instead, the relation between firm seniority and productivity is not necessarily one-way only. Other theories draw on the widespread diffusion of sorting and matching in actual labour markets to emphasize that seniority and experience should not (only) be regarded as the causes of the observed productivity developments but also as their consequences.

The positive link between seniority and productivity may in fact be there for sorting reasons. Given that a worker stays with the firm only if the firm-worker match is good, senior workers presumably belong to the pool of the most productive (e.g. Teulings and Hartog, 1998). Hence, even in the absence of the relation implied by the human capital hypothesis, productivity and seniority may still be correlated in the

---

[3] The available OECD evidence indicates that explicit or implicit seniority-based rules lead earnings to rise even more steeply with age than early on in a career in Austria, France, Japan, South Korea, Luxembourg, and Switzerland. In Finland and the US, the non-wage components of labour costs (for health insurance purposes) rise steeply with age.

data. Moreover, feed-back effects may also be at work, as emphasized by Manning (2000) when the link between experience and productivity is examined. Labour market search, by raising the chance of finding a good job-worker match, may also imply upward sloping experience-earnings profiles in parallel with flat or declining productivity and absent seniority effects. Notice that this search argument would imply a pure effect of experience such that, when age is controlled for, firm-specific seniority would have no impact on wage. Clearly, the feed-back effects implied by sorting and matching models should be taken into account in the empirical analysis.

2.2. Empirically testable questions

To be able to discriminate between the different theories of the functioning of the labour market briefly summarized above, we use our Finnish data set to investigate four main questions on the relation between workforce ageing, seniority, experience, and labour costs:

1. Is age as such related to productivity and wages at all?
2. Is the effect of seniority on productivity and earnings different from the effect of age through the general experience channel?
3. Are the effects of age (and seniority in particular) on productivity and wages significantly different from each other and across industries (in particular, between industries subject to fast technical change and the other industries)?
4. Is the correlation between age and age-related variables, on the one hand, and productivity and wages on the other really the result of causation?

3. WORKFORCE AGEING, SENIORITY AND LABOUR COSTS IN FINLAND: BASIC FACTS

In this section, we present some basic pieces of information on the variables of interest in the statistical analysis below.

In Section 3.1 we argue that Finland shares some common demographic and labour market trends with other European countries, such as the difficult labour market position of old workers. Hence the Finnish case discussed here may be seen as paradigmatic of issues faced by many countries. At the same time, though, the Finnish case also presents some specificity, namely the intensity of the technological and managerial shock in the late 1990s. As discussed above, rapid technological change may accelerate skill depreciation, thereby making the cost-increasing effect of ageing and seniority a more serious concern for firms.

In Section 3.2, directly related to our main object of concern (i.e. investigating how workforce ageing may be a burden for firms), we briefly describe how plant age, seniority and potential experience pair-wise correlate with productivity and wages in our data set of manufacturing plants.

Table 1. The exceptional increase in the share of IT manufacturing goods in total manufacturing in Finland in the second half of the 1990s (1995–2001, percentage points)

Swe	Nor	Den	Jap	USA	UK	Fin	Ger	Net	Ire	Fra	Spa	Ita
−1.4	+0.4	+0.1	+2.0	+2.0	+0.6	+13.4	+1.0	−0.3	+2.3	+0.8	−0.4	−0.8

Source: OECD (2003).

3.1. Workforce ageing and the Finnish IT revolution in the 1990s

Finland is no exception in the OECD as far as the weak labour market situation of older workers is concerned. Old workers in Finland tend to achieve lower labour market participation and employment rates, and suffer from higher unemployment rates than workers in the same age group in other Nordic countries. At the same time, if one compares Finland to countries in Continental Europe, one finds that the old Finns enjoy relatively higher participation and employment and lower unemployment. So Finland is about half-way down the OECD ranking.

These labour market outcomes come with a twist of originality compared to the rest of the OECD, though: throughout the 1990s, the skills of older workers in Finland have also been challenged by the unusually fast pace of the IT revolution in that country.

In the 1990s, the world demand for cellular phones boomed under the push of declining semi-conductor prices. Thanks to Nokia's managerial ability and leadership in the cellular phone industry, the share of electronics (SITC 32–33) in the Finnish GDP markedly rose from about 3.5% of nominal GDP in 1995 to 8.2% in 2000.[4] Throughout the same period of time, the value added of the forest industry (and notably of the industry named 'Pulp, paper and wood products', SITC 20–21) fell from 7.5% in 1995 to 6% in 2000. In parallel – an example of how not all of the so called high-tech industries have gained throughout this period of time – the value added share of 'Industrial machinery and equipment' (SITC 29–31) slightly fell from 5.7% to 5.4% in 2000.

The Nokia-driven technological and managerial shock has been unique in an international landscape. As reported in Table 1, the share of IT goods production over total manufacturing went up by 13.4 percentage points in Finland between 1995 and 2001. This is also remarkable because the beneficial effects of declining semiconductor prices were potentially out there for every country. As shown in Table 2, however, the other OECD countries have seemingly not taken this opportunity or

---

[4] This increase was also the result of the rapid development of a myriad of ancillary manufacturing and high-tech consultancy activities around Nokia. Some of them are first-tier suppliers to Nokia. Some others provide such electronic manufacturing services as component sourcing, equipment renting, production design and testing, and thus bridge the gap between equipment manufacturers and component suppliers. See Ali-Yrkkö *et al.* (2000) and Daveri and Silva (2004) for more detailed renditions.

Table 2. Correlations between averages in 1995–2002

	Age	Experience	Seniority	log of TFP	log of wage
Forest industry					
Age	1				
Experience	0.9939*	1			
Seniority	0.7824*	0.7679*	1		
log of TFP	−0.1747*	−0.1766*	−0.1815*	1	
log of wage	0.4736*	0.4271*	0.6069*		1
Number of observations: 365					
Industrial machinery					
Age	1				
Experience	0.9790*	1			
Seniority	0.6792*	0.6605*	1		
log of TFP		−0.117	−0.1565*	1	
log of wage	0.2317*	0.1127	0.1635*	0.3495*	1
Number of observations: 567					
Electronics					
Age	1				
Experience	0.9528*	1			
Seniority	0.7085*	0.6971*	1		
log of TFP			−0.2118	1	
log of wage	0.2697*			0.2556*	1
Number of observations: 172					

have exploited it differently (perhaps on the IT services side). No doubt, the intensity of the IT technological and managerial shock in the 1990s was of much bigger magnitude in Finland than in any other OECD country.

3.2. Age, seniority, experience, productivity and earnings in Finnish manufacturing plants

To tackle the questions we are interested in before delving into the deeper statistical analysis enabled by multivariate techniques, we describe the main features of our plant-level data set as well as the sample statistics and correlation between age, seniority and potential experience, on the one hand, and the two main components of labour costs, productivity and wages, on the other.

3.2.1. Data set. Similar to the other Nordic countries, Finland is endowed with a rich register data of companies, plants and individuals. The unique identification codes for persons, companies and plants used in the different registers form the backbone of the Finnish administrative register network and the Finnish statistical system, whereby different sources of information can be integrated conveniently for various statistical purposes.[5]

---

[5] Data sources and linking of them are described in the Appendix of this paper and, in greater detail, in Ilmakunnas *et al.* (2001) and Maliranta (2003).

This paper employs linked plant-level information for plants and workforce from the Census of Manufacturing and Employment Statistics between 1990 and 2002 (1995 and 2002, in the main part of our statistical analysis).[6] Thanks to this link, we have valuable information on the characteristics of the labour input for the plants. This includes the average potential experience (the number of years after the last completed degree), seniority (the number of years spent working in the current company) and education (the number of schooling years needed for the degree). On the side of the plant labour costs, we have information about gross wage, value added per hour worked ('labour productivity'), capital stock per hour worked (the 'capital-labour ratio') and the value added shares of capital. These pieces of information, put together as detailed in Box 3, allow us to compute a total factor productivity (TFP) index, a measure of sheer efficiency of each plant.

Box 3. How we computed plant productivity

We numerically compute a TFP (total factor productivity) index – an index of disembodied technical knowledge under constant returns to scale and perfect competition in factor markets, from the standard growth accounting formula in natural logarithms:

$$\ln(TFP)_{pit} = \ln(Y/L)_{pit} - (1 - \bar{a}_i) * \ln(K/L)_{pit}$$

with $\bar{a}_i$ denoting the average industry specific labour share during the period. The average is calculated from the annual industry labour shares preliminarily smoothed by a non-linear filter. Thus we allow the output elasticity of capital and labour to vary between different industries, but not between plants within the same industry. Our TFP index is thus suitable both for analysing both the cross-sectional and time series variation of our data.

In the second step of our empirical analysis, we relate the computed TFP index to the plant characteristics, including average workers characteristics, indicated in the main text.

3.2.2. Summary statistics for Finnish industries and plants.   Tables 2 and 3 show data on the pattern of correlation in our data set, separately for each industry, both for period-averaged plant data (hence along the cross-sectional dimension; see Table 2) and along the time series dimension (see Table 3).

---

[6] The observations between 1990 and 1994 are employed as instruments for data concerning the 1995–2002 period in our statistical analysis.

Table 3. Correlation over time (between variable changes; from 1995 to 2002)

	Age	Experience	Seniority	log of TFP	log of wage
Forest industry					
Age	1				
Experience	0.9784*	1			
Seniority	0.7029*	0.7566*	1		
log of TFP				1	
log of wage					1
Number of observations: 199					
Industrial machinery					
Age	1				
Experience	0.9812*	1			
Seniority	0.7989*	0.7591	1		
log of TFP				1	
log of wage					1
Number of observations: 197					
Electronics					
Age	1				
Experience	0.9922	1			
Seniority			1		
log of TFP				1	
log of wage					1
Number of observations: 49					

Notes: We only report correlation significant at least at the 10% level. * indicates significance at the 1% level. Bonferroni adjustments have been made to significance levels.

As implied by how we measure potential experience, there is a very strong correlation between age and potential experience in all three industries, along both cross-sectional and time dimensions. Not surprisingly either, age and potentially experience have very similar correlations with other variables. The correlation between age and seniority is instead somewhat lower (it ranges between 0.7 and 0.8) but is still clearly statistically significant. The correlation regarding other variables is often statistically insignificant, particularly over time; if this is the case, we omit reporting correlation coefficients.

In the cross-sectional data age and wages are positively correlated, while age is negatively correlated (in the forest industry) or uncorrelated (in Industrial Machinery and Electronics) with TFP. Seniority instead has a negative correlation with TFP in all the three industries but has a positive correlation with the wage level except in Electronics where the correlation is not statistically significant. A positive correlation between the wage level and TFP is there instead for Industrial Machinery and Electronics. We have also computed these correlations separately for declining and expanding plants. Some of the earlier significant correlations turn out to be insignificant but the problem is the small number of observations in some cases (especially in Electronics) which makes it hard to draw further conclusions from these calculations.

4. WORKFORCE AGEING AND THE FIRM: THE EVIDENCE FROM FINNISH MANUFACTURING PLANTS

4.1. Empirical strategy

The aim of our statistical analysis is to identify the plant-wide relation between age and age-related variables (seniority, potential experience) on the one hand and labour costs (productivity and wages) on the other.

The logic of our empirical exercise is straightforward. To evaluate the relation between ageing and plant productivity, we first relate the plant productivity index (computed as in Box 3) to our main variables of interest: age, potential experience and seniority of the plant workforce, and (as indicated in Box 4) to a number of other relevant variables whose statistical significance is of secondary importance for our main purpose in this paper. Then we repeat the same type of exercise with earnings – instead of productivity – as a dependent variable.

Box 4. Two methods for calculating age-productivity profiles at the plant level

Hellerstein and Neumark (1995), Hellerstein *et al.* (1999), Haegeland and Klette (1999) and Ilmakunnas and Maliranta (2005) have used information on the shares of workers in different groups (such as to education, age and the like) to model the quality of the labour input of a plant in a production function estimated from plant level data. By directly estimating this production function jointly with an equation for average wage, they were able to quantify and compare the productivity and wage profiles.

At least with our Finnish data set (but this is known to be a more general problem), this method often tends to produce implausibly low estimates for the capital input coefficients, which may bias the estimated coefficients for age-productivity profiles. Thus, following Griliches and Rinstad (1971) and, more recently, Ilmakunnas *et al.* (2004), we employ a two-step procedure.

First, we numerically compute a TFP (total factor productivity) index (as described in Box 4). Then, in the second step of our empirical analysis, we relate the computed TFP index to the plant characteristics, including average workers characteristics, indicated in the main text. Our variables of interest are seniority (the number of years spent working in the current company), average potential experience (the number of years after the last completed degree) and the number of schooling years (usually needed for the degree). Other included variables are plant age, foreign ownership, and a dummy variable for disappearing plants.

> In the end, our two-step specification, partly based on growth accounting
> techniques, comes at the cost of accepting the – possibly plausible but essen-
> tially untested – constant returns to scale and perfect competition assumptions
> mentioned above. Maliranta (1997) found that the assumption of constant
> returns to scale in the Finnish manufacturing sector is approximately correct.

In our empirical analysis we exploit three industry panels along the cross-plant and time
series dimensions. The three industries have been selected for being representative,
respectively, of an 'average' pre-boom manufacturing industry ('forest'), a non-booming
capital-intensive industry ('industrial machinery') and a booming high-tech industry
('electronics'). As reported in the summary statistics in Table A1 of the appendix, we have
data for 365 plants for the forest industry, 567 plants for 'industrial machinery and equipment' and 172 plants for 'electronics'. For each of these plants, we have a maximum of
eight observations over the years between 1995 and 2002. The unbalanced nature of
our panel is such that, when using the variation of the data over time, we are able to
employ at most respectively 1523, 1717 and 496 observations (hence about 52%, 38%
and 36% of the total potential observations). A fraction of the missing observations is
due to plant 'death' in 1996–2002, which represents about 12% of the forest industry, 20%
of machinery and 22% of electronics. The share of disappearing plants is therefore
one-fourth of the total missing for forest and about one-third for the other industries.

4.1.1. What we hope to learn.

The statistical significance and the size of the estimated
coefficients of the variables of interest give us important information as to whether
and how workforce ageing raises labour costs for the firm or not. Moreover, we want
to learn whether age as such is important or if instead, as predicted by the theories
discussed in the previous section, the productivity-wage implications of seniority
('ageing within the firm') are different from those of potential experience ('ageing
outside the firm'), as predicted by some of the models discussed in the previous section.
Moreover, to understand whether the intuition underlying human capital theories is
borne by the data, we will also check whether ageing has a declining effect on productivity
and wages for older people. Third, to learn whether human capital theories must be
supplemented by the other explanations based on the institutions and incentive considerations discussed above as the deferred compensation hypothesis, we will check
whether the effects of age, seniority and experience are different for productivity and wages.

In addition to that, the cross-industry variation in our data gives us the possibility of
testing whether the industry (more ambitiously, the technological content of industrial
production) makes a difference for age-productivity profiles. If new technologies significantly affect the wage-productivity race, we expect to find industry-specific patterns of
partial correlation, with differences showing up in particular between electronics and
the other industries.

Finally, productivity and wages do not depend on variables such as age, seniority or experience only, but also on education (measured as the number of years of schooling) as well as a few additional other observed and unobserved factors varying across plants but more or less constant over time (such as plant size, foreign ownership and outright time-invariant plant vintage, discussed right below), as well as those factors varying over time but equally for all plants (such as unobserved year-specific effects).[7] Hence, the influence of all these variables together with the effects of ageing is jointly tested in our statistical analysis. In each table, explanatory notes will report the list of the variables employed in the various specifications.

4.2. Implementation difficulties

Our undertaking confronts five main difficulties of implementation: attenuation, reverse causation, unobserved heterogeneity, selectivity and measurement error. We discuss each of them separately, also indicating how we tackle such problems in our empirical analysis.

4.2.1. Attenuation. A very common problem with panels such as the one at hand is that the variation over time of the panel data may be very noisy and subtract precision from the statistical analysis of the underlying phenomenon, giving rise to the so-called attenuation bias. In practice, if this problem is present, the estimated coefficient of age or seniority in the empirical analysis of the determinants of productivity would be artificially biased towards zero. Using plant data averaged over all available years allows one to get rid of this unnecessary noise and, hopefully, concentrate on the underlying long-run relation. This is why, in each table, we present one set of results where standard statistical techniques (such as ordinary least squares) are employed with the cross-section of plants estimated separately for each industry.

4.2.2. Reverse causation. Cross-sectional statistical analysis based on averaged data is not problem-free either, unfortunately. A big problem is potential reverse causation. The statistical relations we intend to analyse posit that age or age-related variables are the independent variables and productivity the dependent variable. But cross-sectional data as such (be they observed at a given point in time or averaged over time) only indicate correlation, not causation. Therefore, if the estimated coefficient linking seniority and productivity is negative (say, after a certain age threshold), this may not indicate that the plants where aged workers are employed are less productive. Rather, the negative correlation may simply signal that senior workers tend to be hired in less productive and older plants, probably featuring outdated machines and methods of production, while new, innovative and high-productivity plants may be

---

[7] Such period effects are appended to the list of the explanatory variables when the time variation of the data is considered, and not when cross-sectional plant data are used.

more often matched to young workers. If this is the case, we would be wrongly interpreting what causes what, attributing to seniority the effect of plant age on plant productivity.

We deal with this problem in two ways. First, in our cross-sectional analysis, we always include an additional explanatory variable: plant age, namely a categorical variable indicating the period of establishment of the plant. If the correlation between seniority or experience and productivity hides a causal correlation from low-productivity old machines onto old (potentially high-productivity) workers, the statistical effect of workers' seniority and experience on plant productivity should disappear once the effect of plant age is accounted for. Second, in another empirical specification (Instrumental Variables, or IV), we supplement the contemporaneous values of the explanatory variables with their lagged values (measured in 1990–94) as additional explanatory variables. If today's plant productivity (say, in 1995–2002) may have a contemporaneous feedback effect onto today's plant seniority, this feedback is less likely to be present when another explanatory variable such as seniority measured yesterday (i.e. in 1990–94) is appended to the list of the productivity determinants.

4.2.3. Unobserved heterogeneity.
Surely, a lot of unobserved heterogeneity in plant productivity is still there in the data even once we have augmented the list of productivity determinants with plant vintage and other lagged variables. Yet the problem of interpreting the statistical results from cross-sectional estimates arises if and only if the unobserved (therefore unmeasured) plant variables are correlated with the included explanatory variables. For example, if managerial ability – a typically unobserved plant variable – were unrelated to hiring decisions, then leaving it out of the empirical analysis would not be a major problem. Unfortunately, instead, an able plant manager may be particularly inclined to hire young productive workers (as Juuti, 2001 pointed out). Then if managerial ability is not observed and therefore omitted from the analysis, its effect may be picked up by the negative estimated relation between senior workers and productivity. We would be misperceiving the effect of managerial ability on hiring decisions as if it were the causal effect of age on productivity. To tackle this problem, we use fixed-effects estimation by appending to the list of explanatory variables terms summarizing the joint effect of the unobserved determinants of plant productivity as long as they are not variable over time (as managerial efficiency is). In this way, the estimated coefficient linking age and productivity is purged of the unwanted influence of unobserved variables constant over time.

By analysing the time variation of our data as well, we can significantly extend sample size, usually associated with enhanced statistical precision.[8] When adopting

---

[8] Clearly, however, the additional observations, being repeated for the same plants, cannot be taken as independent observations. Thus in our statistical analysis, we allow for the error term (the residual unobserved components not captured by the explanatory variable included in our statistical analysis) to be auto-correlated, i.e. to be time-dependent. This serves the purpose of not being misled by the potentially increased gain of precision achieved in capturing the phenomena at hand, thanks to the increased sample size. Accounting for auto-correlation is instead important to correctly appreciate the explanatory power of our model along the time dimension.

the fixed-effects statistical model, however, one effectively relinquishes information contained in the cross-sectional framework and concentrate on the so-called 'within-plant' variation in the panel data set. This may be a good thing if the goal is to answer some questions which – by construction – could not be addressed in the cross-sectional framework, the main of which is whether the relation between the age-related variables, education, productivity and wages is a simultaneous one or whether it operates with some delay.

4.2.4. Selectivity.   Our panel data set also presents selectivity problems, which manifest themselves in two fashions. The first problem is typical of any panel of plants or individuals. Longitudinal studies typically suffer from non-random attrition, that is, the loss of respondents over time tends to generate an upward bias in the age-productivity estimate, given that the plants remaining in the sample are usually positively selected, being very often the best ones. A remedy for this type of selectivity would entail splitting the statistical analysis into two steps. The first step is to estimate the probability that plants (and workers) will disappear from our sample. The second step entails correcting the estimated coefficients, taking into account the bias induced by the omission of the disappeared plants. We do not go that far. Plainly, in evaluating our cross-sectional evidence we check the statistical significance of a variable taking value equal to zero for the plants continuing throughout the period and one for the plants exiting the sample between 1996 and 2002 (as Griliches and Regev, 1995, did in their Israeli study). This variable is not significantly related to productivity or wages in our sample and therefore does not affect our results.

Within continuing plants, though, the between-plant movement of workers may add another bias, whose sign is not clear *a priori*. Those workers who choose to stay and continue to work in a given plant instead of engaging in job shopping to improve their existing match may be the least entrepreneurial (and possibly the least productive) workers. The most able and youngest workers, with a greater scope for job-to-job mobility, may instead be eager to leave the most inefficient firms. Hence, plant productivity may appear to decline as a result of the process of job turnover that leaves behind senior workers rather than being the sheer consequence of declining ability. Therefore a negative statistical correlation in a cross-section of plants may not be the result of skill depreciation of the workforce in each given plant and instead originate from the reallocation effects due to the movement of workers between plants.

By the same token, the rising part of the seniority-productivity profile may not be the result of the higher average productivity of expert workers. Experienced workers may well end up in more productive plants as a result of positive sorting: senior workers may have had the time to sort out plants and choose the best places for work.

Our statistical techniques allow us to evaluate the influence of the host of factors that may be causing attenuation, reverse causation and unobserved heterogeneity. But we are unable to precisely decompose how much of our results are due to reallocation and how much to skill depreciation. Hence, we cannot fully deal with this second type of selectivity issues due to workers' reallocation and sorting. Yet if one simply appends hiring and separation rates (lagged by one period to lessen reverse causation) in our empirical exercises to be discussed below, plant productivity is unrelated to hiring rates and negatively related to separation rates, while the statistical significance of the age-related variables does not change.

This is good news for us, for it implies that our results are not merely the figment of specification mistakes. Yet, given that hiring and separation rates are presumably jointly determined with productivity and wages, we hesitate to interpret our results as definite evidence that our correlations are only due to skill depreciation and not worker reallocation.

4.2.5. Measurement error in value added shares. As explained above, our empirical analysis goes in two steps. First, we numerically calculate productivity from value added data, imputing constant industry-specific value added shares of labour and capital and then we relate our productivity index to its likely determinants. The resulting residual is legitimately interpreted as 'plant productivity' as long as the assumptions of constant returns to scale and perfect competition are accepted. This may be hard-to-swallow assumptions that may bias our results in a direction hard to trace *a priori*. As a shortcut, we simply re-computed our productivity index with somewhat higher and somewhat lower value added shares (by plus and minus 10%). For brevity, we do not report the results of this experiment here. Their thrust, though, is that our findings carry over unchanged, irrespective of the imputed values of the value added shares.

Another way of tackling this issue is by directly estimating production or value added functions. We cannot estimate production functions for our data set does not include data on intermediate products. We did look, however, at the partial correlation between capital per hour worked and our variables of interest on the one hand and value added per hour worked on the other in simple value added regressions that are based on an idea of two inputs in production, labour and capital. The estimated coefficients for capital per hour worked are statistically significant for plants in the forest industry and industrial machinery but much lower than the imputed value for the share of capital in value added (usually about one-third), while they are instead not significantly different from zero for electronics.[9] In any case, the statistical significance of our variables of interest (age, seniority, experience) and education does not change.

4.3. Main results

The main results of this paper revolve around the questions listed at the end of Section 2. Is age related to productivity and wages at all? Is the seniority effect of age

---

[9] The unavailability of data for the intermediate inputs prevents from carrying out the Levinsohn-Petrin correction for the endogeneity of capital in production function and value added regressions.

on productivity and wages different from the effect of age through the general experience channel? Are the effects of age on productivity and wages significantly different from each other and across industries, in particular between 'average' and high-tech industries? And finally, are we capturing causal relations?

Our answers to these questions are presented in industry tables: Table 4 presents the results for the Forest industry, Table 5 for Industrial Machinery and Table 6 for Electronics. Each table is organized in two sub-tables, with the results on the determinants of productivity in the upper panel (panel a) and results for wages in the lower panel (panel b). In turn, each sub-table includes the estimated coefficients for the variables of interest (age, seniority, potential experience and education) computed in various ways, for there is no best statistical method to compute them. The reported results are obtained both averaging data over time (and using Ordinary Least Squares (OLS) and Instrumental Variables (IV) methods of estimation) and also simultaneously exploiting the cross-section and time series variation in the data, with the time-invariant plant-specific unobserved determinants of productivity and wages captured by fixed effects (FE). But, as discussed above, cross-section estimates minimize loss of precision (attenuation bias) at the cost of enhancing reverse causation, unobserved heterogeneity and selectivity biases. IV estimates reduce reverse causation and FE estimates tackle unobserved heterogeneity, but both (IV and FE) methods often entail substantial loss of precision of the estimated coefficients.

In any case, each table is structured so as to make the results from the various twists of our statistical exercises easily comparable. The list of the additionally included variables (potentially important determinants of productivity and wages which are not the main focus of this paper) is also provided at the bottom of each table.

4.3.1. Age as such is not related to productivity but is positively correlated to wages.
The statistical results in columns [1] and [2] in each table account for at least 50% (with a maximum of 60%) of the total variability of plant productivity and wages in the three industries. Most of the explanatory power of the estimated statistical relations comes, however, from two groups of variables which do not represent the main focus of this paper but are anyway possibly important determinants of productivity and earnings: education and plant age (more comments below in the next section).

The main result from columns [1] and [2] is that workforce age *per se* is unrelated to plant productivity. Age is instead positively related to wages in all of the three industries, with some evidence of declining effects of age on wages in industrial machinery. So, as payroll increases but productivity stays constant it means that a firm's profitability declines with ageing of the firm's labour force.

The different pattern of correlation between age, productivity and wages brings about another related point: if wages do not reflect the productivity contribution of older workers, approximating individually unobserved productivity by wages – as sometimes is done – may drive one to misleading conclusions.

Table 4. Statistical analysis of the determinants of plant productivity and wages: forest industry

| | OLS | | | | IV | Fixed effects |
| | Cross-section | | | | Cross-section | Panel |
	[1]	[2]	[3]	[4]	[5]	[6]
Panel a. Productivity						
Age	0.015	0.000				
	(0.154)	(0.011)				
Age²	−0.002					
	(0.019)					
log of tenure			0.181	0.240*	0.373+	−0.198
			(0.305)	(0.099)	(0.221)	(0.122)
[log of tenure]²			0.017			
			(0.076)			
Potential experience			−0.023	−0.022	−0.031	0.019
			(0.016)	(0.015)	(0.025)	(0.012)
Schooling years	−0.048	−0.048	−0.067	−0.063	0.052	0.082
	(0.082)	(0.083)	(0.090)	(0.086)	(0.080)	(0.057)
Schooling y. (t−1)						−0.014
						(0.056)
Schooling y. (t−2)						0.046
						(0.051)
R-squared	0.409	0.409	0.422	0.422	0.191	0.132
Adj. R-squared	0.385	0.387	0.398	0.399	0.157	
R-squared, within						0.089
Observations	365	365	365	365	279	1523
Overident. test					0.813	
Relevance test					0.000	
Panel b. Wages						
Age	−0.025	0.025***				
	(0.046)	(0.003)				
Age²	0.006					
	(0.006)					

Table 4. *Continued*

	OLS Cross-section				IV Cross-section	Fixed effects Panel
	[1]	[2]	[3]	[4]	[5]	[6]
log of tenure			-0.173* (0.085)	0.112*** (0.027)	0.425*** (0.081)	0.136*** (0.030)
[log of tenure]^2			0.081*** (0.023)			
Potential experience			0.009* (0.005)	0.015*** (0.004)	-0.013 (0.009)	0.009** (0.003)
Schooling years	0.159*** (0.024)	0.157*** (0.024)	0.158*** (0.025)	0.174*** (0.025)	0.150*** (0.033)	0.245*** (0.014)
Schooling y. (t-1)						0.179*** (0.014)
Schooling y. (t-2)						0.096*** (0.013)
R-squared	0.520	0.517	0.565	0.546	0.532	0.590
Adj. R-squared	0.500	0.500	0.547	0.528	0.513	0.670
R-squared, within						
Observations	365	365	365	365	279	1523
Overident. test					0.467	
Relevance test					0.000	

Notes: Dependent variable: is logarithm of plant productivity in panel a and log of wages in panel b. Other control variables (results not reported) for models reported in columns [1]–[4] include a dummy variable for foreign-owned plant, one for plants that disappear in 1996–2002 and other dummies for plant vintage groups (6 groups) and size groups (5 groups). In column [5], seniority is instrumented with a set of lagged variables (the average in the period 1990–94). They include schooling years, potential experience, potential experience squared, seniority and seniority squared. In column [5], high *p*-values (> 10%) for the over-identification test (Hansen *J* statistics) indicate that the validity of the instruments cannot be rejected and low *p*-values (< 0.1%) of relevance test (Anderson canonical correspondence LR statistic) gives indication that the employed instruments are relevant both in productivity and wage estimations.
+ *p* < 0.1, * *p* < 0.05, ** *p* < 0.01, *** *p* < 0.001.

Table 5. Statistical analysis of the determinants of plant productivity and wages: Industrial machinery

| | OLS | | | | IV | Fixed effects |
| | Cross-section | | | | Cross-section | Panel |
	[1]	[2]	[3]	[4]	[5]	[6]
Panel a. Productivity						
Age	0.103	0.005				
	(0.079)	(0.005)				
Age²	−0.013					
	(0.010)					
log of tenure			0.135	−0.081	−0.035	0.077
			(0.191)	(0.050)	(0.114)	(0.087)
[log of tenure]²			−0.062			
			(0.051)			
Potential experience			0.014*	0.012+	−0.003	−0.014
			(0.007)	(0.007)	(0.011)	(0.009)
Schooling years	0.124***	0.125***	0.138***	0.137***	0.086**	0.035
	(0.026)	(0.026)	(0.028)	(0.028)	(0.028)	(0.034)
Schooling y. (t−1)						0.001
						(0.037)
Schooling y. (t−2)						0.102**
						(0.036)
R-squared	0.394	0.392	0.397	0.395	0.219	0.212
Adj. R-squared	0.378	0.377	0.380	0.380	0.193	
R-squared, within						0.049
Observations	567	567	567	567	348	1717
Overident. test					0.351	
Relevance test					0.000	
Panel b. Wages						
Age	0.105***	0.015***				
	(0.024)	(0.002)				

Table 5. *Continued*

| | OLS | | | | IV | Fixed effects |
| | Cross-section | | | | Cross-section | Panel |
	[1]	[2]	[3]	[4]	[5]	[6]
Age²	-0.012*** (0.003)					
log of tenure			0.074 (0.073)	-0.012 (0.017)	0.097+ (0.055)	0.056* (0.024)
[log of tenure]²			-0.025 (0.019)			
Potential experience			0.017*** (0.002)	0.016*** (0.002)	0.008 (0.005)	0.003 (0.002)
Schooling years		0.117*** (0.008)	0.133*** (0.008)	0.133*** (0.008)	0.124*** (0.011)	0.065*** (0.010)
Schooling y. (t−1)						0.005 (0.010)
Schooling y. (t−2)						0.019+ (0.010)
R-squared	0.470	0.454	0.457	0.455	0.437	0.836
Adj. R-squared	0.457	0.441	0.442	0.441	0.419	
R-squared, within						0.871
Observations	567	567	567	567	348	1717
Overident. test					0.024	
Relevance test					0.000	

Notes: Dependent variable: is logarithm of plant productivity in panel a and log of wages in panel b. Other control variables (results not reported) for models reported in columns [1]–[4] include a dummy variable for foreign-owned plant, one for plants that disappear in 1996–2002 and other dummies for plant vintage groups (6 groups) and size groups (5 groups). In column [5], seniority is instrumented with a set of lagged variables (the average in the period 1990–94). They include schooling years, potential experience, potential experience squared, seniority and seniority squared. In column [5], high *p*-values (> 10%) for the over-identification test (Hansen *J* statistics) indicate that the validity of the instruments cannot be rejected and low *p*-values (< 0.1%) of relevance test (Anderson canonical correspondence LR statistic) gives indication that the employed instruments are relevant in productivity but not in wage estimation.

+ *p* < 0.1, * *p* < 0.05, ** *p* < 0.01, *** *p* < 0.001.

Table 6. Statistical analysis of the determinants of plant productivity and wages: Electronics

| | OLS | | | | IV | Fixed effects |
| | Cross-section | | | | Cross-section | Panel |
	[1]	[2]	[3]	[4]	[5]	[6]
Panel a. Productivity						
Age	-0.408	0.024				
	(0.377)	(0.026)				
Age^2	0.061					
	(0.053)					
log of tenure			1.741*	-0.062	2.380+	0.937
			(0.749)	(0.232)	(1.443)	(0.599)
[log of tenure]^2			-0.549*		-0.639+	-0.356+
			(0.230)		(0.349)	(0.184)
Potential experience			0.028	0.030	-0.013	-0.010
			(0.035)	(0.036)	(0.045)	(0.032)
Schooling years	0.180**	0.178**	0.182*	0.207**	0.191***	-0.043
	(0.064)	(0.064)	(0.071)	(0.070)	(0.055)	(0.082)
Schooling y. (t-1)						-0.007
						(0.090)
Schooling y. (t-2)						0.182*
						(0.081)
R-squared	0.301	0.290	0.320	0.291	0.308	
Adj. R-squared	0.239	0.232	0.254	0.228	0.211	
R-squared, within						0.086
Observations	172	172	172	172	98	496
Overident. test					0.258	
Relevance test					0.000	
Panel b. Wages						
Age	-0.046	0.019***				
	(0.061)	(0.004)				
Age^2	0.009					
	(0.009)					

Table 6. *Continued*

| | OLS | | | | IV | Fixed effects |
| | Cross-section | | | | Cross-section | Panel |
	[1]	[2]	[3]	[4]	[5]	[6]
log of tenure			0.192+	0.031	0.528	0.250+
			(0.112)	(0.044)	(0.420)	(0.146)
[log of tenure]^2			−0.049		−0.107	−0.068
			(0.033)		(0.105)	(0.045)
Potential experience			0.016*	0.016*	0.008	0.020*
			(0.006)	(0.006)	(0.012)	(0.008)
Schooling years	0.123***	0.123***	0.137***	0.140***	0.145***	0.160***
	(0.010)	(0.009)	(0.011)	(0.011)	(0.015)	(0.020)
Schooling y. (t−1)						0.120***
						(0.022)
Schooling y. (t−2)						0.134***
						(0.020)
R-squared	0.536	0.530	0.537	0.532	0.617	0.493
Adj. R-squared	0.494	0.492	0.492	0.491	0.563	
R-squared, within						0.615
Observations	172	172	172	172	98	496
Overident. test					0.001	
Relevance test					0.000	

Notes: Dependent variable: is logarithm of plant productivity in panel a and log of wages in panel b. Other control variables (results not reported) for models reported in columns [1]–[4] include a dummy variable for foreign-owned plant, one for plants that disappear in 1996–2002 and other dummies for plant vintage groups (6 groups) and size groups (5 groups). In column [5], seniority is instrumented with a set of lagged variables (the average in the period 1990–94). They include schooling years, potential experience, potential experience squared, seniority and seniority squared. In column [5], high p-values ($> 10\%$) for the over-identification test (Hansen J statistics) indicate that the validity of the instruments cannot be rejected and low p-values ($< 0.1\%$) of relevance test (Anderson canonical correspondence LR statistic) gives indication that the employed instruments are relevant in productivity but not in wage estimation.

$+ p < 0.1$, $* p < 0.05$, $** p < 0.01$, $*** p < 0.001$.

4.3.2. Seniority matters for productivity more often than experience, but differently in traditional and high-tech industries. The discussion in Section 2 invites thinking of why age may (or may not) be associated with productivity. It does so suggesting that the process of human capital accumulation takes place within the firm and outside the firm. Lumping together the two effects (as implicitly done in the empirical formulations underlying the results in columns [1] and [2], where age as such is related to productivity) may obscure that the two forms of human capital accumulation need not bear the same returns. The importance of distinguishing these two sources of skills in the analysis of productivity effects is emphasized for instance by Ilmakunnas *et al.* (2004) and Dygalo and Abowd (2005). For example, the accumulation of knowledge that occurs through seniority may be productivity-enhancing while the accumulation of human capital that occurs through the acquisition of overall labour market experience may not contribute positively. In the statistical analysis underlying the results in columns [3]–[6], we dropped this restriction. We find that the statistical significance of seniority and potential experience is indeed different from each other. This also holds across industries and across estimation methods. The overall goodness of fit of IV and FE-based specifications drops significantly.

In the forest industry as well as in electronics, we find that seniority, not potential experience, is positively related to productivity. Our formulation (in logs and logs squared, so as to obtain the best fit of the data) also implies that the effect of seniority on productivity depends on its starting level.

One additional year of seniority for a freshly hired worker adds to productivity less than it adds for a senior worker who has spent a considerable number of years within the same firm. In other words, there are positive but diminishing returns to seniority. In the electronics industry, the returns to seniority decline so much to become negative beyond a certain threshold. These results are well determined when using the period-averaged cross-section of plants and are still there – though less precisely measured – even when seniority is instrumented to allow for possible feedback effects from the lagged values. In the forest industry, the correlation disappears when the time variation of the data is considered through fixed-effects estimation, while a weaker correlation survives for plants in electronics.

In the industrial machinery plants, instead, potential experience positively correlates, though at the usual declining rates, with productivity. Seniority is instead not significantly related to productivity in a statistical sense in this industry. The pattern of partial correlations in this industry is, however, somewhat statistically weaker than for the other industries, for they do not survive when other methods of estimation than the cross-section OLS are employed. This is a symptom that our statistical model that links plant productivity to human capital variables is not equally effective in capturing the determinants of plant productivity in all industries.

4.3.3. Wage and productivity profiles are dissimilar from each other in electronics and similar in the other industries. In our data set, searching for wage determinants is a more successful undertaking than searching for productivity determinants. The line interpolating the data explains more than 50% of the total variability of plant wages in the forest industry and in electronics and more than 40% of the total in industrial machinery, even when the time dimension of the data set is considered. Among the age-related variables, seniority drives wages in forest and experience drives wages in the industrial machinery industry. Notably, the seniority-wage profile in the lower panel is not too far apart from the seniority-productivity profile estimated in the upper panel for the forest industry. The same applies to experience-wage and experience-productivity profiles for industrial machinery, although it should be kept in mind that, as emphasized above, the statistical relation is much less precisely measured for the plants in this industry.

When it comes to electronics, the picture instead changes substantially. Wages depend positively but to a declining extent on both tenure and experience in the cross-section of plants. This result is still there when the time variation of the panel data set is considered through fixed-effects estimation. This correlation is instead not there when variables are instrumented by their lagged values.

We interpret these results as showing that the profiles of wages and productivity with respect to age-related variables are significantly different from each other in electronics. Wages keep going up, though at declining rates, with both seniority and experience, while the seniority-productivity profile follows a very different path made of definite increases when seniority is low and a flattening out which also involves sheer productivity declines as seniority goes beyond a given threshold.

4.4. More results

The statistical analysis underlying Tables 4, 5 and 6 also includes some ancillary results on the determinants of plant productivity and wages, concerning education and plant age. The important implication of these additional results is that the correlations between age-related variables, productivity and wages (discussed above) do not hinge on the omission of other important determinants of plant productivity and wages. Reassuringly, education and plant age affect productivity and wages as expected, but consideration of these additional elements does not cancel our main results.

4.4.1. Education is positively related to productivity and wages. The earnings equations estimated by labour economists routinely include education as an explanatory variable and make inference as to the rate of return on additional years of education. And even the importance of workers' educational levels in determining plant productivity can hardly be overstated.

In our statistical analysis, education turns out always positively related to wages in the three industries, with estimated coefficients ranging between 0.12 and 0.15. Yet the estimated coefficient is bigger in forest than in more technologically advanced industries. As to its effects on productivity, they seem to be instead ranked in decreasing order of the technological level of the industry at hand. Education is positively and sizably related to plant productivity in electronics with a bigger coefficient than in industrial machinery. No relation is there for the forest industry.

When the time series dimension is considered, these effects are present only when the delayed values of the explanatory variables are considered instead of the current ones. Education is indeed positively associated with productivity with a delay of about two years (the lagged value of education is almost significantly related to productivity, though with a small coefficient, even for the forest industry).

Altogether, these effects indicate that high-education workers in more advanced industries are in some way 'exploited', while high-education people in forestry enjoy a rent. The idea that high-education people accept lower wages possibly in exchange for a bright future to buy the lottery of working in dynamic plants and industries is consistent with anecdotal evidence from Finnish newspapers.[10]

4.4.2. Newer plants are more productive.   Another ancillary result underlying Tables 4, 5 and 6 is that older plants tend to be less productive than newer plants. This effect is consistently present for the three industries. These results are not reported in the tables for brevity but are anyway singled out and pictured in Figure 1.

Figure 1 shows a graphical illustration of productivity and wage effects of plant vintage, whereas the horizontal bars indicate the average effects of plant vintage on productivity (printed light grey) and wages (printed dark grey), with 95% confidence intervals appended. The evidence in the graph points to the marked quantitative relevance of such effects. Younger plants are indeed definitely more productive in all industries. This also holds for wages, though the effect is much less marked. These results are consistent with the literature briefly surveyed in Box 5.[11]

4.5. Implications of our main results: a numerical illustration

If theory and the related empirical findings were to imply that the effect of age-related variables on productivity is always the same irrespective of age, seniority or experience, one might easily compute the numerical effect of ageing on productivity. The estimated coefficient would tell us by how many percentage points productivity varies as a result of a unit change in the age or seniority of a given person (or the average age of a typical worker in a given plant).

Unfortunately, psychometric studies and the economics of human capital teach us that the world is more complicated and the effect of age on productivity may change its sign from positive into negative starting from some threshold age onwards. This raises the empirical questions of *where* (*at which year of age, seniority or experience*) this

---

[10] A more academic argument following more or less the same lines is in Moen (2005).

[11] Maliranta (1999) experimented with alternative capital stock measures (perpetual inventory method vs. fire insurance value of capital stock). They yielded quite similar results for the plant vintage effects. More recent Finnish evidence of the plant vintage effects include Ilmakunnas *et al.* (2004) and Ilmakunnas and Maliranta (2005).

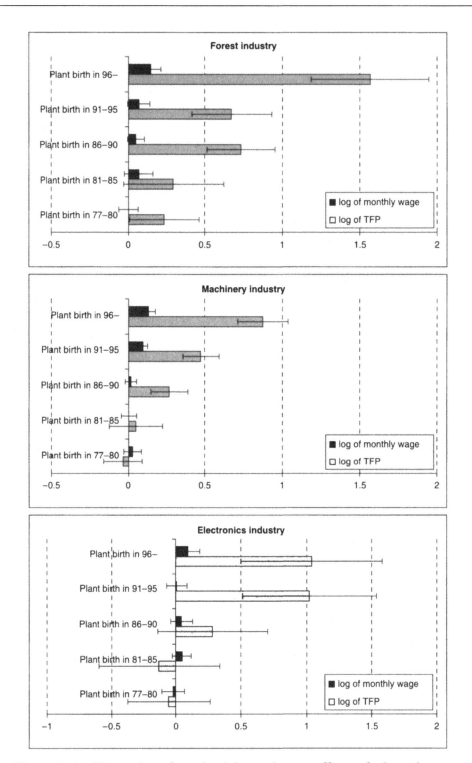

Figure 1. An illustration of productivity and wage effects of plant vintage

Notes: Bars indicate the log difference of total factor productivity and monthly wage with respect to the reference group (plants established in 1976 or earlier). Error bars around the mean bars indicate 95% confidence intervals. The estimates are from the models presented in column [3] of Tables 4–6.

threshold is. Moreover, having found that the returns to seniority decline with seniority or, as in electronics, actually become negative, it remains unclear *by how much* they decline.

Box 5. Old plants, old workers, productivity and wages

Old-aged firms may be less productive and disproportionately hire old-age workers. The evidence on the relation between firm age and productivity is not abundant, though. Dunne *et al.* (1989) report that manufacturing plants that have been in business longer are less likely to close, and Brock and Evans (1986) show that older firms are less likely to fail (controlling for plant and firm size, respectively). This may partly explain why older workers tend to stick with these probably less productive but more financially sound firms.

On the other hand, it has often been found that older firms pay higher wages, after controlling for other relevant firm characteristics. This is often taken to reflect the quality (and thus the higher productivity) of the workers they hire, as well as the working conditions they offer. Yet, as discussed in the main text, this need not be the case. Older firms may pay higher wages to extend fringe benefits, such as pensions or health insurance, to their most faithful workers or, more subtly, because they cannot deny pay raises to people who have developed a good knowledge of the company's ability to pay throughout the years.

Davis and Haltiwanger (1991) find that older manufacturing plants indeed pay higher wages, and age remains a significant determinant of wages once industry, region and size differences are accounted for, with and without controlling for the probability that the plant will close (usually lower for older firms). Troske (1999, Table 11.11) reports similar results: controlling for employer size and location, workers in plants that are less than 5 years old earn nearly 20% less than workers in plants that have been in business 15 years or more. Blanchflower and Oswald (1988) find no significant relationship between wages and years in operation in British data, while Winter-Ebmer (2001) found a positive relation with Austrian data. The very careful study by Kölling *et al.* (2005) shows that, in Germany, older firms pay on average higher wages for workers with the same broadly defined degree of formal qualification. More recently, Brown and Medoff (2003) have analysed the relationship between how long an employer has been in business (firm age) and wages. According to their analysis, firms that have been in business longer pay higher wages (as previous studies have found), but pay if anything lower wages after controlling for worker characteristics. There is some evidence that the relationship is not monotonic, with wages falling and then rising with the number of years in business.

Finally, regarding evidence with Finnish data, Nurmi (2004) finds that old and large firms are less likely to fail and less sensitive to exogenous shocks than young and small firms.

In this section, we employ statistical simulation – a quantitative technique that allows one to describe complicated phenomena in a flexible way (how is described in the top part of Box 5) – to illustrate these issues.

The simulation results are then translated out of the jargon using CLARIFY, the user-friendly software developed by Harvard political scientists Gary King, Michael Tomz and Jason Wittenberg (King *et al.*, 2000; Tomz *et al.*, 2003) expressly for delivering the results of the application of even complicated quantitative techniques to a wider audience not necessarily trained in statistics but still interested in achieving a rather precise knowledge of the quantitative aspects of economic and social issues (see more details in the bottom part of Box 6).

Box 6. Numerical simulations through CLARIFY

a. The issue

The starting point may be a standard multivariate regression exercise where the statistical relation between a dependent variable (say, productivity) and a host of potential explanatory variables (say: age, education and so on) is investigated. The result of a regression exercise usually consists of quantitative information ('estimated coefficients') on the sensitivity of the dependent variable to each of the explanatory variables, while holding the other explanatory variables constant. This piece of information is, however, subject to various sources of uncertainty (the statistical model may be wrong or incomplete; the available information on the explanatory variables may be incomplete as well; some variables of interest may be outright unobserved). Hence, this 'partial correlation' may thus be more or less precisely estimated. If the researcher obtains a precise estimate, the quantitative implication of his-her research may be trusted; otherwise not.

b. Simulation-based approach to interpreting statistical results

Among other things, numerical (so called 'Montecarlo') simulation essentially applies survey sampling techniques to proxy complicated (but presumably more realistic) mathematical relations and eventually determines how trustworthy the results of a given regression are. In surveys, random sampling from the population of interest is commonly used to estimate key features (such as mean and variance) of such population, with the precision of the estimate increasing in sample size. Simulation essentially follows the same logic to learn about probability distributions of estimated coefficients, not populations. In the same fashion as with real samples, approximations can be computed to any desired level of precision by varying the number of simulations.

c. How statistical simulation works in practice through the software CLARIFY

Start from a set of point-wise estimated coefficients of age, education and the other variables set out to explain productivity. Each of these coefficients has a sampling distribution. The central limit theorem guarantees that, for a large enough sample, one can randomly draw ('simulate') coefficient ('parameter') values from a multivariate normal distribution, with mean equal to the point estimates of the coefficients and variances equal to the estimated variance and covariance matrix of the point-wise estimates. By random drawing, one can obtain a realization of the estimated coefficients on average consistent with their point-wise estimates. This is the result of one simulation round. This experiment can be repeated many times at will (clearly, if the coefficient were precisely known, each draw would be identical) and many values for the estimated coefficient of interest computed. Each coefficient can then be multiplied by the value of its corresponding explanatory variable (age). The variability in the values of the simulated coefficients translates in variability (randomness) of the expected value of productivity (the dependent variable), while the effects of the other variables on productivity are held constant at their means.

As a result, we can compute (and graph) the average partial effect of age on productivity and also confidence intervals that delimit the degree of trustworthiness of such an average. To sum up, in our case, the true relation between age and productivity is likely complicated, for the effect of age on productivity may be positive or negative depending on age. If this is the case, describing the results of statistical analysis becomes rapidly cumbersome and only imperfectly related to the question at hand. King *et al.* (2000) have developed a software program (CLARIFY) that, without changing any underlying data or statistical assumption, provides interpretation-friendly and graphical answers to the questions of interest.

Figures 2 and 3 are the outputs of **CLARIFY** and concern, respectively, the seniority and experience profiles of productivity and wages estimated *through Ordinary Least Squares from the period-averaged cross-section of plants.*[12] Being OLS cross-sectional OLS estimates, they suffer from many of the biases whose shortcomings have been extensively discussed above. Although precisely tracking the overall direction of the biases is not easy, the reported results likely represent upper bound estimates, and they include both skill depreciation and worker reallocation effects.

The statistical simulations underlying Figures 2 and 3 and Table 7 (based on those figures) revolve around the multivariate statistical analysis whose point-wise results and significance are reported in Table A2 in the appendix. To maximize the goodness

---

[12] To compute the necessary confidence intervals, CLARIFY requires relatively precisely estimated coefficients be imputed. This is why we use OLS cross-sectional estimates, with the caveats in the main text.

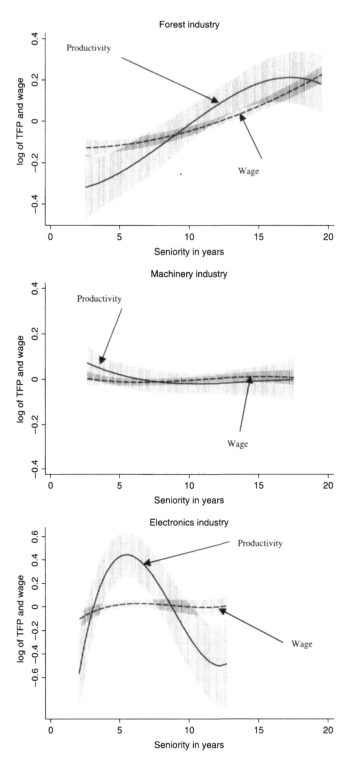

Figure 2. Productivity and wage responses to seniority: simulation analysis from estimates in Table A2

Notes: See Box 6 for a detailed explanation of how such profiles are constructed.

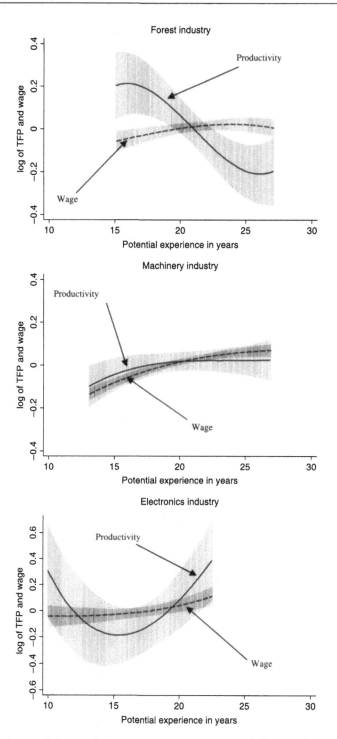

Figure 3. Productivity and wage responses to potential experience: simulation analysis from estimates in Table A2

Notes: See Box 6 for a detailed explanation of how such profiles are constructed.

Table 7. Simulations of cumulated productivity and wage responses under various settings

	Difference . . .		. . . in log of TFP			. . . in log of monthly wage		
	from . . .	to . . .	Mean	Std. err.	t-value	Mean	Std. err.	t-value
Seniority								
Forest								
Seniority in years and other variables	7 at their means	17 at their means	0.38	0.15	2.60	0.23	0.04	5.81
Machinery								
Seniority in years and other variables	7 at their means	17 at their means	0.00	0.08	0.01	0.02	0.03	0.73
Electronics								
Seniority in years and other variables	2 at their means	6 at their means	1.07	0.32	3.31	0.13	0.07	1.83
Seniority in years and other variables	6 at their means	10 at their means	−0.68	0.20	−3.34	−0.03	0.05	−0.61
Potential Experience								
Forest								
Experience in years and other variables	15 at their means	25 at their means	−0.40	0.17	−2.33	0.08	0.05	1.69
Machinery								
Experience in years and other variables	13 at their means	20 at their means	0.12	0.07	1.77	0.15	0.02	7.76
Electronics								
Experience in years and other variables	10 at their means	16 at their means	−0.48	0.22	−2.22	0.02	0.05	0.46
Experience in years Other variables	16 at their means	22 at their means	0.49	0.25	1.95	0.12	0.06	2.13

Table 7. *Continued*

	Difference...		...in log of TFP			...in log of monthly wage		
	from...	to...	Mean	Std. err.	t-value	Mean	Std. err.	t-value
Seniority and experience combined								
Forest								
Seniority in years	7	17	−0.02	0.12	−0.16	0.31	0.04	8.22
and experience in years	15	25						
and other variables	at their means	at their means						
Machinery								
Seniority in years	3	10	0.04	0.07	0.53	0.15	0.02	6.62
and experience in years	13	20						
and other variables	at their means	at their means						
Electronics								
Seniority in years	2	6	0.61	0.29	2.11	0.14	0.05	2.71
and experience in years	10	14						
and other variables	at their means	at their means						
Seniority in years	6	12	−0.69	0.25	−2.77	0.05	0.05	1.06
and experience in years	14	20						
and other variables	at their means	at their means						

Notes: Simulations are based on the same regression models (results in Table A2) used for drawing Figures 2–3. 'Mean' indicates the log difference of productivity (or wage) levels. Multiplying the number by 100 provides an approximation of percentage difference in productivity (or wage) levels in the different hypothetical situations. For more details on how these figures are computed, see Box 6.

of fit of the interpolating line, the empirical specification underlying the graphs is more flexible than those in Tables 4, 5 and 6. This boils down to appending more polynomial terms of the same variables to the list of the productivity and wage determinants, in addition to the linear and squared terms present in the tables seen above.

In each figure, along the vertical axis, one reads the marginal response of the dependent variables (logarithms of TFP and wages) to changes in seniority, experience and education years, measured along the horizontal axis. Such responses are defined over the interval of values taken by each explanatory variable in the industry at hand. The thick and dotted lines indicate, respectively, the average marginal response of TFP and wages (with the average taken over the very many potential values of the coefficients of interest). The dot-shaded and line-shaded intervals around such estimated average responses represent confidence intervals, which provide an indication of the degree of precision of the simulated estimates.

4.5.1. Seniority profiles (Figure 2). Productivity and wage responses to the cross-section variability in the number of seniority years are very similar to each other in the forest industry (both growing fast) and in industrial machinery (both essentially flat, once confidence intervals are taken into account). From the figures reported in the upper part of Table 7, one learns that, moving from a plant with a seniority of 7 years for the average worker to a plant with seniority equal to 17, having set the other determinants of productivity to their means results in a productivity increase of 38% in the forest industry. In electronics, the seniority-productivity profile follows a well-defined inverted-U shape, while the wage is mildly increasing. These trends correspond to a swift positive productivity response of cumulated 107% as one shift from plants with an average worker seniority of two years to plants with worker seniority equal to six years (with wages going up more moderately). If one moves further by another four years from plants with seniority equal to six to plants with seniority equal to ten, productivity undergoes a (relative) shortfall of cumulative 68%, with roughly unchanged wages. These are huge numbers. As mentioned in the caveat above, however, they are upper bound estimates also inclusive of worker reallocation effects. It should be noted, though, that very drastic declines in relative productivity levels with age have been documented for other countries such as France in the literature (see e.g. Figure 4.4 in Productivity Commission, 2005).

4.5.2. Experience profiles (Figure 3). Productivity and wage responses to the cross-section variability in the years of potential experience are much less precisely estimated, particularly for productivity. This may be the result of multi-collinearity between experience and seniority, which may be at the origin of the initially downward sloping response of productivity to experience in the forest industry and in electronics. In industrial machinery, one finds instead plausible results with positive wage and productivity responses to experience (with wages and productivity by 15% and 12% respectively over 7 years; see Table 7). A possible way out is to compute the implied productivity response of both higher experience and seniority (after all, if a worker stays with the same plant, he/she acquires both experience and seniority at once). When this is done (see the results in the lower panel of Table 7, 'Seniority and experience combined'), one finds an essentially flat productivity response to the combination of seniority and experience and a moderately positive wage response for a cumulated 15% over 7 years of time. The combination of seniority and experience leaves the results for electronics qualitatively unchanged, instead. When the number of seniority and experience years is relatively low, moving from low-seniority and low-experience plants to high-seniority and high-experience plants corresponds to a cumulated productivity increase of about 60%. When this is done moving from intermediate to high levels of seniority and experience, the productivity shortfall is of about 70%. Wages do not follow suit, instead, but keep going up.

4.6. Summing up and discussion

Our statistical analysis provides a reasonably coherent picture of the empirical relation between age, seniority and experience, on the one hand, and plant productivity and wages, on the other, in Finland in the years of the IT revolution.

At first sight, our results seem to support the view that workforce ageing as such has adverse effects on labour costs. Age is essentially unrelated to productivity while it is positively correlated with wages. As we distinguish the effects of seniority on productivity and wages from those of general experience, though, we find that the picture is more complicated and sharply differs across industries (see Box 7 for a survey of other studies emphasizing industry differences in productivity and wage profiles).

Box 7. Previous statistical evidence on age, seniority, experience, productivity and wages

About 25 years ago, Medoff and Abraham (1980, 1981) used performance evaluation to gauge separate information about individual productivity and wage profiles. They found that wages do not necessarily reflect productivity. Bishop (1987) and Flabbi and Ichino (2001) also put together measures of individual productivity, following the Medoff and Abraham methodology and confirming their results with other data sets.

Hellerstein *et al.* (1999), using US data, find that productivity and wages increase with age, except for the oldest age group in some specifications, and their patterns are fairly similar. Crépon *et al.* (2002) use French data and conclude that the relationship of productivity and age follows an inverted U-shape, but wage is increasing in age. In manufacturing, wage increases with skill level, but productivity increases even more. In non-manufacturing, wage increases more than productivity as skill levels go up. Haegeland and Klette (1999) use Norwegian data and find that productivity and wage increase with education and the highly educated go hand in hand by productivity. Medium-level potential experience (age minus education years) gave higher productivity than short experience, but with long experience productivity declined although still stayed higher than with short experience. Medium-level experience was underpaid, but the wage premium for long experience corresponded to the productivity premium. They concluded that the wage-experience profile only partly reflected the productivity profile.

Only a few scholars have looked at cross-industry heterogeneity of productivity and wage responses. Aubert and Crépon (2004) estimated average earnings relations for France and found evidence of declining productivity after the age of 55, but they found that the age-productivity profile (as captured by such earnings functions) does not differ much across industries. In contrast, Aubert *et al.* (2004) estimated labour demand curves by using wage bill shares conditioned on value added as well as old and new economy capital; they did find significant evidence that innovative firms and work-practices present lower wage bill shares.

The same result seemingly applies within occupational groups for other countries. Similarly to our findings here, Neuman and Weiss (1995) found that earnings peaks are located earlier in age in the high-tech sector. Hellerstein and Neumark (1995), using Israeli data, find that earnings and productivity profiles are fairly similar for the relatively less skilled workers (the group that covers most of the workforce).

Other studies have in turn found that the relation has changed over time. The seniority-wage profile has seemingly become steeper and its peak moved forwards in Denmark as a result of the decentralization of wage determination (Bingley and Westergaard-Nielsen, 2003). Eriksson and Jäntti (1997) found that in 1971 the peak of the wage profile was at the age group 35–39 years but has then moved forward, being at the age group 45–49 years in 1990 in Finland.

Finally, a host of previous studies indeed highlights the productivity-enhancing role of worker mobility between plants. The mobility of workers has an additional important productivity effect that goes beyond the 'within firm' effect discussed above and examined in this paper. 'Churning' of plants/firms (i.e. simultaneous entries and exits) has been found to have a dominant role in industry productivity growth. Thanks to this mechanism, a worker's productivity may improve greatly when she moves from a low productivity plant/firm to a high productivity plant/firm (Foster *et al.*, 2001; Disney *et al.*, 2003). With the data from the Finnish manufacturing sector, Maliranta (2003) finds that the average productivity growth rate of the plants is typically 50–70% of the industry productivity growth rate, which is due to the fact that entries, but especially exits and the reallocation of labour and capital between the continuing plants have an important role to play as well. This gap between industry and plant productivity growth has been particularly pronounced in the Finnish electronics industry since the latter part of the 1980s, but has also been substantial for instance in the textile and wearing industry during the latter half of the 1980s and in the basic metal industry during the latter half of the 1980s and the first half of the 1990s.

Returns to seniority are usually positive but declining with the level of seniority in the forest industry plants; about the same applies to earnings profiles. Similar considerations hold for the productivity and wage effects of general experience in industrial machinery, although the estimated relation is statistically less solid. The similarity of the productivity and wages responses to the accumulation of human capital indicates that, in 'average' industries, skill depreciation does not seemingly lead to higher labour costs. And given that these industries are still quantitatively important in the Finnish economy, wage-productivity misalignments cannot be the main explanation for the bad labour market performance of the elderly in Finland.

The picture is quite different for the high-tech plants. In electronics – the industry where people are exposed to rapid technological and managerial changes – the responses of plant productivity and wages to seniority are very different from each other. The seniority-productivity profile shows a positive relation first and then negative as one looks at plants with higher average seniority, while wages instead keep going up with seniority.[13] This holds for plants with similar education, plant age and size and other conditions and is thus not related to plant differences in these other respects. How negative the productivity returns to seniority may become cannot be said with certainty. Numerical simulations based on our OLS cross-sectional results indicate that the change of sign in the seniority-productivity profile may be pronounced.

Altogether, our results are consistent with the idea that fast technical change brings about accelerated skill depreciation of senior workers. We cannot honestly rule out, however, that our correlations may also be the result of worker movements across plants. The negative correlation between seniority and productivity may in fact also reflect the reallocation away of younger (and more productive) workers who leave behind older plants attracted by the career prospects offered in newly born high-productivity firms and plants.[14] We cannot precisely quantify the relative importance

---

[13] This is not too surprising: as recently discussed at length by Uusitalo and Vartiainen (2005), the combination of highly centralized collective agreements with relatively autonomous but still highly unionized industry wage setting has resulted in a very low weight (4.4%, on average) given to performance-related firm-level corrections of wages.

[14] Evidence on the importance of reallocation for productivity purposes was indeed provided by Ilmakunnas et al. (2005) for the Finnish manufacturing sector, where it was shown that the churning of workers (i.e. simultaneous hiring and separation of workers within a plant) speeds up plant productivity growth, while holding back seniority.

of the two effects in our statistical analysis. Both skill depreciation and worker reallocation appear to affect the relation between seniority and productivity in the Finnish high-tech industry.

It looks as though the deferred compensation hypothesis, perhaps amended with the insights from sorting and matching theories, fits better the labour market facts in high-tech industries than the human capital hypothesis. Yet the evidence for the 'average' industries is not consistent with this hypothesis. This is an open issue that we briefly discuss further in the concluding section.

5. CONCLUSIONS

We started this paper asking ourselves whether we could explain the weak labour market position of older workers. The simultaneous presence of a relatively aged – and still rapidly ageing – workforce and a major external shock (such as the IT revolution of the late 1990s) makes Finland a nice experiment to address this question investigating the diverse responses of wages and productivity to age, seniority and experience patterns across industries.

Our results do not indicate that age as such is responsible for the bad labour market outcomes of the elderly. The differential effect of seniority and experience on productivity and earnings is minor for two of the three Finnish manufacturing industries (the 'average' ones) we chose to analyse. These productivity and wage patterns probably reflect the relatively more valuable role of tacit knowledge in traditional industries. Productivity and wage profiles differ just in electronics, not in the other industries. We interpret this as implying that exposure to rapid technological and managerial changes seems to make a difference for plant productivity, less so for wages for the high-tech plants. Yet this productivity-wage discrepancy is not associated with age but rather with seniority, hence with a variable which can be affected by individual and policy decisions to a greater extent than age, that is largely exogenous for the individual (though not for the plant manager).

In the end, our results give support to at least two important policy implications. First, the similar shapes of productivity and wage profiles in 'average industries' indicate that the weak labour market performance of older workers in Finland is not because they are a burden for the average firm in the economy. Leaving high-tech plants aside, the bad labour market outcomes of the elderly in the rest of the economy are presumably driven by two other causes, such as discriminatory attitudes on the employer side and public incentives schemes easing the way towards early retirement. To ameliorate the labour market performance of the elderly, policy should address these issues. Second, higher seniority is instead associated with higher labour costs in high-tech plants. This is consistent with the anecdotal evidence from Wal-Mart and Ericsson that we have reported. It is also consistent with the beliefs – entertained by many Finnish employers – that older people could not adapt as easily as younger ones to the arrival of the new technology.[15] And indeed a survey conducted by the Ministry of Labour in 2002 indicates that as much as 10% of prime-aged workers (and 15% of workers above 50) agree that 'workplace discriminates against old workers'.[16] In spite of government-mandated media campaigns to counteract such attitudes, the possibility that a negative employer bias against old workers has affected hiring and firing practices in the late 1990s cannot thus be easily ruled out. Our results suggest that this effect is not present in the Finnish economy at large but mainly in high-tech plants.

To improve the employability of older workers in these industries, public policy should divert resources away from preserving existing jobs and lend more attention on the retraining of old workers to ease their reallocation away from less productive plants (or plants where they have become less productive) into new jobs. Some governments are more worried and more interventionist than others in this respect. In the last few years, for instance, the Finnish Government has already embarked on a programme ('The National Programme on Ageing Workers'; see OECD, 2004, p. 119) aimed at deferring retirement and, in parallel, improving the so called 'employability' of older workers. It is unclear, however, to what extent grand plans may be effective to bring about a solution to these problems. Policies aimed at easing reallocation across plants even within the same industry would probably be a useful complementary tool in this respect.

Finally, our results are also somehow puzzling in at least one respect. They are not fully consistent with any of the existing theories that we know. The results for the high-tech plants are consistent with the deferred compensation hypothesis and not with the human capital hypothesis. As surveyed in the theoretical section of the paper, the human capital hypothesis would predict a negative discrepancy in plants with an older labour force where we instead find the opposite results. But even the Lazear hypothesis is not fully consistent with our Finnish data because the results found for electronics are not there for the other industries.

This begs the question of why the Lazear model is more relevant in high-tech plants than in the other plants. One possibility is that productivity is less easily observable in high-tech industries. This would make the asymmetric information mechanism envisaged by Lazear more sensible in those industries. This explanation would probably do if our results were there for plants producing immaterial 'weightless' services whose output is typically hard to measure. Our discussion here instead concerns plants producing 'concrete' manufacturing goods for which productivity mis-measurement is presumably a less serious concern. An alternative possibility is

---

[15] Juuti (2001) reports that young line managers with a good educational background often harboured prejudice against the ability of older workers to cope with new things. This is potentially important for hiring and firing practices. Although discriminating attitudes are rarely shared by top-level managers, recruitment decisions happen to be taken by the mid-management level.

[16] Kouvonen (1999) reports somewhat lower figures, with a 5% share of people above 45 having experienced age at discrimination at work for the average firm.

that seniority, being the other side of impeded resource reallocation, is particularly damaging in industries where changes – requiring flexibility and ability to quickly adapt – come about all the time. Hence, the adverse consequences of seniority manifest themselves in these industries and less so in other industries where changes are smoother. Under these circumstances, a less mobile ageing workforce might constitute an impediment to productivity growth of firms and their plants. To the extent that low productivity (and low immobility) is a consequence of declining ability to incessantly adopt new technologies due to weak basic education, public policy should focus on efforts to increase the quantity and improve the quality of the adult education. If, however, the main reason for staying still too long is not the inability of older workers to adopt new technologies, policy-makers should seek ways to encourage the mobility of the ageing workforce to maintain the scope for continued productivity enabled by learning-by-doing. Greater mobility of workers might also facilitate the diffusion of technologies and thereby speed up productivity growth of the firms – and stimulating 'creative destruction' (i.e. productivity-enhancing churning of plants and firms within industry) to boot.

Finally, how special are our results? Insofar as the use of ICT will spread to other industries in the years to come, it can be expected that the productivity patterns observed in electronics will emerge in other industries in the future. The findings for electronics may be foretelling more general developments in the other industries of the Finnish economy – and possibly other economies. For sure, in a world where innovation forces, as opposed to catching up forces, have become the key engine of growth (see Acemoglu *et al.*, 2003, and the Sapir Report, 2004), companies and governments will be more and more involved in such problems as the ones discussed in this paper.

Discussion

Wendy Carlin
University College London and CEPR

Four facts about the advanced economies provide the motivation for this paper: the poor labour market performance of older workers (unemployment and employment rates); the ageing of the labour force; evidence measured in surveys of a decline in physical and mental performance at higher ages; and finally, the change in industry structure toward 'high tech' industries. This raises the question of whether the employability of older workers declines because they become too costly (diminishing productivity is not compensated by lower wages) and whether this is especially marked in high-tech sectors of the economy. The authors of this paper do not find evidence supporting either of these hypotheses in their data from three Finnish manufacturing industries. However, their findings suggest that there is a hump-shaped relationship between a measure of productivity and the seniority (not age) of workers in plants in the high-tech industry in their sample: electronics. There is no corresponding pattern for wages. This is interpreted as signalling a potential problem in the matching of workers to jobs in industries with rapid technological progress in the context of constraints on worker mobility (e.g. costs of firing).

Channels through which ageing can affect economic performance are the average quality of the direct labour input, the effect on capital deepening because of the implications of ageing for private and public saving and its impact on technological progress (new ideas and diffusion). Older people may be less creative, entrepreneurial and risk-taking and the depreciation of their skill set may imply less adaptation and diffusion of new knowledge. On the other hand, an ageing population may create bigger incentives for labour and memory saving innovation.

In order to evaluate the economic impact of age-related variables, it is essential to specify whose perspective we are taking. From the perspective of workers, the decision is whether to remain in their job, to search for a new one, to leave the labour force or to invest in (re)training. And the key question is how age and or seniority affect wage and employment prospects, as well as training opportunities within and outside the firm. For firms, the question is how age or seniority affects the profitability of existing production and the firm's investment in human and physical capital and in innovation. What are the constraints on the wage structure they can deploy and on firing? From the perspective of a policy-maker concerned with welfare, the question is the impact of age-related variables on total factor productivity and the role of policy-related barriers to the reallocation of workers, training and early retirement programmes.

In this paper, Daveri and Maliranta take one slice of this question, focusing on the impact of age-related variables on the quality of direct labour input:

- How are productivity and wages related to age structure and seniority at the plant level in manufacturing?
- Does this relationship vary according to the innovativeness or technology intensiveness of the industry?

To answer these questions, it is necessary to have matched employer-employee data and a clear contrast in industry characteristics. This makes the use of data from Finland an appropriate choice: there is high-quality matched data and looking at the period of the late 1990s to the early 2000s provides a nice contrast among the traditional industry of 'forest products', a neutral one of industrial machinery and a high-tech industry, electronics.

The method is to use plant-level data to estimate an index of total factor productivity and to calculate the average wage. Each of these is then used as the dependent variable in a separate regression for each industry with various combinations of the age-related variables on the right-hand side along with a set of plant-level control variables (including years of schooling, a dummy for a foreign-owned plant and dummies for different vintages of plants including those that exit during the observation period). The age-related variables are worker age, seniority (i.e. years in the current firm) and labour market potential experience (age minus age when completed last qualification/degree) averaged for workers in each plant. It is somewhat odd that TFP is the productivity variable of choice when an initial motivation was the impact of age-related variables on firm profitability via labour costs, which suggests that it is labour productivity that is relevant, not TFP.[17]

Neither age nor age squared is ever significant in a productivity regression. In electronics but in neither of the other industries, there is a positive coefficient on seniority and a negative coefficient on the squared term in seniority. This says that when looking across plants, TFP initially rises as the average tenure of workers in the plant goes up but then falls in plants with higher levels of average seniority. The effects of age-related variables on wages are mainly (but not always) positive in forest products, hump-shaped for age (but with no robust tenure effects) in machinery and positive for age and weakly positive for tenure and experience in electronics.

The authors conclude that it is not age *per se* but seniority that affects TFP and that this effect is found only in the high-tech sector, electronics. In order to make their results more easily interpretable, they estimate modified versions of their equations and produce graphs showing the average partial effect of the variable of interest. From these equations they calculate the effect on TFP of a change in, for example, seniority. As acknowledged by the authors, the estimate that plant productivity doubles when average seniority of the workforce goes from 2 to 6 years and then falls by two-thirds as average seniority goes from 6 to 10 years is very large. My main concern with this central result in the paper is that it may reflect the dynamics of a rapidly growing industry rather than the inherent characteristics of long-tenure workers in electronics.

In electronics, a plant where the average tenure is six years is estimated to be at the 'turning point' from rising to falling TFP. As Table A1 shows, the mean tenure in the sample for electronics plants is six years, which reflects the rapid growth of the industry: it is 11 years and 9 years respectively in the forest products and machinery industries. The likely role of industry dynamics in generating tenure/productivity profiles of the kind shown in the paper can be illustrated by a simple example. If we assume that initially there are three industries, F, M and W with identical plants in terms of TFP, age and seniority structure. In particular, we assume there is no causal link from the average age or seniority of workers in a plant to the plant's TFP. We now introduce a different demand shock for each industry: a negative demand shock for industry F, no change for M and a positive shock for E. We assume that there is unobserved heterogeneity in managerial ability across plants. As a consequence of the

---

[17] TFP is calculated using a simple growth accounting framework with the assumption of a constant labour share (WL/Y). If the aim is to test whether seniority or ageing affects labour costs, which are measured by the ratio of wages to labour productivity, then this is perhaps not an ideal choice.

AGE, SENIORITY AND LABOUR COSTS

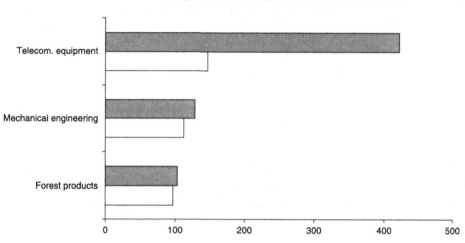

Figure 4. Contrasting industry dynamics in Finland, 1995–2002

Note: Telecommunications equipment = ISIC322; Mechanical engineering = ISIC29; Forest products = ISIC20+21.

Source: Groningen Growth and Development Centre, 60-Industry Database, October 2005, http://www.ggdc.net/, updated from O'Mahony and van Ark (2003).

differential demand shocks and assuming there are costs of entry and exit, we will observe disequilibrium in the F and E industries. Good managers in E will expand output, increase hiring and raise TFP relative to other plants in E. Since hires have zero seniority, average seniority in these expanding, higher TFP plants will fall: lower seniority is associated with higher TFP but by assumption, this is independent of any relationship between individual human capital (and TFP) and tenure. Similarly, good managers in F identify the decline in their industry earlier and cease hiring sooner, with the result that higher TFP firms end up with on average longer tenure workers. This produces a positive relationship between seniority and TFP in the 'declining' industry and a negative relationship in the 'expanding' industry. In the industry where there is no shock, there is no relationship. This pattern is consistent with the contrast between the three industries shown in Figure 2 of the paper.[18]

Figure 4 provides some illustrative data showing that employment grew in telecommunications equipment and shrank in forest products over the time period considered in the paper.

[18] A similar story could be told to account for the within firm pattern that is shown in column [6] of Table 6. Using fixed effects estimation, the relationship between changes in TFP over time and in the age-related variables is uncovered, controlling for time invariant characteristics of plants such as managerial quality. A similar although a much weaker hump-shaped relationship between TFP and seniority is reported. If we now assume that a new higher TFP technology emerges in electronics during the period of observation but not in forest products, production in electronics becomes more profitable and each firm expands. The increase in hiring reduces seniority and we associate a within-firm rise in TFP with a fall in seniority.

The authors undertake a number of tests to check the robustness of their results but they are not able to separate out the possible impact of industry dynamics driven by exogenous demand or technology shocks from the causality of seniority producing a change in efficiency that they seek to identify. Another approach to identifying such an effect would be to focus on those who switch jobs. The Daveri–Maliranta story implies that in electronics longer tenure workers are worse substitutes for otherwise equivalent workers than is the case in the other two industries. This suggests that they should get a bigger wage cut if they switch jobs as compared with similar workers in one of the other industries.[19]

Hence although the results in the paper are suggestive, I think further investigation is required before we can be confident that there really is a causal link of policy-relevant magnitude in a high-tech industry from seniority (longer tenure in a given firm) to lower TFP.

Rudolf Winter-Ebmer
University of Linz, Institute for Advanced Studies (IHS), Vienna and CEPR

Daveri and Maliranta have produced a very interesting paper on the impact of age and seniority on wages and productivity in Finland. The main idea is that the effects of ageing on firm productivity are very different in traditional industries as compared to high-tech or information technology industries (electronics in their empirical analysis). Psychometric studies have shown that physical, cognitive and verbal abilities have different age gradients: whereas physical and cognitive skills, such as mathematical and logical skills decay pretty fast, organizational and verbal skills show no particular ageing pattern at all (Skirbekk, 2003). Daveri and Maliranta argue that ageing of the workforce is more problematic in high-tech industries because of a faster technical change, faster changes in production technologies and faster product development. While most psychometric and other studies relate to age as such, Daveri and Maliranta concentrate their argument on the impact of job tenure within a particular firm: while there is no difference between the productivity-experience and wage-experience paths in the electronics industry – nor in the machinery industry by the way – there is a significant divergence in the development of productivity and wages as seniority in a firm increases. This pattern cannot be seen in more traditional industries like forestry and machinery.

While the general pattern of a higher interdependence between firm seniority, technology adaptation and learning – and in turn productivity – in high-tech firms is sensible, the main empirical results seem to be out of line. Productivity in electronics firms increases by 61 log points in the first 4 years of tenure (in fact from year 2 to

---

[19] Using Finnish data, Uusitalo and Vartiainen (2005) report that firm exits and promotions increase earnings up to age 50, after which such events do not on average improve a person's relative position. Whether this is true of tenure and whether it differs across industries would be relevant evidence for the Daveri–Maliranta hypothesis.

year 6) but decreases in the following 6 years again by 69 log points (see Table 7). A literal interpretation of these results would be that workers who stay with their firms for more than 6 years lose more than half of their productivity; they become such a burden to the firm, that everybody would have to be fired otherwise the managers would be acting completely irresponsibly. This is probably not what we are seeing in these firms.

Moreover, the measured effect is basically a product of a simple OLS cross-section regression; it is much reduced and less well statistically determined if other methods or data are used. Some other possible explanations come to my mind which could have produced such an outcome. The data relate to mean characteristics of the workforce, such as mean age and mean tenure of workers. As the IT boom in Finland did not start before the mid 1990s, I suspect that there are not many firms with mean tenure of its workforce of more than 7 years – and if they exist, they might be fairly different firms with a different technology and firm organization. As Daveri and Maliranta correctly state, the causal impact of mean tenure on productivity cannot be properly distinguished from matching and selection problems: it is by no means a coincidence that some workers stay with the firm longer, others don't; it is no coincidence why some firms stick to their complete workforce longer or to phrase it differently, why workers want to stay longer with a particular firm. Good workers stay with good firms and vice versa. All these matching arguments make the strong point that a simple correlation between job seniority and productivity will be an upward biased estimate of the real causal effect of job seniority on productivity. Related labour economics studies on the causal effect of seniority on wages come to the conclusion that OLS estimates overestimate the true causal effect by a factor between two and four (Topel, 1991; Altonji and Shakotko, 1987).

It has to be said, though, that finding convincing estimates of the relation between firm employment structure and productivity is very difficult: simple fixed effects models using variation in the composition of the workforce over time to determine the variation of productivity fall again prey to the criticism of reverse causality: why do, and how can, firms change the composition of their workforce? Only by changing recruitment and lay-off policies, policies which are obviously related to past and expected productivity. While the causal impact is very difficult to establish in such studies, any work in this direction using new data sets is very interesting. Further important questions come to my mind, for instance concerning inter-firm mobility within the industry which seems to contribute to productivity growth throughout the industry (Parent, 2000). It seems that inter-firm mobility is higher in the high-tech sector which could contribute to explain the diverging pattern between seniority-productivity and experience-productivity profiles. Another important issue concerns wage-setting schemes: If indeed high-tech sectors have a higher prevalence of deferred payment schemes like stock options or profit sharing in some sort or the other, the relation between age or tenure and wages would be steeper and the divergence between wage and productivity development would shrink.

The personnel economics and firm organization literature has also stressed complementarities in the composition of the workforce: a good mix of old and young workers might be better for firm productivity than employing only young or only old workers (Lazear, 1998; Grund and Westergård-Nielsen, 2005). It might be interesting to see whether these results hold also in the high-tech industry. Such an analysis would require looking at the age and tenure composition of the workforce in more detail by using the underlying micro data.

In my view, policy conclusions are still difficult to draw from this paper. Maybe Finland was not such a good experiment in this respect, because its high-tech sector had an explosive growth after 1995, which is too short and too turbulent a period to draw firm conclusions about the effects of firm seniority and the like. Replicating the study for another country with a more smooth development of its high-tech sector might be a welcome complement.

APPENDIX: DATA SET AND VARIABLE DESCRIPTION

Similarly to the other Nordic countries, Finland is endowed with a rich register data of companies, plants and individuals (see Statistics Denmark *et al.*, 2003). The unique identification codes for persons, companies and plants used in the different registers form the backbone of the Finnish administrative register network and the Finnish statistical system, whereby different sources of information can be integrated conveniently for various statistical purposes.[20] By using this system, Statistics Finland has constructed the Finnish Longitudinal Employer-Employee Database (FLEED), which is tailored for various needs of economic research. Its most comprehensive and detailed version is maintained at Statistics Finland. It contains information of companies, plants and individuals. Plants are linked to their companies, and individuals to their employer plants and companies. Data are collected from Business Register (plants and companies in the business sector), Census of Manufacturing (manufacturing plants), Financial Statements Statistics (companies in the business sector), R&D survey and ICT survey (companies in the business sector), and Employment Statistics (individuals aged between 16 and 69 years). These data include a wide variety of detailed information on these units. A large proportion of variables are available from 1990 to 2002. These data cover essentially the whole target population of companies, plants and individuals. Due to confidentiality concerns, outside researchers do not have direct access to it. For the outside researchers, Statistics Finland has constructed a separate version of it. The variable set is more limited and some of the categorical variables are broader (many industries are combined, for example).

This paper employs plant level information for plants and workforce. Productivity measures, plant age, plant size originate from the Census of Manufacturing. We do not have information of the levels of value added, hours worked or capital stock as

---

[20] Data sources and linking of them is described in greater detail in Ilmakunnas *et al.* (2001) and Maliranta (2003).

Table A1. Descriptive statistics of data on plants by industry, plant averages in 1995–2002

Variables	Forest industry					Machinery industry					Electronics industry				
	Mean	Sd	p5	Median	95p	Mean	Sd	p5	Median	95p	Mean	Sd	p5	Median	95p
Log of TFP index	1.80	0.74	0.88	1.66	3.28	2.83	0.59	2.08	2.72	4.00	2.27	1.04	0.99	2.05	4.58
Log of monthly wage (in euros)	7.61	0.24	7.23	7.59	8.02	7.69	0.19	7.36	7.69	8.00	7.65	0.23	7.27	7.67	8.03
Schooling years	11.0	0.4	10.3	11.0	11.7	11.6	0.9	10.6	11.4	13.6	12.2	1.2	10.6	11.9	14.5
Age in years	39.6	3.8	33.3	40.1	45.0	39.3	4.0	31.8	39.8	45.0	35.6	3.8	29.4	35.8	41.6
Potential experience in years	21.6	3.9	15.1	22.1	27.1	20.7	4.2	13.1	21.1	26.9	16.4	4.0	9.3	16.6	22.5
Seniority in years	10.9	5.6	2.6	10.8	19.5	9.2	4.8	2.7	8.9	17.5	6.3	3.3	2.1	5.3	12.69
	Proportion (%)					Proportion (%)					Proportion (%)				
Plant birth before 1977	57.0					34.57					27.91				
Plant birth 1977–1980	6.3					8.47					7.56				
Plant birth 1981–1985	5.5					6.88					4.07				
Plant birth 1986–1990	10.7					16.58					23.26				
Plant birth 1991–1995	9.9					18.87					19.77				
Plant birth 1996–	10.7					14.64					17.44				
Plant size 5–9 persons	1.8					3.14					3.17				
Plant size 10–19 persons	9.0					10.20					6.85				
Plant size 20–49 persons	30.9					41.08					33.51				
Plant size 50–99 persons	21.7					20.56					20.65				
Plant size 100– persons	36.7					25.02					35.81				
Foreign-owned plant	6.2					19.86					12.95				
Plant death during 1996–2002	11.8					19.22					22.09				
Number of plants	365					567					172				

Notes: The data are constructed in the Research Laboratory of Statistics Finland by linking the plants in the Finnish Manufacturing Census and individuals in the Employment Statistics with plant codes.

Source: Authors' own calculations.

FRANCESCO DAVERI AND MIKA MALIRANTA

Table A2. Statistical analysis behind the simulation graphs, between plants estimation

	Forest TFP	Forest wage	Machinery TFP	Machinery wage	Elect. TFP	Elect. wage
Schooling years	-3.386	-0.073	0.826+	0.182	1.481	0.310
	(2.491)	(0.815)	(0.470)	(0.140)	(1.294)	(0.210)
[Schooling years]^2	1.503	0.095	-0.285	-0.020	-0.511	-0.070
	(1.113)	(0.368)	(0.194)	(0.057)	(0.524)	(0.084)
Potential experience	1.017**	-0.014	0.171	0.082+	-0.785	0.007
	(0.371)	(0.118)	(0.151)	(0.044)	(0.616)	(0.110)
[Potential experience]^2	-0.513**	0.021	-0.072	-0.024	0.364	-0.012
	(0.187)	(0.057)	(0.081)	(0.022)	(0.390)	(0.071)
[Potential experience]^3	0.081**	-0.005	0.010	0.002	-0.047	0.005
	(0.030)	(0.009)	(0.014)	(0.004)	(0.078)	(0.015)
Seniority in years	-0.013	-0.003	-0.045	-0.020	1.276***	0.131*
	(0.086)	(0.027)	(0.054)	(0.018)	(0.272)	(0.062)
[Seniority in years]^2	0.070	0.012	0.033	0.022	-1.665***	-0.161+
	(0.081)	(0.026)	(0.056)	(0.017)	(0.365)	(0.083)
[Seniority in years]^3	-0.025	-0.000	-0.008	-0.007	0.622***	0.061+
	(0.022)	(0.007)	(0.017)	(0.005)	(0.153)	(0.034)
Plant birth in 77–80	0.237*	0.003	-0.051	0.019	-0.088	-0.027
	(0.119)	(0.032)	(0.066)	(0.029)	(0.154)	(0.044)
Plant birth in 81–85	0.247*	0.059	0.057	0.014	-0.210	0.032
	(0.117)	(0.041)	(0.079)	(0.021)	(0.257)	(0.043)
Plant birth in 86–90	0.658***	0.040	0.255***	0.013	0.094	0.019
	(0.104)	(0.027)	(0.057)	(0.018)	(0.209)	(0.046)
Plant birth in 91–95	0.575***	0.026	0.432***	0.083***	0.680**	-0.012
	(0.144)	(0.037)	(0.060)	(0.017)	(0.232)	(0.042)
Plant birth in 96–	0.969***	0.052	0.629***	0.077**	0.677*	0.029
	(0.196)	(0.037)	(0.088)	(0.025)	(0.286)	(0.052)
R-squared	0.545	0.647	0.486	0.516	0.527	0.581
Adj. R-squared	0.510	0.620	0.461	0.493	0.442	0.505
Number of plants	365	365	567	567	172	172

Notes: Other control variables include dummies for plant size (5 groups), foreign-ownership and death during 1996–2002. Robust standard errors are shown in parentheses.
+ $p < 0.1$, * $p < 0.05$, ** $p < 0.01$, *** $p < 0.001$.

such, but we do have the ratio of value added to the number of hours worked (by which we identify labour productivity) and the capital stock per hour worked (a measure of the capital-labour ratio). The capital stock measure is calculated through the perpetual inventory method (for more details, see Maliranta, 2003).

Since 1995 (our main period of analysis), all plants owned by firms that employ no less than 20 persons are included. Therefore, since 1995 the data also include the very small plants of multi-unit firms, but, on the other hand, the plants of small single-unit firms are left outside. Some plants are dropped from the sample because of failure of linking some plants in the Manufacture Census to other sources of information. Thanks to the link between Census of Manufacturing and Employment Statistics, we have information about plant workforce. This includes the average potential experience (the number of years after the last completed degree), seniority (the number of years spent working in the current company) and the number of schooling years (usually needed for the degree). The labour characteristics of the plants are computed in Statistics Finland by using the comprehensive version of the database. About 80–90% of individuals can be linked to their plants so that our variables should be measured with a reasonable accuracy. In the analysis, we have also dropped some outliers.[21]

REFERENCES

Acemoglu, D., P. Aghion and F. Zilibotti (2003). 'Vertical integration and distance to frontier', *Journal of the European Economic Association*, 1(2/3), 630–38.

Ali-Yrkkö, J., L. Paija, C. Reilly and P. Ylä-Anttila (2000). *Nokia: A Big Company in a Small Country*. ETLA, The Research Institute of the Finnish Economy, Series B162, Helsinki.

Altonji, J.G. and R.A. Shakotko (1987). 'Do wages rise with job seniority?', *Review of Economic Studies*, 54, 437–39.

Aubert, P. and B. Crépon (2004). *Age Salaire Et Productivité: La Productivité Des Salariés Décline-T-Elle En Fin De Carrière*. Technical report. Mimeo, Economie et Statistiques.

Aubert, P., E. Caroli and M. Roger (2004). *New Technologies, Workplace Organisation and the Age Structure of the Workforce: Firm-Level Evidence*. INSEE, Paris.

Autor, D.H., F. Levy and R.J. Murnane (2003). 'The skill content of recent technological change: An empirical exploration', *Quarterly Journal of Economics*, 118(4), 1279–333.

Becker, G.S. (1962). 'Investment in human capital: A theoretical analysis', *Journal of Political Economy*, 70(5, Part 2: Investment in Human Beings), 9–49.

Bingley, P. and N. Westergaard-Nielsen (2003). 'Returns to tenure, firm-specific human capital and worker heterogeneity', *International Journal of Manpower*, 24(7), 774–88.

Bishop, J. (1987). 'The recognition and reward of employee performance', *Journal of Labor Economics*, 5(4), s36–s56.

Blanchflower, D.G. and A.J. Oswald (1988). 'Internal and external influences upon pay settlements', *British Journal of Industrial Relations*, 26(3), 363–70.

Brock, W.A. and D.S. Evans (1986). *The Economics of Small Business*. Holmes & Meier, New York.

Brown, C. and J.L. Medoff (2003). 'Firm age and wages', *Journal of Labor Economics*, 21(3), 677–97.

---

[21] In the estimation, some extreme outliers are removed from the regression analysis. Identification has been carried out by using the method of Hadi (1992; 1994). The variables used in this procedure are the log of labour productivity, the log of monthly wage, the log of capital intensity, schooling years and potential experience. Overall, a couple of percentages of plants were dropped for being deemed outliers.

Crépon, B., N. Deniau and S. Pérez-Duarte (2002). *Wages, Productivity, and Worker Characteristics: A French Perspective*, January, INSEE. http://www.crest.fr/pageperso/crepon/CreponDeniauPerezDuarte2002.pdf

Daveri, F. and O. Silva (2004). 'Not only Nokia: What Finland tells us about new economy growth', *Economic Policy*, 19(38), 117–63.

Davis, S.J. and J. Haltiwanger (1991). 'Wage dispersion between and within U.S. manufacturing plants, 1963–86', *Brookings Papers on Economic Activity, Microeconomics 1991*, 115–80.

Disney, R., J. Haskel and Y. Heden (2003). 'Restructuring and productivity growth in UK manufacturing', *Economic Journal*, 113(489), 666–94.

Dunne, T., M.J. Roberts and L. Samuelson (1989). 'The growth and failure of U.S. manufacturing plants', *Quarterly Journal of Economics*, 104(4), 671–98.

Dygalo, N.N. and J.M. Abowd (2005). 'Estimating experience-productivity profiles from earnings over employment spells', unpublished manuscript, 27 November.

Eriksson, T. and M. Jäntti (1997). 'The distribution of earnings in Finland 1971–1990', *European Economic Review*, 41(9), 1763–79.

Flabbi, L. and A. Ichino (2001). 'Productivity, seniority and wages: New evidence from personnel data', *Labour Economics*, 8(3), 359–87.

Foster, L., J. Haltiwanger and C.J. Krizan (2001). 'Aggregate productivity growth: Lessons from microeconomic evidence', in C.R. Hulten, E.R. Dean & M.J. Harper (eds.), *New Developments in Productivity Analysis* (pp. 303–63). University of Chicago Press, Chicago.

Griliches, Z. (1995). 'R&D and productivity: Econometric results and measurement issues', in P. Stoneman (Ed.), *Handbook of the Economics of Innovation and Technological Change* (pp. 52–89). Blackwell Publishers Ltd, Oxford.

Griliches, Z. and V. Ringstad (1971). *Economics of Scale and the Form of the Production Function*. North Holland, Amsterdam, 1971.

Griliches, Z. and H. Regev (1995). 'Productivity and firm turnover in Israeli industry: 1979–1988', *Journal of Econometrics*, 65, 175–203.

Grund, C. and N. Westergård-Nielsen (2005). 'Age structure of the workforce and firm performance', IZA Working Paper No. 1816, Bonn.

Hadi, A.S. (1992). 'Identifying multiple outliers in multivariate data', *Journal of the Royal Statistical Society, Series (B)*, 54, 761–71.

— (1994). 'A modification of a method for the detection of outliers in multivariate samples', *Journal of the Royal Statistical Society, Series (B)*, 56, 393–96.

Haegeland, T. and T.J. Klette (1999). 'Do higher wages reflect higher productivity? Education, gender and experience premiums in a matched plant-worker data set', in *The Creation and Analysis of Employer-Employee Matched Data* (pp. 231–59). Elsevier Science, North-Holland, Amsterdam.

Hellerstein, J.K. and D. Neumark (1995). 'Are earnings profiles steeper than productivity profiles?' *Journal of Human Resources*, 30(1), 89.

Hellerstein, J.K., D. Neumark and K.R. Troske (1999). 'Wages, productivity, and worker characteristics: Evidence from plant-level production functions and wage equations', *Journal of Labor Economics*, 17(3), 409–46.

Ilmakunnas, P. and M. Maliranta (2005). 'Technology, labour characteristics and wage-productivity gaps', *Oxford Bulletin of Economics and Statistics*, 67(5), 623–44.

Ilmakunnas, P., M. Maliranta and J. Vainiomäki (2001). 'Linked employer-employee data on Finnish plants for the analysis of productivity, wages and turnover', in T. Jensen and A. Holm (eds.), *Nordic Labour Market Research on Register Data* (pp. 205–46). TemaDord, Nordic Council of Ministers, Coperhagen.

— (2004). 'The roles of employer and employee characteristics for plant productivity', *Journal of Productivity Analysis*, 21, 249–76.

— (2005). 'Worker turnover and productivity growth', *Applied Economics Letters*, 12(7), 395–98.

Juuti, P. (2001). *Ikäjohtaminen*. Kansallinen ikäohjelma, Työministeriö, JTO-tutkimuksia No. 13. Helsinki.

Kanazawa, S. (2003). 'Why productivity fades with age: The crime-genius connection', *Journal of Research in Personality*, 37, 257–72.

King, G., M. Tomz and J. Wittenberg (2000). 'Making the most of statistical analyses: Improving interpretation and presentation', *American Journal of Political Science*, 44(2), 347–61.

Kouvonen, A. (1999). *Ikäsyrjintäkokemukset Työssä Ja Työhönotossa*. Työpoliittinen tutkimus No. 203.

Kölling, A., C. Schnabel and J. Wagner (2005). 'Establishment age and wages: Evidence from German linked employer-employee data', in L. Bellmann, O. Hübler, W. Meyer and

G. Stephan (eds.), *Institutionen, Löhne Und Beschäftigung* (pp. 81–99). Nürnberg. http://www.wiso.uni-erlangen.de/forschung/forschungsberichte/forschungsbericht2005.pdf

Lazear, E.P. (1981). 'Agency, earnings profiles, productivity, and hours restrictions', *American Economic Review*, 71(4), 606–20.

— (1998). *Personnel Economics for Managers*, John Wiley and Sons, New York.

Maliranta, M. (1997). 'Plant Productivity in Finnish Manufacturing – Characteristics of High Productivity Plants', The Research Institute of the Finnish Economy (ETLA), Discussion Paper No. 612, Helsinki.

— (1999). 'Factors of performance by plant generation: Some findings from Finland', in S. Biffignandi (ed.), *Micro- and Macrodata of Firms: Statistical Analysis and International Comparison* (pp. 391–424). Physica, Heidelberg.

— (2003). *Micro Level Dynamics of Productivity Growth. An Empirical Analysis of the Great Leap in Finnish Manufacturing Productivity in 1975–2000*. The Research Institute of the Finnish Economy (ETLA), Series A 38 (available at http://www.etla.fi/files/1075_micro_level_dynamics.pdf), Helsinki.

Maliranta, M. and P. Rouvinen (2004). 'ICT and business productivity: Finnish micro-level evidence', in *The Economic Impact of ICT; Measurement, Evidence and Implications* (pp. 213–40). OECD, Paris.

Manning, A. (2000). 'Movin on up: Interpreting the earnings-experience profile', *Bulletin of Economic Research*, 52, 261–95.

Medoff, J.L. and K.G. Abraham (1980). 'Experience, performance, and earnings', *Quarterly Journal of Economics*, 95(4), 703–36.

— (1981). 'Are those paid more really more productive? The case of experience', *Journal of Human Resources*, 16(2), 186–216.

Moen, J. (2005). 'Is mobility of technical personnel a source of R&D spillovers?', *Journal of Labor Economics*, 23(1), 81–114.

Neuman, S. and A. Weiss, (1995). 'On the effects of schooling vintage on experience-earnings profiles: Theory and evidence', *European Economic Review*, 39(5), 943–55.

Nurmi, S. (2004). *Essays on Plant Size, Employment Dynamics and Survival*. Helsinki School of Economics, A-230, Helsinki.

OECD (2003). *OECD Science, Technology and Industry Scoreboard*. OECD, Paris.

— (2004). *Ageing and Employment Policies: Finland*. OECD, Paris.

— (2006). *Live Longer, Work Longer*. OECD, Paris.

O'Mahony, M. and B. Van Ark (eds.) (2003). *EU Productivity and Competitiveness: An Industry Perspective: Can Europe Resume the Catching-Up Process*. European Commission, Enterprise Publications.

Parent, D. (2000). 'Industry-specific capital and the wage profile: Evidence from the NLSY and the PSID', *Journal of Labor Economics*, 18(2), 306–23.

Productivity Commission (2005). *Economic Implications of an Ageing Australia*. Research Report, Canberra (http://www.pc.gov.au/study/ageing/finalreport/).

Sapir Report (2004). *An Agenda for a Growing Europe*: Oxford University Press, Oxford.

Skirbekk, V. (2003). *Age and Individual Productivity: A Literature Survey*. MPIDR, Working Paper No. 2003-028.

Statistics Denmark, Statistics Finland, Statistics Iceland, Statistics Norway and Statistics Sweden (2003). *Access to Microdata in the Nordic Countries*. Statistics Sweden, Örebro.

Teulings, C. and J. Hartog (1998). *Corporatism or Competition?* Cambridge University Press, Cambridge.

Tomz, M., J. Wittenberg and G. King (2003). *Clarify: Software for Interpreting and Presenting Statistical Results* (Version 2.1), Stanford University, University of Wisconsin, and Harvard University, 5 January. Available at http://gking.harvard.edu/.

Topel, R.H. (1991). 'Specific capital, mobility and wages: Wages rise with job seniority', *Journal of Political Economy*, 99, 145–76.

Troske, K.R. (1999). 'Evidence on the employer size-wage premium from worker-establishment matched data', *Review of Economics and Statistics*, 81(February), 15–26.

Uusitalo, R. and J. Vartiainen (2005). 'Finland: Firm factors in wages and wage changes', unpublished manuscript, 9 June.

Verhaegen, P. and T.A. Salthouse (1997). 'Meta-analyses of age-cognition relations in adulthood. Estimates of linear and nonlinear age effects and structural models'. *Psychological Bulletin*, 122(3), 231–49.

Winter-Ebmer, R. (2001). 'Firm size, earnings, and displacement risk', *Economic Inquiry*, 39(3), 474–86.

Valuing ecosystem services

SUMMARY

This paper explores two methods for valuing ecosystems by valuing the services that they yield to various categories of user and that are not directly valued in the market, and illustrates the usefulness of these methods with an application to the valuation of mangrove ecosystems in Thailand. The first method is known as the production function approach and relies on the fact that ecosystems may be inputs into the production of other goods or services that are themselves marketed, such as fisheries. I discuss issues that arise in measuring the input into fisheries, particularly those due to the fact that the fishery stock is changing over time, and the shadow value of the ecosystem consists in its contribution to the maintenance of the stock as well as its contribution to current output. The second method is known as the expected damage approach and is used to value the services of storm protection in terms of the reduction in expected future storm damage that the ecosystem can provide. These two methods are shown to yield very different valuations of ecosystems from those that would be derived by the methods typically used in cost-benefit analyses. I argue that they represent a significant improvement on current practice.

— *Edward B. Barbier*

Economic Policy January 2007 Printed in Great Britain
© CEPR, CES, MSH, 2007.

Valuing ecosystem services as productive inputs

Edward B. Barbier

University of Wyoming

1. INTRODUCTION

Global concern over the disappearance of natural ecosystems and habitats has prompted policymakers to consider the 'value of ecosystem services' in environmental management decisions. These 'services' are broadly defined as 'the benefits people obtain from ecosystems' (Millennium Ecosystem Assessment, 2003, p. 53).

However, our current understanding of key ecological and economic relationships is sufficient to value only a handful of ecological services. An important objective of this paper is to explain and illustrate through numerical examples the difficulties faced in valuing natural ecosystems and their services, compared to ordinary economic or financial assets. Specifically, the paper addresses the following three questions:

1. What progress has been made in valuing ecological services for policy analysis?
2. What are the unique measurement issues that need to be overcome?
3. How can future progress improve upon the shortcomings in existing methods?

I am grateful to David Aadland, Carlo Favero, Geoff Heal, Omer Moav and three anonymous referees for helpful comments. The Managing Editor in charge of this paper was Paul Seabright.

Economic Policy January 2007 pp. 177–229 Printed in Great Britain

1.1. Key challenges and policy context

As a report from the US National Academy of Science has emphasized, 'the fundamental challenge of valuing ecosystem services lies in providing an explicit description and adequate assessment of the links between the structure and functions of natural systems, the benefits (i.e., goods and services) derived by humanity, and their subsequent values' (Heal *et al.*, 2005, p. 2). Moreover, it has been increasingly recognized by economists and ecologists that the greatest 'challenge' they face is in valuing the ecosystem services provided by a certain class of key ecosystem functions – regulatory and habitat functions. The diverse benefits of these functions include climate stability, maintenance of biodiversity and beneficial species, erosion control, flood mitigation, storm protection, groundwater recharge and pollution control (see Table 1 below).

One of the natural ecosystems that has seen extensive development and application of methods to value ecosystem services has been coastal wetlands. This paper focuses mainly on valuation approaches applied to these systems, and in particular their role as a nursery and breeding habitat for near-shore fisheries and in providing storm protection for coastal communities.

The paper employs a case study of mangrove ecosystems in Thailand to compare and contrast approaches to valuing habitat and storm protection services. Global mangrove area has been declining rapidly, with around 35% of the total area lost in the past two decades (Valiela *et al.*, 2001). Mangrove deforestation has been particularly prevalent in Thailand and other Asian countries. The main cause of global mangrove loss has been coastal economic development, especially aquaculture expansion (Barbier and Cox, 2003). Yet ecologists maintain that global mangrove loss is contributing to the decline of marine fisheries and leaving many coastal areas vulnerable to natural disasters. Concern about the deteriorating 'storm protection' service of mangroves reached new significance with the 26 December 2004 Asian tsunami that caused widespread devastation and loss of life in Thailand and other Indian Ocean countries.

The Thailand case study also illustrates the importance of valuing ecosystem services to policy choices. Because these services are 'non-marketed', their benefits are not considered in commercial development decisions. For example, the excessive mangrove deforestation occurring in Thailand and other countries is clearly related to the failure to measure explicitly the values of habitat and storm protection services of mangroves. Consequently, these benefits have been largely ignored in national land use policy decisions, and calls to improve protection of remaining mangrove forests and to enlist the support of local coastal communities through legal recognition of their *de facto* property rights over mangroves are unlikely to succeed in the face of coastal development pressures on these resources (Barbier and Sathirathai, 2004). Unless the value to local coastal communities of the ecosystem services provided by protected mangroves is estimated, it is difficult to convince policymakers in Thailand and other countries to consider alternative land use policies.

Thus, as the Thailand case study reveals, the challenge of valuing ecosystem services is also a policy challenge. Because the benefits of these services are important and should be taken into account in any future policy to manage coastal wetlands in Thailand and other countries, it is equally essential that economics continues to develop and improve existing methodologies to value ecological services.

1.2. Outline and main results

The paper makes three contributions. The first is to demonstrate that valuing ecological services as productive inputs is a viable methodology for policy analysis, and to illustrate the key steps through a detailed case study of mangroves in Thailand. The second contribution is to identify the measurement issues that make valuation of non-marketed ecosystem services a unique challenge, yet one that is important for many important policy decisions concerning the management of natural ecosystems. The third contribution of the paper is to show, using the examples of habitat and storm protection services, that improvements in methods for valuing these services can correct for some shortcomings and measurement errors, thus yielding more accurate valuation estimates. But even the preferred approaches display measurement weaknesses that need to be addressed in future developments of ecosystem valuation methodologies.

Section 2 discusses in more detail the importance of valuing ecosystem services, especially those arising from the regulatory and habitat functions to environmental decision-making. Section 3 reviews various methods for valuing these services. Because the benefits arising from ecological regulatory and habitat functions mainly support or protect valuable economic activities, the production function (PF) approach of valuing these benefits as environmental inputs is a promising methodology. However, the latter approach faces its own unique measurement issues. To illustrate the PF approach as well as its shortcomings, the section discusses recent advances using the examples of the habitat and storm protection services of coastal wetland ecosystems. Section 4 compares the application of the different methods to valuing mangroves in Thailand. The case study indicates the importance of considering the key ecological-economic linkages underlying each service in choosing the appropriate valuation approach, and how each approach influences the final valuation estimates. In the case of valuing the mangroves' habitat-fishery linkage, modelling the contribution of this linkage to growth in fish stocks over time appears to be a key consideration. The case study also demonstrates the advantages of the expected damage function approach as an alternative to the replacement cost method of valuing the storm protection service of coastal wetlands. Section 5 concludes the paper by discussing the key areas for further development in ecosystem valuation methodologies, such as incorporating the effects of irreversibilities, uncertainties and thresholds, and the application of integrated ecological-economic modelling to reflect multiple ecological services and their benefits. Although substantial progress has been made in valuing some ecosystem services, many difficulties still remain. Future progress in ecosystem valuation for policy analysis requires understanding the key flaws in existing methods that need correcting.

2. BACKGROUND: VALUATION OF ECOSYSTEM SERVICES

The rapid disappearance of many ecosystems has raised concerns about the loss of beneficial 'services'. This raises two important questions. What are ecosystem services, and why is it important to value these environmental flows?

2.1. Ecosystem services

Although in the current literature the term 'ecosystem services' lumps together a variety of 'benefits', economics normally classifies these benefits into three different categories: (i) 'goods' (e.g. products obtained from ecosystems, such as resource harvests, water and genetic material); (ii) 'services' (e.g. recreational and tourism benefits or certain ecological regulatory functions, such as water purification, climate regulation, erosion control, etc.); and (iii) cultural benefits (e.g., spiritual and religious, heritage, etc.).[1] This paper focuses on methods to value a sub-set of the second category of ecosystem 'benefits' – the services arising from regulatory and habitat functions. Table 1 provides some examples of the links between regulatory and habitat functions and the resulting ecosystem benefits.

2.2. Valuing environmental assets

The literature on ecological services implies that natural ecosystems are assets that produce a flow of beneficial goods and services over time. In this regard, they are no different from any other asset in an economy, and in principle, ecosystem services should be valued in a similar manner. That is, regardless of whether or not there exists a market for the goods and services produced by ecosystems, their social value must equal the discounted net present value (NPV) of these flows.

However, what makes environmental assets special is that they give rise to particular measurement problems that are different for conventional economic or financial assets. This is especially the case for the benefits derived from the regulatory and habitat functions of natural ecosystems.

For one, these assets and services fall in the special category of 'nonrenewable resources with renewable service flows' (Just *et al.*, 2004, p. 603). Although a natural ecosystem providing such beneficial services is unlikely to increase, it can be depleted, for example through habitat destruction, land conversion, pollution impacts and so

---

[1] See Daily (1997), De Groot *et al.* (2002) and Millennium Ecosystem Assessment (2003) for the various definitions of ecosystem services that are prevalent in the ecological literature.

Table 1. Some services provided by ecosystem regulatory and habitat functions

Ecosystem functions	Ecosystem processes and components	Ecosystem services (benefits)
Regulatory functions		
Gas regulation	Role of ecosystems in biogeochemical processes	Ultraviolet-B protection / Maintenance of air quality / Influence of climate
Climate regulation	Influence of land cover and biologically mediated processes	Maintenance of temperature, precipitation
Disturbance prevention	Influence of system structure on dampening environmental disturbance	Storm protection / Flood mitigation
Water regulation	Role of land cover in regulating run-off, river discharge and infiltration	Drainage and natural irrigation / Flood mitigation / Groundwater recharge
Soil retention	Role of vegetation root matrix and soil biota in soil structure	Maintenance of arable land / Prevention of damage from erosion and siltation
Soil formation	Weathering of rock and organic matter accumulation	Maintenance of productivity on arable land
Nutrient regulation	Role of biota in storage and recycling of nutrients	Maintenance of productive ecosystems
Waste treatment	Removal or breakdown of nutrients and compounds	Pollution control and detoxification
Habitat functions		
Niche and refuge	Suitable living space for wild plants and animals	Maintenance of biodiversity / Maintenance of beneficial species
Nursery and breeding	Suitable reproductive habitat andnursery grounds	Maintenance of biodiversity / Maintenance of beneficial species

Sources: Adapted from Heal *et al.* (2005, Table 3-3) and De Groot *et al.* (2002).

forth. Nevertheless, if the ecosystem is left intact, then the flow services from the ecosystem's regulatory and habitat functions are available in quantities that are not affected by the rate at which they are used.

In addition, whereas the services from most assets in an economy are marketed, the benefits arising from the regulatory and habitat functions of natural ecosystems generally are not. If the aggregate willingness to pay for these benefits is not revealed through market outcomes, then efficient management of such ecosystem services requires explicit methods to measure this social value (e.g., see Freeman, 2003; Just *et al.*, 2004). A further concern over ecosystem services is that their beneficial flows are threatened by the widespread disappearance of natural ecosystems and habitats across the globe. The major cause of this disappearance is conversion of the land to other uses, degradation of the functioning and integrity of natural ecosystems through resource exploitation, pollution, and biodiversity loss, and habitat fragmentation (Millennium Ecosystem Assessment, 2003). The failure to measure explicitly the aggregate willingness to pay for otherwise non-marketed ecological services exacerbates these problems, as the benefits of these services are 'underpriced' in development decisions as a consequence. Population and development pressures in many areas of the world result in increased land demand by economic activities, which mean that the opportunity cost of maintaining the land for natural ecosystems is rarely zero. Unless the benefits arising from ecosystem services are explicitly measured, or 'valued', then these non-marketed flows are likely to be ignored in land use decisions. Only the benefits of the 'marketed' outputs from economic activities, such as agricultural crops, urban housing and other commercial uses of land, will be taken into account, and as a consequence, excessive conversion of natural ecosystem areas for development will occur.

A further problem is the uncertainty over their future values of environmental assets. It is possible, for example, that the benefits of natural ecosystem services may increase in the future as more scientific information becomes available over time. In addition, if environmental assets are depleted irreversibly through economic development, their value will rise relative to the value of other economic assets (Krutilla and Fisher, 1985). Because ecosystems are in fixed supply, lack close substitutes and are difficult to restore, their beneficial services will decline as they are converted or degraded. As a result, the value of ecosystem services is likely to rise relative to other goods and services in the economy. This rising, but unknown, future scarcity value of ecosystem benefits implies an additional 'user cost' to any decision that leads to irreversible conversion today.

Valuation of environmental assets under conditions of uncertainty and irreversibility clearly poses additional measurement problems. There is now a considerable literature advocating various methods for estimating environmental values by measuring the additional 'premium' that individuals are willing to pay to avoid the uncertainty surrounding such values (see Ready, 1995 for a review). Similar methods are also advocated for estimating the user costs associated with irreversible development, as this also amounts to valuing the 'option' of avoiding reduced future choices for individuals (Just et al., 2004). However, it is difficult to implement such methods empirically, given the uncertainty over the future state of environmental assets and about the future preferences and income of individuals. The general conclusion from studies that attempt to allow for such uncertainties in valuing environmental assets is that 'more empirical research is needed to determine under what conditions we can ignore uncertainty in benefit estimation ...where uncertainty is over economic parameters such as prices or preferences, the issues surrounding uncertainty may be empirically unimportant' (Ready, 1995, p. 590).

3. VALUING THE ENVIRONMENT AS INPUT

Uncertainty and irreversible loss are important issues to consider in valuing ecosystem services. However, as emphasized by Heal et al. (2005), a more 'fundamental challenge' in valuing these flows is that ecosystem services are largely not marketed, and unless some attempt is made to value the aggregate willingness to pay for these services, then management of natural ecosystems and their services will not be efficient. The following section describes advances in developing the 'production function' approach, compared to other valuation methods, as a means to measuring the aggregate willingness to pay for the largely non-marketed benefits of ecosystem services.

3.1. Methods of valuing ecosystem services

Table 2 indicates various methods that can be used for valuing ecological services.[2] However, some approaches are limited to specific benefits. For example, the travel cost method is used principally for environmental values that enhance individuals' enjoyment of recreation and tourism, averting behaviour models are best applied to the health effects arising from pollution, and hedonic wage and property models are used primarily for assessing work-related hazards and environmental impacts on property values, respectively.

In contrast, stated preference methods, which include contingent valuation methods, conjoint analysis and choice experiments, have the potential to be used widely in valuing ecosystem goods and services. These valuation methods involve surveying individuals who benefit from an ecological service or range of services, and analysing the responses to measure individuals' willingness to pay for the service or services.

For example, choice experiments of wetland restoration in southern Sweden revealed that individuals' willingness to pay for the restoration increased if the result enhanced overall biodiversity but decreased if the restored wetlands were used mainly for the introduction of Swedish crayfish for recreational fishing (Carlsson *et al.*, 2003). In some cases, stated preference methods are used to elicit 'non-use values', that is, the additional 'existence' and 'bequest' values that individuals attach to ensuring that a well-functioning system will be preserved for future generations to enjoy. A contingent valuation study of mangrove-dependent coastal communities in Micronesia demonstrated that the communities 'place some value on the existence and ecosystem functions of mangroves over and above the value of mangroves' marketable products' (Naylor and Drew, 1998, p. 488).

However, to implement a stated-preference study two key conditions are necessary: (1) the information must be available to describe the change in a natural ecosystem in terms of service that people care about, in order to place a value on those services; and (2) the change in the natural ecosystem must be explained in the survey instrument in a manner that people will understand and not reject the valuation scenario (Heal *et al.*, 2005). For many of the services arising from ecological regulatory and habitat

---

[2] It is beyond the scope of this paper to discuss all the valuation methods listed in Table 2. See Freeman (2003), Heal *et al.* (2005) and Pagiola *et al.* (2004) for more discussion of these various valuation methods and their application to valuing ecosystem goods and services.

Table 2. Various valuation methods applied to ecosystem services

Valuation method[a]	Types of value estimated[b]	Common types of applications	Ecosystem services valued
Travel cost	Direct use	Recreation	Maintenance of beneficial species, productive ecosystems and biodiversity
Averting behaviour	Direct use	Environmental impacts on human health	Pollution control and detoxification
Hedonic price	Direct and indirect use	Environmental impacts on residential property and human morbidity and mortality	Storm protection; flood mitigation; maintenance of air quality
Production function	Indirect use	Commercial and recreational fishing; agricultural systems; control of invasive species; watershed protection; damage costs avoided	Maintenance of beneficial species; maintenance of arable land and agricultural productivity; prevention of damage from erosion and siltation; groundwater recharge; drainage and natural irrigation; storm protection; flood mitigation
Replacement cost	Indirect use	Damage costs avoided; freshwater supply	Drainage and natural irrigation; storm protection; flood mitigation
Stated preference	Use and non-use	Recreation; environmental impacts on human health and residential property; damage costs avoided; existence and bequest values of preserving ecosystems	All of the above

[a] See Freeman (2003), Heal et al. (2005) and Pagiola et al. (2004) for more discussion of these various valuation methods and their application to valuing ecosystem goods and services.
[b] Typically, use values involve some human 'interaction' with the environment whereas non-use values do not, as they represent an individual valuing the pure 'existence' of a natural habitat or ecosystem or wanting to 'bequest' it to future generations. Direct use values refer to both consumptive and non-consumptive uses that involve some form of direct physical interaction with environmental goods and services, such as recreational activities, resource harvesting, drinking clean water, breathing unpolluted air and so forth. Indirect use values refer to those ecosystem services whose values can only be measured indirectly, since they are derived from supporting and protecting activities that have directly measurable values, such as many of the services listed in Table 1.
Source: Adapted from Heal et al. (2005, Table 4-2) and Table 1.

functions, one or both of these conditions may not hold. For instance, it has proven very difficult to describe accurately through the hypothetical scenarios required by stated-preference surveys how changes in ecosystem processes and components affect ecosystem regulatory and habitat functions and thus the specific benefits arising from these functions that individuals value. If there is considerable scientific uncertainty surrounding these linkages, then not only is it difficult to construct such hypothetical scenarios but also any responses elicited from individuals from stated-preference surveys are likely to yield inaccurate measures of their willingness to pay for ecological services.

In contrast to stated-preference methods, the advantage of PF approaches is that they depend on only the first condition, and not both conditions, holding. That is, for those regulatory and habitat functions where there is sufficient scientific knowledge of how these functions link to specific ecological services that support or protect economic activities, then it may be possible to employ the PF approach to value these services. However, PF methods have their own measurement issues and limitations. These are also discussed further in the rest of this section, and illustrated using examples of key ecological services from coastal and estuarine wetlands.

3.2. The production function approach

Many of the beneficial services derived from regulatory and habitat functions are commonly classified by economists as indirect use values (Barbier, 1994). The benefits attributed to these services arise through their support or protection of activities that have directly measurable values (see Table 2). For example, coastal and estuarine wetlands, such as tropical mangroves and temperate marshlands, act as 'natural barriers' by preventing or mitigating storms and floods that could affect property and land values, agriculture, fishing and drinking supplies, as well as cause sickness and death. Similarly, coastal and estuarine wetlands may also provide a nursery and breeding habitat that supports the productivity of near-shore fisheries, which in turn may be valued for their commercial or recreational catch.

Because the benefits of these ecosystem services appear to enhance the productivity of economic activities, or protect them from possible damages, one possible method of measuring the aggregate willingness to pay for such services is to estimate their value as if they were a factor input in these productive activities. This is the essence of the PF valuation approaches, also called 'valuing the environment as input' (Barbier, 1994 and 2000; Freeman, 2003, ch. 9).[3]

The basic modelling approach underlying PF methods is similar to determining the additional value of a change in the supply of any factor input. If changes in the regulatory and habitat functions of ecosystems affect the marketed production activities of an economy, then the effects of these changes will be transmitted to individuals through the price system via changes in the costs and prices of final goods and services. This means that any resulting 'improvements in the resource base or environmental quality' as a result of enhanced ecosystem services, 'lower costs and prices and increase the quantities of marketed goods, leading to increases in consumers' and perhaps producers' surpluses' (Freeman, 2003, p. 259). The sum of consumer and producer surpluses in turn provides a measure of the willingness to pay for the improved ecosystem services.

---

[3] The concept of 'valuing' the environment as input is not new. Dose-response and change-in-productivity models, which have been used for some time, can be considered special cases of the PF approach in which the production responses to environmental quality changes are greatly simplified (Freeman, 1982).

An adaptation of the PF methodology is required in the case where ecological regulatory and habitat functions have a protective value, such as the storm protection and flood mitigation services provided by coastal wetlands. In such cases, the environment may be thought of producing a non-marketed service, such as 'protection' of economic activity, property and even human lives, which benefits individuals through limiting damages. Applying PF approaches requires modelling the 'production' of this protection service and estimating its value as an environmental input in terms of the expected damages avoided.

Although this paper focuses mainly on applications of the PF approach to coastal wetland ecosystems, as Table 2 indicates PF approaches are being increasingly employed for a diverse range of environmental quality impacts and ecosystem services. Some examples include maintenance of biodiversity and carbon sequestration in tropical forests (Boscolo and Vincent, 2003); nutrient reduction in the Baltic Sea (Gren *et al.*, 1997); pollination service of tropical forests for coffee production in Costa Rica (Ricketts *et al.*, 2004); tropical watershed protection services (Kaiser and Roumasset, 2002); groundwater recharge supporting irrigation farming in Nigeria (Acharya and Barbier, 2000); coral reef habitat support of marine fisheries in Kenya (Rodwell *et al.*, 2002); marine reserves acting to enhance the 'insurance value' of protecting commercial fish species in Sicily (Mardle *et al.*, 2004) and in the northeast cod fishery (Sumaila, 2002); and nutrient enrichment in the Black Sea affecting the balance between invasive and beneficial species (Knowler *et al.*, 2001).

3.3. Measurement issues for modelling habitat-fishery linkages

Applying PF methods to valuing ecosystem services has its own demands in terms of ecological and economic data. To highlight these additional measurement issues, this section draws on the example of valuing coastal wetlands as a nursery and breeding habitat for commercial near-shore fisheries.

First, application of the PF approach requires properly specifying the habitat-fishery PF model that links the physical effects of the change in this service to changes in market prices and quantities and ultimately to consumer and producer surpluses. As with many ecological services, it is difficult to measure directly changes in the habitat and nursery function of coastal wetlands. Instead, the standard approach adopted in coastal habitat-fishery PF models is to allow the wetland area to serve as a proxy for the productivity contribution of the nursery and habitat function (see Barbier, 2000 for further discussion). It is then relatively straightforward to estimate the impacts of the change in the coastal wetland area input on fishery catch, in terms of the marginal costs of fishery harvests and thus changes in consumer and producer surpluses.

Second, market conditions and regulatory policies for the marketed output will influence the values imputed to the environmental input (Freeman, 1991). For instance, the offshore fishery supported by coastal wetlands may be subject to open access. Under these conditions, profits in the fishery would be dissipated, and equilibrium prices would be equated to average and not marginal costs. As a consequence, there is no producer surplus, and the welfare impact of a change in wetland habitat is measured by the resulting change in consumer surplus only.

Third, if the ecological service supports a harvested natural resource system, such as a fishery, forestry or a wildlife population, then it may be necessary to model how changes in the stock or biological population may affect the future flow of benefits. If the natural resource stock effects are not considered significant, then the environmental changes can be modelled as impacting only current harvest, prices and consumer and producer surpluses. If the stock effects are significant, then a change in an ecological service will impact not only current but also future harvest and market outcomes. In the PF valuation literature, the first approach is referred to as a 'static model' of environmental change on a natural resource production system, whereas the second approach is referred to as a 'dynamic model' because it takes into account the intertemporal stock effects of the environmental change (Barbier, 2000; Freeman, 2003, ch. 9).

Finally, most natural ecosystems provide more than one beneficial service, and it may be important to model any trade-offs among these services as an ecosystem is altered or disturbed. Integrated economic-ecological modelling could capture more fully the ecosystem functioning and dynamics underlying the provision of key services, and can be used to value multiple services arising from natural ecosystems. For instance, integrated modelling of an entire wetland-coral reef-sea grass system could measure simultaneously the benefits of both the habitat-fishery linkage and the storm protection service provided by the system. Examples of such multi-service ecosystem modelling include analysis of salmon habitat restoration (Wu *et al.*, 2003); eutrophication of small shallow lakes (Carpenter *et al.*, 1999); changes in species diversity in a marine ecosystem (Finnoff and Tschirhart, 2003); and introduction of exotic trout species (Settle and Shogren, 2002).

To illustrate the first three of the above issues, I next explore two ways of measuring the welfare effects of an environmental change on a productive natural resource system with the example of the coastal habitat-fishery linkage. I will return to the issue of integrated ecological-economic modelling of multiple ecological services in Section 5.

3.3.1. Habitat-fishery linkages: static approaches.
This section illustrates the use of a static model to value how a change in coastal wetland habitat area affects the market for commercially harvested fish. Many initial PF methods to value habitat-fishery linkages have relied on this static approach. For example, using data from the Lynne *et al.* (1981), Ellis and Fisher (1987) constructed such a model to value the support by Florida marshlands for Gulf Coast crab fisheries in terms of the resulting changes in consumer and producer surpluses from the marketed catch. Freeman (1991) then extended Ellis and Fisher's approach to show how the values imputed to

the wetlands in the static model is influenced by whether or not the fishery is open access or optimally managed. Sathirathai and Barbier (2001) also used a static model of habitat-fishery linkages to value the role of mangroves in Thailand in supporting near-shore fisheries under both open access and optimally managed conditions.

As most near-shore fisheries are not optimally managed but open access, the following illustration of the static model of habitat-fishery linkages assumes that the fishery is open access. Any profits in the fishery will attract new entrants until all the profits disappear, and in equilibrium, the welfare change in coastal wetland is in terms of its impact on consumer surplus only.

As noted above, the general PF approach treats an ecological service, such as coastal wetland habitat, as an 'input' into the economic activity, and like any other input, its value can be equated with its impact on the productivity of any marketed output. More formally, if h is the marketed harvest of the fishery, then its production function can be denoted as:

$$h = h(E_i \ldots E_k, S) \tag{1}$$

The area of coastal wetlands, S, may therefore have a direct influence on the marketed fish catch, h, which is independent from the standard inputs of a commercial fishery, $E_i \ldots E_k$.

A standard assumption in most static habitat-fishery models is that the production function (1) takes the Cobb–Douglas form, $h = AE^a S^b$, where E is some aggregate measure of total effort in the off-shore fishery and S is coastal wetland habitat area. It follows that the optimal cost function of a cost-minimizing fishery is:

$$C^* = C(h, w, S) = wA^{-1/a}h^{1/a}S^{-b/a} \tag{2}$$

where w is the unit cost of effort. Assuming an iso-elastic market demand function, $P = p(h) = kh^\eta$, $\eta = 1/\varepsilon < 0$, then the market equilibrium for catch of the open access fishery occurs where the total revenues of the fishery just equals cost, or price equals average cost, i.e. $P = C^*/h$, which in this model becomes:

$$kh^\eta = wA^{-1/a}h^{1-a/a}S^{-b/a} \tag{3}$$

which can be rearranged to yield the equilibrium level of fish harvest:

$$h = \left[\frac{w}{k}\right]^{a/\beta} A^{-1/\beta}S^{-b/\beta}, \ \beta = (1 + \eta)a - 1 \tag{4}$$

It follows from (4) that the marginal impact of a change in wetland habitat is:

$$\frac{dh}{dS} = -\frac{b}{\beta}\left[\frac{w}{k}\right]^{a/\beta} A^{-1/\beta}S^{-(b+\beta)/\beta} \tag{5}$$

The change in consumer surplus, CS, resulting from a change in equilibrium harvest levels (from h^0 to h^1) is:

$$\Delta CS = \int_{h^0}^{h^1} p(h)dh - [p^1h^1 - p^0h^0] = \frac{k[(h^1)^{\eta+1} - (h^0)^{\eta+1}]}{\eta + 1} - k[(h^1)^{\eta+1} - (h^0)^{\eta+1}]$$

$$= -\frac{\eta[p^1h^1 - p^0h^0]}{\eta + 1}. \qquad (6)$$

By utilizing (5) and (6) it is possible to estimate the new equilibrium harvest and price levels and thus the corresponding changes in consumer surplus associated with a change in coastal wetland area, for a given demand elasticity, γ.

Figure 1 is the diagrammatic representation of the welfare measure of a change in wetland area on an open access fishery corresponding to Equation (6). As shown in the figure, a change in wetland area that serves as a breeding ground and nursery for an open access fishery results in a shift in the average cost curve, AC, of the fishery. The welfare impact is the change in consumer surplus (area P*ABC).

3.3.2. Habitat-fishery linkages: dynamic approaches.

If the stock effects of a change in coastal wetlands are significant, then valuing such changes in terms of the impacts on current harvest and market outcomes is a flawed approach. To overcome this shortcoming, a dynamic model of coastal habitat-fishery linkage incorporates the change in wetland area within a multi-period harvesting model of the fishery. The standard approach is to model the change in coastal wetland habitat as affecting the biological growth function of the fishery (Barbier, 2003). As a result, any value impacts of a change in this habitat-support function can be determined in terms of changes in the long-run equilibrium conditions of the fishery. Alternatively, the welfare analysis could be conducted in terms of the harvesting path that approaches this equilibrium or the path that is moving away from initial conditions in the fishery.

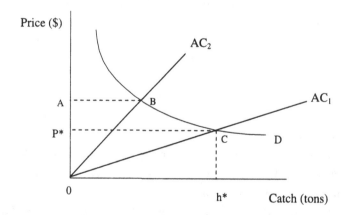

Figure 1. The economic value effects of increased wetland area on an open access fishery

Notes: AC: average cost; D: demand curve; P*: price per tonne; h*: fish catch in tonnes after change; P*ABC: change in consumer and producer surplus.

Source: Adapted from Freeman (1991).

Most attempts to value habitat-fishery linkages via a dynamic model that incorporates stock effects have assumed that the fishery affected by the habitat change is in a long-run equilibrium. Such a model has been applied, for example, in case studies of valuing habitat fishery linkages in Mexico (Barbier and Strand, 1998), Thailand (Barbier *et al.*, 2002; Barbier, 2003) and the United States (Swallow, 1994). Similar 'equilibrium' dynamic approaches have been used to model other coastal environmental changes, including the impacts of water quality on fisheries in the Chesapeake Bay (Kahn and Kemp, 1985; McConnell and Strand, 1989) and the effects of mangrove deforestation and shrimp larvae availability on aquaculture in Ecuador (Parks and Bonifaz, 1997).

However, valuing the change in coastal wetland habitat in terms of its impact on the long-run equilibrium of the fishery raises additional methodological issues. First, the assumption of prevailing steady state conditions is strong, and may not be a realistic representation of harvesting and biological growth conditions in the near-shore fisheries. Second, such an approach ignores both the convergence of stock and harvest to the steady state and the short-run dynamics associated with the impacts of the change in coastal habitat on the long-run equilibrium. The usual assumption is that this change will lead to an instantaneous adjustment of the system to a new steady state, but this in turn requires local stability conditions that may not be supported by the parameters of the model.

There are examples of pure fisheries models that assume that the dynamic system is not in equilibrium but is either on the approach to a steady state or is moving away from initial fixed conditions. The latter approach has proven particularly useful in the case of open access or regulated access fisheries (Bjørndal and Conrad, 1987; Homans and Wilen, 1997). The following model shows how this approach can be adopted here to the case of valuing a change in wetland habitat in terms of the dynamic path of an open access fishery.

Defining X_t as the stock of fish measured in biomass units, any net change in growth of this stock over time can be represented as:

$$X_t - X_{t-1} = F(X_{t-1}, S_{t-1}) - h(X_{t-1}, E_{t-1}), \frac{\partial^2 F}{\partial X_{t-1}^2} > 0, \frac{\partial F}{\partial S_{t-1}} > 0. \tag{7}$$

Thus, net expansion in the fish stock occurs as a result of biological growth in the current period, $F(X_{t-1}, S_{t-1})$, net of any harvesting, $h(X_{t-1}, E_{t-1})$, which is a function of the stock as well as fishing effort, E_{t-1}. The influence of the wetland habitat area, S_{t-1}, as a breeding ground and nursery habitat on growth of the fish stock is assumed to be positive, $\partial F/\partial S_{t-1} > 0$, as an increase in wetland area will mean more carrying capacity for the fishery and thus greater biological growth.

As before, it is assumed that the near-shore fishery is open access. The standard assumption for an open access fishery is that effort next period will adjust in response to the real profits made in the past period (Clark, 1976; Bjørndal and Conrad, 1987). Letting $p(h)$ represent landed fish price per unit harvested, w the unit cost of effort and $\phi > 0$ the adjustment coefficient, then the fishing effort adjustment equation is:

$$E_t - E_{t-1} = \phi[\, p(h_{t-1}) h(X_{t-1}, E_{t-1}) - wE_{t-1}],\ \frac{\partial p(h_{t-1})}{\partial h_{t-1}} < 0. \tag{8}$$

Assume a conventional bioeconomic fishery model with biological growth characterized by a logistic function, $F(X_{t-1}, S_{t-1}) = rX_{t-1}[1 - X_{t-1}/K(S_{t-1})]$, and harvesting by a Schaefer production process, $h_t = qX_tE_t$, where q is a 'catchability' coefficient, r is the intrinsic growth rate and $K(S_t) = \alpha \ln S_t$, is the impact of coastal wetland area on carrying capacity, K, of the fishery. The market demand function for harvested fish is again assumed to be iso-elastic, i.e. $p(h) = kh^\eta$, $\eta = 1/\varepsilon < 0$. Substituting these expressions into (7) and (8) yields:

$$X_t = rX_{t-1}\left[1 - \frac{X_{t-1}}{\alpha \ln S_{t-1}}\right] - h_{t-1} + X_{t-1} \tag{9}$$

$$E_t = \phi R_{t-1} + (1 - \phi w)E_{t-1},\ R_{t-1} = kh_{t-1}^{1+\eta}. \tag{10}$$

Both X_t and E_t are predetermined, and so (9) and (10) can be estimated independently (see Homans and Wilen, 1997). Following Schnute (1977), define the catch per unit effort as $c_t = h_t/E_t = qX_t$. If X_t is predetermined so is c_t. Substituting the expression for catch per unit effort in (9) produces:

$$\frac{c_t - c_{t-1}}{c_{t-1}} = r - \frac{r}{q\alpha}\frac{c_{t-1}}{\ln S_{t-1}} - qE_{t-1}. \tag{11}$$

Thus Equations (10) and (11) can also be estimated independently to determine the biological and economic parameters of the model. For given initial effort, harvest and wetland data, both the effort and stock paths of the fishery can be determined for subsequent periods, and the consumer plus producer surplus can be estimated for each period. Alternative effort and stock paths can then be determined as wetland area changes in each period, and thus the resulting changes in consumer plus producer surplus in each period are the corresponding estimates of the welfare impacts of the coastal habitat change.[4]

3.4. Replacement cost and cost of treatment

In circumstances where an ecological service is unique to a specific ecosystem and is difficult to value, then economists have sometimes resorted to using the cost of replacing the service as a valuation approach.[5] This method is usually invoked because of the lack of data for many services arising from natural ecosystems.

For example, the presence of a wetland may reduce the cost of municipal water treatment because the wetland system filters and removes pollutants. It is therefore

[4] As along its dynamic path the open access fishery is not in equilibrium, producer surpluses, or losses, are relevant for the welfare estimate of a change in coastal wetland habitat.

[5] Such an approach to approximating the benefits of a service by the cost of providing an alternative is not used exclusively in environmental valuation. For example, in the health economics literature this approach is referred to as 'cost of illness' (Dickie, 2003). This involves adding up the costs of treating a patient for an illness as the measure of the benefit to the patient of staying disease-free.

tempting to use the cost of an alternative treatment method, such as the building and operation of an industrial water treatment plant, to represent the value of the wetland's natural water treatment service. Such an approach does not measure directly the benefit derived from the wetland's waste treatment service; instead, the approach is estimating this benefit with the cost of providing the ecosystem service that people value. Herein lies the main problem with the replacement cost method: it is using 'costs' as a measure of economic 'benefit'. In economic terms, the implication is that the ratio of costs to benefit of an ecological service is always equal to one.

The problems posed by the replacement cost method are illustrated in Figure 2, in the case of waste water treatment service provided by an existing wetland ecosystem. The cost of the waste water treatment service provided by the wetlands is 'free' and thus corresponds to the horizontal axis, MC_S. Given the demand curve for water, Q_1 amount of water is consumed. However, if the wetland is destroyed the marginal cost of an alternative, human-built waste treatment facility is MC_H. Thus, the 'replacement cost' of using the treatment facility to provide Q_1 amount of water in the absence of the wetlands is the difference between the two supply curves, or area $0BDQ_1$. However, this overestimates the benefit of having the wetlands provide the waste treatment service. The true benefit of this ecosystem service is the demand curve, or total willingness to pay, for Q_1 amount of water less the costs of providing it, or area $0ACQ_1$.

For these reasons, economists consider that the replacement cost approach should be used with caution. Shabman and Batie (1978) suggested that this method can provide a reliable valuation estimation for an ecological service if the following conditions are met: (1) the alternative considered provides the same services; (2) the alternative compared for cost comparison should be the least-cost alternative; and (3) there should be substantial evidence that the service would be demanded by society if it were provided by that least-cost alternative. In the absence of any information on benefits, and a decision has to be made to take some action, then treatment costs become a way of looking for a cost-effective action.

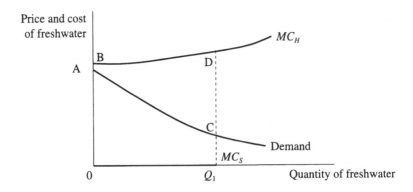

Figure 2. Replacement cost estimation of an ecosystem service

Source: Adapted from Ellis and Fisher (1987).

One of the best-known examples of a policy decision based on using the 'replacement cost' method to assess the value of an ecosystem service is the provision of clean drinking water by the Catskills Mountains for New York City (Heal *et al.*, 2005). In 1996, New York City faced a choice: either it could build water filtration systems to clean its water supply or the city could restore and protect the Catskill watersheds to ensure high-quality drinking water. Because estimates indicated that building and operating the filtration system would cost $6–8 billion whereas protecting and restoring the watersheds would cost $1–1.5 billion, New York chose to protect the Catskills. In this case, it was sufficient for the policy decision simply to demonstrate the cost-effectiveness of restoring and protecting the ecological integrity of the Catskills watersheds compared to the alternative of the human-constructed water filtration system. Thus, clearly this is an example where the criteria established by Shabman and Batie (1978) apply.

The main reason why economists have resorted to replacement cost approaches to valuing an ecosystem service, however, is that there is often a lack of data on the linkage between the initial ecological function, the processes and components of ecosystems that facilitate this function, and the eventual ecological service that benefits humans. The lack of such data makes it extremely difficult to construct reliable hypothetical scenarios through stated preference surveys and similar methods to elicit accurate responses from individuals about their willingness to pay for ecological services. As an illustration, in the Catskills case study, a stated preference survey may have elicited an estimate of the total willingness-to-pay by New York City residents for the amount of freshwater provided – for example, the total demand for freshwater Q_1 in Figure 2 – but it would have been very difficult to obtain a measure of the willingness-to-pay to avoid losses in the water treatment service that occur through *changes* in the land use in Catskills watershed that affect the free provision of this ecological service.

Similarly, as pointed out by Chong (2005), it is very difficult to use stated preference methods in tropical developing areas to assess the benefits to local communities of the storm protection service of mangrove systems. Although there is sufficient scientific evidence suggesting that such a service occurs, there is a lack of ecological data on how loss of mangroves in specific locations will affect their ability to provide storm protection to neighbouring communities. To date, the few studies that have attempted to value the storm prevention and flood mitigation services of the 'natural' storm barrier function of mangrove systems have employed the replacement cost method by simply estimating the costs of replacing mangroves with constructed barriers that perform the same services (Chong, 2005). Unfortunately, such estimates not only make the classic error of estimating a 'benefit' by a 'cost' but also may yield unrealistically high estimates, given that removing all the mangroves and replacing them with constructed barriers is unlikely to be the least-cost alternative to providing storm prevention and flood mitigation services in coastal areas.

3.5. Expected damage function approach

For some ecological services, an alternative to employing replacement cost methods might be the *expected damage function* (EDF) approach.[6]

The EDF approach, which is a special category of 'valuing' the environment as 'input', is nominally straightforward; it assumes that the value of an asset that yields a benefit in terms of reducing the probability and severity of some economic damage is measured by the reduction in the expected damage. The essential step to implementing this approach, which is to estimate how changes in the asset affect the probability of the damaging event occurring, has been used routinely in risk analysis and health economics, for example, as in the case of airline safety performance (Rose, 1990); highway fatalities (Michener and Tighe, 1992); drug safety (Olson, 2004); and studies of the incidence of diseases and accident rates (Cameron and Trivedi, 1998; Winkelmann, 2003). Here we show that the EDF approach can also be applied, under certain circumstances, to value ecological services that also reduce the probability and severity of economic damages.

Recall that one of the special features of many regulatory and habitat services of ecosystems is that they may protect nearby economic activities, property and even human lives from possible damages. As indicated in Table 1, such services include storm protection, flood mitigation, prevention of erosion and siltation, pollution control and maintenance of beneficial species. The EDF approach essentially 'values' these services through estimating how they mitigate damage costs.

The following example illustrates how the expected damage function (EDF) methodology can be applied to value the storm protection service provided by a coastal wetland, such as a marshland or mangrove ecosystem. The starting point is the standard 'compensating surplus' approach to valuing a quantity or quality change in a non-market environmental good or service (Freeman, 2003).

Assume that in a coastal region the local community owns all economic activity and property, which may be threatened by damage from periodic natural storm events. Assume also that the preferences of all households in the community are sufficiently identical so that it can be represented by a single household. Let $m(p^x, z, u^0)$ be the expenditure function of the representative household, that is, the minimum expenditure required by the household to reach utility level, u^0, given the vector of prices, p^x, for all market-purchased commodities consumed by the household, the expected number or incidence of storm events, z^0.

Suppose the expected incidence of storms rises from z^0 to z^1. The resulting expected damages to the property and economic livelihood of the household, $E[D(z)]$, translates into an exact measure of welfare loss through changes in the minimum expenditure function:

[6] The expected damage function approach predates many of the PF methods discussed so far, and has been used extensively to estimate the risk of health impacts from pollution (Freeman, 1982, chs. 5 and 9).

$$E[D(z)] = m(p^x, z^1, u^0) - m(p^x, z^0, u^0) = c(z) \tag{12}$$

where $c(z)$ is the compensating surplus. It is the minimum income compensation that the household requires to maintain it at the utility level u^0, despite the expected increase in damaging storm events. Alternatively, $c(z)$ can be viewed as the minimum income that the household needs to avoid the increase in expected storm damages.

However, the presence of coastal wetlands could mitigate the expected incidence of damaging storm events. Because of this storm protection service, the area of coastal wetlands, S, may have a direct effect on reducing the 'production' of natural disasters, in terms of their ability to inflict damages locally. Thus the 'production function' for the incidence of potentially damaging natural disasters can be represented as:

$$z = z(S), \; z' < 0, \; z'' > 0. \tag{13}$$

It follows from (12) and (13) that $\partial c(z)/\partial S = \partial E[D(z)]/\partial S < 0$. An increase in wetland area reduces expected storm damages and therefore also reduces the minimum income compensation needed to maintain the household at its original utility level. Alternatively, a loss in wetland area would increase expected storm damages and raises the minimum compensation required by the household to maintain its welfare. Thus, we can define the marginal willingness to pay, $W(S)$, for the protection services of the wetland in terms of the marginal impact of a change in wetland area on expected storm damages:

$$W(S) = -\frac{\partial E[D(z(S))]}{\partial S} = -E\left[\frac{\partial D}{\partial z}z'\right], W' < 0. \tag{14}$$

The 'marginal valuation function', $W(S)$, is analogous to the Hicksian compensated demand function for marketed goods. The minus sign on the right-hand sign of (14) allows this 'demand' function to be represented in the usual quadrant, and it has the normal downward-sloping property (see Figure 3). Although an increase in S reduces z and thus enables the household to avoid expected damages from storms, the additional value of this storm protection service to the household will fall as wetland area increases in size. This relationship should hold across all households in the coastal community. Consequently, as indicated in Figure 3, the marginal willingness to pay by the community for more storm protection declines with S.

The value of a non-marginal change in wetland area, from S_0 to S_1, can be measured as:

$$-\int_{S_0}^{S_1} W(S)dS = E[D(z(S))] = c(S). \tag{15}$$

If there is an increase in wetland area, then the value of this change is the total amount of expected damage costs avoided. If there is a reduction in wetland area, as shown in Figure 3, then the welfare loss is the total expected damages resulting from the increased incidence of storm events. As indicated in (15), in both instances the

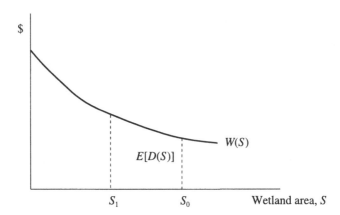

Figure 3. Expected damage costs from a loss of wetland area

valuation would be a compensation surplus measure of a change in the area of wetlands and the storm protection service that they provide.

As indicated in (14), an estimate of the marginal impact of a change in wetland area on expected storm damages has two components: the influence of wetland area on the expected incidence of economically damaging natural disaster events, z', and some measure of the additional economic damage incurred per event. Thus the right-hand expression in (14) can be estimated, provided that there are sufficient data on past storm events, and preferably across different coastal areas, and some estimate of the economic damages inflicted by each event. The most important step in the analysis is the first one, using the data on the incidence of past natural disasters and changes in wetland area in coastal areas to estimate $z(S)$. One way this analysis can be done is through employing *count data models*.

Count data models explain the number of times a particular event occurs over a given period. In economics, count data models have been used to explain a variety of phenomenon, such as explaining successful patents derived from firm R&D expenditures, accident rates, disease incidence, crime rates and recreational visits (Cameron and Trivedi, 1998; Greene, 2003, ch. 21; Winkelmann, 2003). Count data models could be used to estimate whether a change in the area of coastal wetlands, S, reduces the expected incidence of economically damaging storm events. The basic methodology for such an application of count data models is described further in the appendix.

However, applying the EDF method to estimating the storm protection value of coastal wetlands raises two additional measurement issues.

First, as the 2004 Asian tsunami and recent hurricanes in the United States have demonstrated, the risks to vulnerable populations living in coastal areas from the economic damages of storm events can be very large. This suggests that coastal populations will display a degree of risk aversion to such events, in the sense that they would like to see the least possible variance in expected storm damages. Applying standard techniques, such as the capital-asset pricing model, this implies in turn that there should be a 'risk premium' attached to the storm protection value of coastal wetlands that reduces the variance in expected economic damages from storm events (Hirshleifer and Riley, 1992).

Second, estimating how coastal wetlands affect the expected number of economic damaging events from the count data model and then multiplying the effect by the average economic damages across events could be misleading under some extreme circumstances. For instance, suppose a loss in wetland area is associated with a situation in which there is a change in the incidence of storms from one devastating storm to two relatively minor storms per year. The count data model would then be interpreted as not providing evidence against the null that the change in the wetland area increases expected storm damages. Clearly, there needs to be a robustness check on the count data model to ensure that such situations do not dominate the application of the EDF approach.

4. CASE STUDY OF MANGROVE ECOSYSTEMS IN THAILAND

This section illustrates the application of the PF approach and the EDF approach to valuation of ecological services with a case study of mangrove ecosystems in Thailand. The two services of interest are the provision of a breeding and nursery habitat for fisheries and the storm protection service of mangroves.

Both the dynamic and static PF approaches are used to estimate the value of the mangrove-fishery habitat service. The EDF approach to estimating the storm protection service of mangroves is contrasted with the replacement cost method.

4.1. Case study background

Many mangrove ecosystems, especially those in Asia, are threatened by rapid deforestation. At least 35% of global mangrove area has been lost in the past two decades; in Asia, 36% of mangrove area has been deforested, at the rate of 1.52% per year (Valiela et al., 2001). Although many factors are behind global mangrove deforestation, a major cause is aquaculture expansion in coastal areas, especially the establishment of shrimp farms (Barbier and Cox, 2003). Aquaculture accounts for 52% of mangrove loss globally, with shrimp farming alone accounting for 38% of mangrove deforestation; in Asia, aquaculture contributes 58% to mangrove loss with shrimp farming accounting for 41% of total deforestation (Valiela et al., 2001).

Mangrove deforestation has been particularly prevalent in Thailand. Some estimates suggest that over 1961–96 Thailand lost around 2050 km^2 of mangrove forests, or about 56% of the original area, mainly due to shrimp aquaculture and other coastal developments (Charuppat and Charuppat, 1997). Since 1975, 50–65% of Thailand's mangroves have been converted to shrimp farms (Aksornkoae and Tokrisna, 2004).

Figure 4 shows two long-run trend estimates of mangrove area in Thailand. In 1961, there were approximately 3700 km^2 of mangroves, which declined steadily to

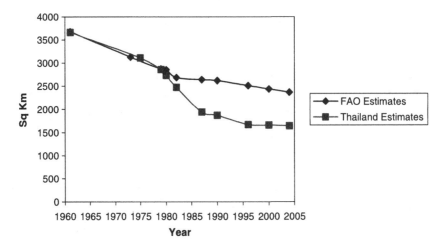

Figure 4. Mangrove area (km²) in Thailand, 1961–2004

Notes: FAO estimates from FAO (2003). 2000 and 2004 data are estimated from 1990–2000 annual average mangrove loss of 18.0 km². Thailand estimates from various Royal Thailand Forestry Department sources reported in Aksornkoae and Tokrisna (2004). 2000 and 2004 data are estimated from 1993–96 annual average mangrove loss of 3.44 km².

Sources: Based on FAO (2003), Aksornkoae and Tokrisna (2004) and author's estimates.

around 2700 to 2900 km² by 1980. Since then, mangrove deforestation has continued, although there are disagreements over the rate of deforestation. For example, FAO estimates based on long-run trend rates suggest a slower rate of decline, and indicate that there may be almost 2400 km² of mangroves still remaining. However, estimates based on Thailand's Royal Forestry Department studies suggest that rapid shrimp farm expansion during the 1980s and early 1990s accelerated mangrove deforestation, and as a consequence, the area of mangroves in 2004 may be much lower, closer to 1,645 km².

Mangrove deforestation in Thailand has focused attention on the two principal services provided by mangrove ecosystems, their role as nursery and breeding habitats for offshore fisheries and as natural 'storm barriers' to periodic coastal storm events, such as wind storms, tsunamis, storm surges and typhoons. In addition, many coastal communities exploit mangroves directly for a variety of products, such as fuelwood, timber, raw materials, honey and resins, and crabs and shellfish. One study estimated that the annual value to local villagers of collecting these products was $88 per hectare (ha), or approximately $823/ha in net present value terms over a 20-year period and with a 10% discount rate (Sathirathai and Barbier, 2001).

4.1.1. Breeding and nursery habitat for fisheries. An extensive literature in ecology has emphasized the role of coastal wetland habitats in supporting neighbouring marine fisheries (for a review, see Mitsch and Gosselink, 1993; World Conservation Monitoring Center; World Resources Institute 1996). Mangroves in Thailand also provide this important habitat service (Aksornkoae *et al.*, 2004).

Thailand's coastline is vast, stretching for 2815 km, of which 1878 km is on the Gulf of Thailand and 937 km on the Andaman Sea (Indian Ocean) (Kaosa-ard and Pednekar, 1998). Since 1972, the 3 km offshore coastal zone in southern Thailand has been reserved for small-scale, artisanal marine fisheries. The Gulf of Thailand is divided into four such major zones, and the Andaman Sea comprises a fifth zone.[7] The mangroves along these coastal zones are thought to provide breeding grounds and nurseries in support of several species of demersal fish and shellfish (mainly crab and shrimp) in Thailand's coastal waters.[8] The artisanal marine fisheries of the five major coastal zones of Thailand depend largely on shellfish but also some demersal fish. For example, in 1994 shrimp, crab, squid and cuttlefish alone accounted for 67% of all catch in the artisanal marine fisheries, and demersal fish accounted for 5.3% (Kaosa-ard and Pednekar, 1998).

The coastal artisanal fisheries of Thailand are characterized by classic open access conditions (Kaosa-ard and Pedneker, 1998; Wattana, 1998). Since the 1970s, there have been approximately 36 000–38 000 households engaged in small-scale fishing activities. Although there are 2500 fishing communities scattered over the 24 coastal provinces of Thailand, 90% of the artisanal fishing households are concentrated in communities spread along the Southern Gulf of Thailand and Andaman Sea coasts. While the number of households engaged in small-scale fishing has remained fairly stable since 1985, the use of motorized boats has increased by more than 30% (Wattana, 1998). Gill nets still remain the most common form of fishing gear used by artisanal fishers. Although a licence fee and permit are required for fishing in coastal waters, officials do not strictly enforce the law and users do not pay. Currently, there is no legislation for supporting community-based fishery management (Kaosa-ard and Pednekar, 1998).

4.1.2. Storm protection. The 26 December 2004 Indian Ocean tsunami disaster has focused attention on the role of natural barriers, such as mangroves, in protecting vulnerable coastlines and populations in the region from such storm events (UNEP, 2005; Wetlands International, 2005). Mangrove wetlands, which are found along sheltered tropical and subtropical shores and estuaries, are particularly valuable in minimizing damage to property and loss of human life by acting as a barrier against tropical storms, such as typhoons, cyclones, hurricanes and tsunamis (Chong, 2005; Massel *et al.*, 1999; Mazda *et al.*, 1997). Evidence from the 12 Indian Ocean countries affected by the tsunami disaster, including Thailand, suggests that those coastal areas

[7] The four Gulf of Thailand zones consist of the following coastal provinces: Trat, Chantaburi and Rayong (Zone 1); Chon Buri, Chachoengsao, Samut Parkakan, Samut Sakhon, Samut Songkhram, Phetchaburi, Prachaup Khiri Khan (Zone 2); Chumphon, Surat Thani, Nakhon Si Thammarat (Zone 3); and Songkhla, Patthani, Narathiwart (Zone 4). The fifth zone on the Indian Ocean (Andaman Sea) consists of the following coastal provinces: Ranong, Phangnga, Phuket, Krabi, Trang and Satun (Zone 5).

[8] Mangrove-dependent demersal fish include those belonging to the *Clupeidae*, *Chanidae*, *Ariidae*, *Pltosidae*, *Mugilidae*, *Lujanidae* and *Latidae* families. The shellfish include those belonging to the families of *Panaeidae* for shrimp and *Grapsidae*, *Ocypodidae* and *Portnidae* for crab.

that had dense and healthy mangrove forests suffered fewer losses and less damage to property than those areas in which mangroves had been degraded or converted to other land uses (Dahdouh-Guebas *et al.*, 2005; Harakunarak and Aksornkoae, 2005; Kathiresan and Rajendran, 2005; UNEP, 2005; Wetlands International, 2005).

In Thailand, the Asian tsunami affected all six coastal provinces along the Indian Ocean (Andaman Sea) coast: Krabi, Phang Nga, Phuket, Ranong, Satun and Trang. In Phang Nga, the most affected province, post-tsunami assessments suggest that large mangrove forests in the north and south of the province significantly mitigated the impact of the Tsunami. They suffered damage on their seaside fringe, but reduced the tidal wave energy, providing protection to the inland population (UNEP, 2005; Harakunarak and Aksornkoae, 2005). Similar results were reported for those shorelines in Ranong Province protected by dense and thriving mangrove forests. In contrast, damages were relatively extensive along the Indian Ocean coast where mangroves and other natural coastal barriers were removed or severely degraded (Harakunarak and Aksornkoae, 2005).

With the overwhelming evidence of the storm protection service provided by intact and healthy mangrove systems, since the tsunami disaster increased emphasis has been placed on replanting degraded and deforested mangrove areas in Asia as a means to bolstering coastal protection. For example, the Indonesian Minister for Forestry has announced plans to reforest 600 000 hectares of depleted mangrove forest throughout the nation over the next 5 years. The governments of Sri Lanka and Thailand have also stated publicly intentions to rehabilitate and replant mangrove areas (UNEP, 2005; Harakunarak and Aksornkoae, 2005).

Although the Asian tsunami has called attention to the storm protection service provided by mangroves, the benefits of this service extends to protection against many types of periodic coastal natural disaster events. As one post-tsunami assessment noted: 'It is important to recognize that any compromising of mangrove "protection function" is relevant to a wide variety of storm events, and not just tsunamis. Whereas the Indian Ocean area counted "only" 63 tsunamis between 1750 and 2004, there were more than three tropical cyclones per year in roughly the same area' (Dahdouh-Guebas *et al.*, 2005, pp. 445–6).

The EM-DAT International Disaster Database shows that the number of coastal natural disasters in Thailand has increased in both the frequency of occurrence and in the number of events per year (see Figure 5). Over 1975–87, Thailand experienced on average 0.54 coastal natural disasters per year, whereas between 1987–2004 the incidence increased to 1.83 disasters per year. Thus, a recent World Bank report identified the coastal and delta areas of Thailand as potentially high fatality (more than 1000 deaths per event) and other damage 'hotspots' at risk from storm surge events (Dilley *et al.*, 2005, pp. 101–3).

The EM-DAT database also calculates the economic damage incurred per event. Figure 6 plots the damages per coastal natural disaster in Thailand for 1975–2004. The 2004 Asian tsunami with estimated damages of US$240 million (1996 prices)

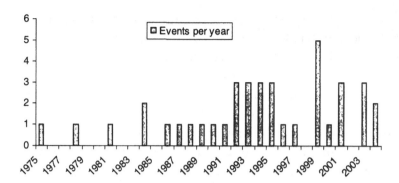

Figure 5. Coastal natural disasters in Thailand, 1975–2004

Notes: Over 1975–2004, coastal natural disasters included wave/surge (tsunami and tidal wave), wind storm (cyclone/typhoon and tropical storm) and flood (significant rise of water level in coastal region. In order for EM-DAT (2005) to record an event as a disaster, at least one or more of the following criteria must be fulfilled: 10 or more people reported killed; 100 people reported affected; declaration of a state of emergency; call for international assistance.

Source: EM-DAT (2005). EM-DAT: The OFDA/CRED International Disaster Database. www.em-dat.net – Université Catholique de Louvain, Brussels, Belgium.

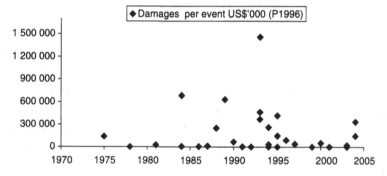

Figure 6. Real damages per coastal natural disaster in Thailand, 1975–2004

Notes: The EM-DAT (2005) estimate of the economic impact of a disaster usually consists of direct (e.g. damage to infrastructure, crops, housing) and indirect (e.g. loss of revenues, unemployment, market destabilization) consequences on the local economy. However, the estimate of 'zero' economic damages may indicate that no economic damages were recorded for an event. The estimates of economic damages are in thousands of US$ and converted to 1996 prices using Thailand's GDP deflator.

Source: EM-DAT (2005). EM-DAT: The OFDA/CRED International Disaster Database. www.em-dat.net – Université Catholique de Louvain, Brussels, Belgium.

was not the most damaging event to occur in Thailand. In fact, although the incidence of coastal damages has increased since 1987, in recent years the real damages per event has actually declined. For example, from 1979 to 1996, the economic damages per event were around US$190 million whereas from 1996 to 2004, real damages per event averaged US$61 million.

In sum, over the past two decades the rise in the number and frequency of coastal natural disasters in Thailand (Figure 5) and the simultaneous rapid decline in coastal mangrove systems over the same period (Figure 4) is likely to be more than a coincidence. Natural disasters occur when large numbers of economic assets are damaged or destroyed during a natural hazard event. Thus an increase in the incidence of coastal disasters is likely to have two sets of causes: the first is the natural hazards themselves – tsunamis and other storm surges, tidal waves, typhoons or cyclones, tropical storms and floods – but the second set is the increasing vulnerability of coastal populations, infrastructure and economic activities to being harmed or damaged by a hazard event.[9] The widespread loss of mangroves in coastal areas of Thailand may therefore have increased the vulnerability of these areas to more incidences of natural disasters.

4.2. Valuation of habitat-fishery linkage service

This subsection compares and contrasts the static and dynamic approaches outlined in Section 3.3 to valuing the habitat-fishery support service of mangroves in Thailand. As discussed above, in Thailand the near-shore artisanal fisheries supported by this ecological service are not optimally managed but largely open access.

To conduct the static production function analysis of the mangrove-fishery linkage, the methodology of Section 3.3.1 is applied to the same shellfish, demersal fishery and mangrove data over 1983–96 as in Barbier (2003). These comprise pooled time-series and cross-sectional data over the 1983–96 period for Thailand's artisanal and shellfish fisheries, as well as the extent of mangrove area, corresponding to the five coastal zones along the Gulf and Thailand and Indian Ocean (Andaman Sea). Evidence from domestic fish markets in Thailand suggest that the demand for fish is fairly inelastic, and an elasticity of -0.5 was assumed for the iso-elastic market demand function. Thus the static analysis calculation of the marginal impact of a change in wetland area in Equation (5) requires specifying the unknown parameters of the Cobb–Douglas production function for the fishery, $h = AE^a S^b$. Section A1 in the appendix explains the approach used to estimate the unknown parameters (A, a, b) of the log-linear version of the Cobb–Douglas production function and reports the resulting preferred estimations (see Table A1). Using these results in Equations (5) and (6) allows calculation of the welfare impacts of mangrove deforestation on Thailand's two artisanal fisheries. The results are depicted in Table 3, which displays both the point estimates and the 95% confidence bounds on these estimates through use of the standard errors. All price and cost data for the fisheries used in the welfare analysis are in 1996 real terms.

---

[9] This view that natural disasters should not be viewed solely as 'acts of God' but clearly have an important anthropogenic component to their cause is reflected in much of the current expert opinion on natural disaster management. This is summarized succinctly by Dilley *et al.* (2005, p. 115): 'Hazards are not the cause of disasters. By definition, disasters involve large human or economic losses. Hazard events that occur in unpopulated areas and are not associated with losses do not constitute disasters. Losses are created not only by hazards, therefore, but also by the intrinsic characteristics of the exposed infrastructure, land uses, and economic activities that cause them to be damaged or destroyed when a hazard strikes. The socioeconomic contribution to disaster causality is potentially a source of disaster reduction. Disaster losses can be reduced by reducing exposure or vulnerability to the hazards present in a given area.'

Table 3. Valuation of mangrove-fishery linkage service, Thailand, 1996–2004 (US$)

Production function approach	Average annual mangrove loss	
	FAO (18.0 km^2)[a]	Thailand (3.44 km^2)[b]
Static analysis:		
Annual welfare loss	99 004 (12 704–814 504)	18 884 (2425–154 307)
Net present value	570 167	108 756
(10% discount rate)	(55 331–4 690 750)	(10 563–888 657)
Net present value	527 519	100 621
(12% discount rate)	(52 233–4 339 883)	(9972–822 186)
Net present value	472 407	90 108
(15% discount rate)	(48 080–3 886 476)	(9179–736 288)
Dynamic analysis:		
Net present value	1 980 128	373 404
(10% discount rate)	(403 899–2 390,728)	(164 506–691 573)
Net present value	1 760 374	331 995
(12% discount rate)	(357 462–2 104 176)	(147 571–614 058)
Net present value	1 484 461	279 999
(15% discount rate)	(299 411–1 747 117)	(126 178–516 691)

Notes: All valuations are based on mangrove-fishery linkage impacts on artisanal shellfish and demersal fisheries in Thailand at 1996 prices. The demand elasticity for fish is assumed to be −0.5. Figures in parentheses represent upper and lower bound welfare estimates based on the standard errors of the estimated parameters in each model (see Section A1 in the appendix).
[a] FAO estimates from FAO (2003). 2000 and 2004 data are estimated from 1990–2000 annul average mangrove loss of 18.0 km^2.
[b] Thailand estimates from various Royal Thailand Forestry Department sources reported in Aksornkoae and Tokrisna (2004). 2000 and 2004 data are estimated from 1993–96 annual average mangrove loss of 3.44 km^2.
Sources: Author's calculations.

As Figure 4 shows, there are two different estimates of the 1996–2004 annual mangrove deforestation rates in Thailand, namely the FAO estimate of 18.0 km^2 and the Royal Thai Forestry Department estimate of 3.44 km^2. For the welfare impacts arising from the FAO estimates of annual average mangrove deforestation rates in Thailand over 1996–2004, the static analysis suggests that the annual loss in the habitat-fishery support service is around US$99 000 ($13 000 to 815 000 with 95% confidence). The net present value of these losses over the entire period is between US$0.47 and 0.57 million ($48 000 to 4.7 million with 95% confidence). For the much lower Thailand deforestation estimates, the annual welfare loss is just under $19 000 ($2400 to 154 000 with 95% confidence) and the net present value of these losses over the 1996–2004 period is US$90 000 to 108 000 ($9000 to 0.9 million with 95% confidence).

Following the methodology of Section 3.3.2, we can also apply a dynamic production function model to mangrove-fishery linkages in Thailand. As explained in the section, this approach involves estimating the parameters of the dynamic mangrove-fishery model, and then using these parameters to simulate the dynamic path of the fishery and the corresponding consumer and surplus changes resulting from mangrove deforestation. Because there are no data on the biomass stock, X_t, for

Thailand's near-shore fisheries, the appropriate dynamic model is the version indicating the change over time in fishing effort, E_t, and catch per unit effort, c_t, i.e. Equations (10) and (11). To compare with the static analysis, we use the same shellfish, demersal fisheries and mangrove data, as well as assume the same iso-elastic demand, from Barbier (2003) to estimate Equations (10) and (11) (see Section A2 in the appendix). For example, the estimated parameters in the appendix correspond to the following parameters of the dynamic production function model: $b_0 = r$, $b_1 = -r/q\alpha$, $b_2 = -q$, $b_0/(b_1*b_2) = \alpha$, $a_1 = \phi$, $a_2 = 1-\phi w$ and $-(a_2 - 1)/a_1 = w$. These estimated parameters are then employed to simulate the dynamic effort and stock paths (9) and (10) of each fishery, starting from an initial level of effort, catch per unit effort and mangrove area, and assuming a constant elasticity of demand of -0.5.[10] By using 1996 data as the initial starting point in the simulation, i.e. for X_0, E_0, S_0 and h_0, the dynamic paths yield effort, stock and harvest for each subsequent year from 1996–2004.

In the base case dynamic simulation, mangrove area is held constant at 1996 levels. Two alternative paths for stock, effort and thus harvest are then also simulated, corresponding to the two different estimates of the 1996–2004 annual mangrove deforestation rates in Thailand, namely the FAO estimate of 18.0 km^2 and the Royal Thai Forestry Department estimate of 3.44 km^2 respectively. The resulting changes in consumer plus producer surpluses in each year over 1996–2004, between each deforestation simulation and the base case, provide the estimates of the welfare impacts of the decline in the mangrove-fishery support service. That is, the changes in consumer and producer surplus resulting from mangrove deforestation in each subsequent year of the simulation are discounted to obtain a net present value estimate of the resulting welfare loss. As in the static analysis, the discount rate is varied from 10% to 15% (see Table 3). The standard errors for the parameters of the model estimated from Equations (10) and (11) were also used to construct both lower and upper confidence bounds on the simulation paths, and thus also on the welfare estimates of the impacts of deforestation on the mangrove-fishery linkage.

The results for the dynamic mangrove-fishery linkage analysis are also depicted in Table 3, which indicates the welfare calculations associated with both the FAO and Thailand deforestation estimates over 1996–2004. The table reports calculations arising from the simulations based on the point estimates of the parameters of the dynamic mangrove-fishery model. The ranges of values indicated in parentheses for the dynamic analysis represent the lower and upper bound confidence intervals

---

[10] Although there are no reliable stock data for Thailand's near-shore fisheries, the Schaefer harvesting function, $h_t = qE_tX_t$, assumed in the model allows stock to be determined from catch per unit effort for a given estimated parameter q. That is, $X_t = c_t/q$, where $c_t = h_t/E_t$. See Schnute (1977) for further details. The procedure employed here is to use the known harvest and effort levels, as well as the estimated parameter q, for each fishery in the initial year 1996 to estimate the initial unknown stock level, X_0. Equations (9) and (10) were then used to simulate the dynamic path for X_t and E_t in the subsequent years (1997–2004), as well as the subsequent harvest, $h_t = qE_tX_t$. The dynamic simulation approach employed here is standard for an open access fishery model (see Bjørndal and Conrad, 1987; Clark, 1976; Homans and Wilen, 1997).

derived from the standard errors of the estimated model parameters (see Section A2 in the appendix). If the FAO estimate of mangrove deforestation over 1996–2004 is used, then the net present value of the welfare loss ranges from around US$1.5 to 2.0 million ($0.3 to 2.4 million in the upper and lower bound simulation estimates). In contrast, the lower Thailand deforestation estimation for 1996–2004 suggests that the net present value welfare loss from reduced mangrove support for fisheries is around US$0.28 to 0.37 million ($0.13 to 0.69 million in the upper and lower bound simulation estimates).

The welfare estimates in Table 3 indicate that the losses in the habitat-fishery support service caused by mangrove deforestation in Thailand over 1996–2004 are around three times greater for the dynamic production function approach compared to the static analysis. In addition, the confidence bounds on the welfare estimates produced with the static analysis are significantly larger, suggesting that the static approach yields much more variable estimates of the welfare losses. Given the disparity in estimates between the two approaches, a legitimate question to ask is whether or not one approach should be preferred to the other in valuing habitat-fishery linkages.

It has been argued in the literature that, on the methodological grounds, the 'dynamic' PF approach is more appropriate for valuing how coastal wetland habitats support offshore fisheries because this service implies that fish populations are more likely to be affected over time (Barbier, 2000). If this is the case, then the environmental 'input' of mangroves serving as breeding and nursery habitat for near-shore fisheries should be modelled as part of the growth function of the fish stock. In contrast, the static analysis, by definition, ignores stock effects and focuses exclusively on the impact of changes in mangrove area on fishing effort and costs in the same period in which the habitat service changes. The comparison of the dynamic and static analysis in the Thailand case study of mangrove-fishery linkages confirms that, by incorporating explicitly the multi-period stock effects resulting from mangrove loss, the dynamic model produces much larger estimates for the value of changes in the habitat-fishery support service. Since in this case study at least these stock effects appear to be considerable, then they are clearly an important component of the impacts of mangrove deforestation on the habitat-fishery service in Thailand.

In sum, the Thailand case study suggest caution in using the static analysis in preference to the dynamic production function approach in valuing the ecological service of coastal wetlands as breeding and nursery habitat for offshore fisheries. As Table 3 indicates, the static approach could underestimate the value of this service as well as yield more variable estimates. This may prove misleading for policy analysis, particularly when considering options to preserve as opposed to convert coastal wetlands. Certainly, the perception among coastal fishing communities throughout Thailand is that the habitat-fishery service of mangroves is vital, and local fishers in these communities have reported substantial losses in coastal fish stocks and yields, which they attribute to recent deforestation (Aksornkoae et al., 2004; Sathirathai and Barbier, 2001).

4.3. Valuation of storm protection service

To date, the most prevalent method of valuing the storm protection service provided by coastal wetlands is the replacement cost approach (Chong, 2005). This paper has suggested the use of an alternative methodology, the EDF approach. The purpose of the following subsection is to compare and contrast both approaches, using the Thailand case study.

Sathirathai and Barbier (2001) employed the replacement cost method to estimate the value of coastal protection and stabilization provided by mangroves in southern Thailand. The same approach and data will be employed here. According to the Harbor Department of the Royal Thai Ministry of Communications and Transport, the unit cost of constructing artificial breakwaters to prevent coastal erosion and damages from storm surges is estimated to be US$1011 (in 1996 prices) per metre of coastline. Based on this estimate, the authors calculate the equivalent cost of protecting the shoreline with a 75-metre width stand of mangrove is approximately US$13.48 per m^2, or US$134 801 per ha (1996 prices). Over a 20-year period and assuming a 10% discount rate, the annualized value of this cost amounts to $14 169 per ha. This is the 'replacement cost' value of the storm protection function per ha of mangrove.

The analysis for this paper uses this replacement cost value to calculate the annual and net present value welfare losses associated with the two mangrove deforestation estimates for Thailand over 1996–2004. The results are depicted in Table 4.

For the FAO mangrove deforestation estimate of 18.0 km^2 per year over 1996–2004, the annual welfare loss in storm protection service is around US$25.5 million, and the net present value of this loss over the entire period ranges from US$121.7 to 146.9 million. For the Thailand deforestation estimation of 3.4 km^2 per year, the annual welfare loss in storm protection is about US$4.9 million, and the net present value of this loss over the entire period ranges from US$23.2 to 28 million.

Section 3.5 describes the methodology for the EDF approach to estimating the value of the storm protection service of coastal wetlands such as mangroves. As emphasized in the appendix, the key step to this approach is to estimate the influence of changes in coastal wetland area on the expected incidence of economically damaging natural disaster events. The application of the EDF approach here employs a count data model for this purpose. The details of the estimation are contained in Section A3 of the appendix.

The analysis for Thailand over 1979–96 shows that loss of mangrove area in Thailand increases the expected number of economically damaging natural disasters affecting coastal provinces. Using this estimated 'marginal effect' (−0.00308), it is possible to estimate the resulting impact on expected damages of natural coastal disasters. For example, EM-DAT (2005) data show that over 1979–96 the estimated real economic damages per coastal event per year in Thailand averaged around US$189.9 million (1996 prices). This suggests that the marginal effect of a one-km^2

Table 4. Valuation of storm protection service, Thailand, 1996–2004 (US$)

Valuation approach	Average annual mangrove loss	
	FAO (18.0 km²)[a]	Thailand (3.44 km²)[b]
Replacement cost method:[c]		
Annual welfare loss	25 504 821	4 869 720
Net present value (10% discount rate)	146 882 870	28 044 836
Net present value (12% discount rate)	135 896 056	25 947 087
Net present value (15% discount rate)	121 698 392	23 236 280
Expected damage function approach:		
Annual welfare loss	3 382 169	645 769
	(2 341 686–5 797 339)	(447 106–1 106 905)
Net present value	19 477 994	3 718 998
(10% discount rate)	(13 485 827–33 387 014)	(2 574 894–6 374 694)
Net present value	18 021 043	3 440 818
(12% discount rate)	(12 477 089–30 889 671)	(2 382 292–5 897 868)
Net present value	16 138 305	3 081 340
(15% discount rate)	(11 173 553–27 662 490)	(2 133 404–5 281 692)

Notes: Figures in parentheses represent upper and lower bound welfare estimates based on the 95% confidence interval for the estimated coefficients in the model (see Section A3 in the appendix).
[a] FAO estimates from FAO (2003). 2000 and 2004 data are estimated from 1990–2000 annual average mangrove loss of 18.0 km².
[b] Thailand estimates from various Royal Thailand Forestry Department sources reported in Aksornkoae and Tokrisna (2004). 2000 and 2004 data are estimated from 1993–96 annual average mangrove loss of 3.44 km²
[c] Re-calculated based on Sathirathai and Barbier (2001).
Sources: Author's calculations.

loss of mangrove area is an increase in expected storm damages of about US$585 000 per km². In Table 4, this latter calculation is combined with the FAO and Thailand estimates of the average annual rates of deforestation to compute the welfare losses in storm protection service for Thailand over 1996–2004. The table shows the welfare calculations based both on the point estimates of the count data regression and on using the standard errors to construct 95% confidence bounds on these estimates.

Table 4 shows that, for the FAO mangrove deforestation estimate of 18.0 km² per year over 1996–2004, the EDF approach estimates the annual welfare loss in storm protection service to be around US$3.4 million ($2.3 to 5.8 million with 95% confidence), and the net present value of this loss over the entire period ranges from US$16.1 to 19.5 million ($11.2 to 33.4 million with 95% confidence). For the Thailand deforestation estimation of 3.4 km² per year, the annual welfare loss in storm protection is over US$0.65 million ($0.45 to 1.1 million with 95% confidence), and the net present value of this loss over the entire period ranges from US$3.1 to 3.7 million ($2.1 to 6.4 million with 95% confidence).

Comparing the EDF approach and the replacement cost method of estimating the welfare impacts of a loss of the storm protection service due to mangrove deforestation confirms that the replacement cost method tends to produce extremely high estimates – almost 4 times greater than even the largest upper-bound estimate calculated using the EDF approach. This suggests that the replacement cost method should be used with caution, and when data are available, the EDF approach may provide more reliable values of the storm protection service of coastal wetlands.

4.4. Land use policy implications

Valuation of the ecosystem services provided by mangroves are important for two land use policy decisions in Thailand. First, although declining in recent years, conversion of remaining mangroves to shrimp farm ponds and other commercial coastal developments continues to be a major threat to Thailand's remaining mangrove areas. Second, since the December 2004 tsunami disaster, there is now considerable interest in rehabilitating and restoring mangrove ecosystems as 'natural barriers' to future coastal storm events.

To illustrate how improved and more accurate valuation of ecosystems can help inform these two policy decisions, Table 5 compares the per hectare net returns to shrimp farming, the costs of mangrove rehabilitation and the value of mangrove services. All land uses are assumed to be instigated over 1996–2004 and are valued in 1996 US dollars. The net economic returns to shrimp farming are based on non-declining yields over a 5-year period of investment, with the pond abandoned in subsequent years (Sathirathai and Barbier, 2001). These returns to shrimp aquaculture are estimated to be $1078 to $1220 per ha. In comparison, the costs rehabilitating mangrove ecosystems on land that has been converted to shrimp farms and then abandoned are $8812 to $9318 per ha. Thus valuing the goods and services of mangrove ecosystems can help to address two important policy questions: Do the net economic returns to shrimp farming justify further mangrove conversion to this economic activity, and is it worth investing in mangrove replanting and ecosystem rehabilitation in abandoned shrimp farm areas?

As indicated in Table 5, if the older methods of valuing habitat-fishery linkages with the static approach and storm protection with the replacement cost method are employed, then mangrove ecosystem benefits are considerably higher than the net economic returns to shrimp farming and the costs of replanting and rehabilitating mangroves in abandoned farm areas. However, the static analysis undervalues the habitat-fishery linkage of mangroves whereas the replacement cost method over-inflates storm protection. The replacement cost method estimates storm protection at $67 610 to 81 602 per ha, which is 99% of the value of all mangrove ecosystem benefits. In contrast, the net income to local coastal communities from collected forest products and the value of habitat-fishery linkages total to only $730 to $881 per ha, which suggests that these two benefits of mangroves are insufficient on their own to justify either halting conversion to shrimp farms or replanting and rehabilitating these ecosystems on abandoned pond land.

If improved methods of valuing habitat-fishery linkages by the dynamic approach and storm protection by the expected damage function method are employed, then

Table 5. Comparison of land use values per hectare, Thailand, 1996–2004 (US$)

Land use	Net present value per hectare (10–15% discount rate)	
Shrimp farming:[a]		
Net economic returns	1078–1220	
Mangrove ecosystem rehabilitation:[b]		
Total cost	8812–9318	
Ecosystem goods and services	*Older methods*	*Improved methods*
Net income from collected forest products[c]	484–584	484–584
Habitat-fishery linkage	246–297[d]	708–987[e]
Storm protection service	67 610–81 602[f]	8966–10 821[g]
Total	68 341–82 484	10 158–12 392

[a] Based on Sathirathai and Barbier (2001), updated to 1996 US$.
[b] Based on costs of rehabilitating abandoned shrimp farms, replanting mangrove forests and maintaining and protecting mangrove seedlings. From Sathirathai and Barbier (2001), updated to 1996 US$.
[c] Based on Sathirathai and Barbier (2001), updated to 1996 US$.
[d] Based on marginal value per ha based on the static analysis of this study (see Section 4.2).
[e] Based on average value per hectare over 1996–2004 based on the dynamic analysis of this study and assuming the estimated Thailand deforestation rate of 3.44 sq km per year (see Section 4.2).
[f] Based on average value per hectare of replacement cost method of this study (see Section 4.3).
[g] Based on marginal value per hectare of expected damage function approach of this study (see Section 4.3).
Sources: Author's calculations.

the outcome is somewhat different. Although the total value of mangrove ecosystem services is lowered to $10 158 to $12 392 per ha, it still exceeds the net economic returns to shrimp farming. Storm protection service is still the largest benefit of mangroves, but it no longer dominates the land use value comparison. The net income to local coastal communities from collected forest products and the value of habitat-fishery linkages total to $1192 to $1571 per ha, which now are greater than the net economic returns to shrimp farming. The value of the storm protection, however, is critical to the decision as to whether or not to replant and rehabilitate mangrove ecosystems in abandoned pond areas. As shown in Table 5, storm protection benefits make mangrove rehabilitation an economically feasible land use option.

5. CONCLUSIONS

The case study of valuing mangroves in Thailand illustrates the potential use of the PF approach to modelling key ecological regulatory and habitat services. The study also indicates the importance of choosing the appropriate PF method for modelling the key ecological-economic linkages underlying each service.

For example, the case study confirms that, if coastal wetlands such as mangroves serve as a breeding and nursery habitat for a variety of near-shore fisheries, then it seems more appropriate to model this environmental input as part of the growth function of the fish stock. In comparison, not accounting for the stock effects of a change in coastal nursery and breeding grounds may lead to an underestimation of the value of this habitat-fishery linkage. The case study also illustrates how the EDF approach can be applied to valuing the storm protection service provided by mangroves, and demonstrates why this method should be preferred to the less-reliable replacement cost method, which has been used extensively in the literature to date (Chong, 2005).

The case study also points to some important policy implications for Thailand. In recent decades, considerable mangrove deforestation has taken place in Thailand, mainly as a result of shrimp farm expansion and other coastal economic developments (see Figure 4). Over this period, mangrove conversion for these development activities was systematically encouraged by government land use policies (Aksornkoae and Tokrisna, 2004; Barbier, 2003; Sathirathai and Barbier, 2001). Such policies were designed without consideration of the value of the ecological services provided by mangroves, such as their habitat support for coastal fisheries and storm protection. The case study of valuing these ecological services for Thailand illustrates that their benefits are significant, and should certainly not be ignored in future mangrove land management decisions.

The case study applications in this paper of valuing coastal storm protection and habitat services have policy implications beyond Thailand as well. Even before Hurricanes Katrina and Rita devastated the central Gulf Coast of the United States in 2005, the US Army Corps of Engineers had proposed a $1.1 billion multi-year programme to slow the rate of wetland loss and restore some wetlands in coastal Louisiana. In the aftermath of these hurricanes, the US Congress is now considering expanding the programme substantially to a $14 billion restoration effort (Zinn, 2005). As noted in Section 4, in the wake of the 2004 Asian tsunami, mangrove restoration projects for enhanced coastal protection are underway in many countries throughout the region. International donor groups are also supporting mangrove restoration projects in Asia, especially in countries and regions devastated by the tsunami (Check, 2005). In addition, there is mounting scientific evidence that near-shore fisheries throughout the world are undergoing rapid decline, with loss of coastal habitat and nursery grounds for these fisheries a contributory cause (Jackson et al., 2001; Myers and Worm, 2003). Valuing the storm protection and habitat services of coastal wetlands, as illustrated by the Thailand case study in this paper, can therefore play a vital role in current and future debates about the state of coastal ecosystems worldwide and the assessment of the costs and benefits of restoring these vital ecosystems.

Thus, valuing the non-market benefits of ecological regulatory and habitat services is becoming increasingly important in assisting policymakers to manage critical environmental assets. However, further progress applying production function approaches and other methods to value ecological services faces two challenges.

First, for these methods to be applied effectively to valuing ecosystem services, it is important that the key ecological and economic relationships are well understood. Unfortunately, our knowledge of the ecological functions, let alone the ecosystem processes and components, underlying many of the services listed in Table 1 is still incomplete.

Second, natural ecosystems are subject to stresses, rapid change and irreversible losses, they tend to display threshold effects and other non-linearities that are difficult to predict, let alone model in terms of their economic impacts. These uncertainties can affect the estimation of values from an *ex ante* ('beforehand') perspective. The economic valuation literature recognizes that such uncertainties create the conditions for *option values*, which arise from the difference between valuation under conditions of certainty and uncertainty (e.g., see Freeman, 2003 and Just *et al.*, 2004). The standard approach recommended in the literature is to estimate this additional value separately, through various techniques to measure an *option price*, that is, the amount of money that an individual will pay or must be compensated to be indifferent from the status quo condition of the ecosystem and the new, proposed condition. However, in practice, estimating separate option prices for unknown ecological effects is very difficult. Determining the appropriate risk premium for vulnerable populations exposed to the irreversible ecological losses is also proving elusive. These are problems currently affecting all economic valuation methods of ecosystem services, and not just the production function approach. As one review of these studies concludes: 'Given the imperfect knowledge of the way people value natural ecosystems and their goods and services, and our limited understanding of the underlying ecology and biogeochemistry of aquatic ecosystems, calculations of the value of the changes resulting from a policy intervention will always be approximate' (Heal *et al.*, 2005, p. 218).

Finally, Section 3 noted recent attempts to extend the production function approach to the ecosystem level through integrated ecological-economic modelling. This allows the ecosystem functioning and dynamics underlying the provision of ecological services to be modelled and can be used to value multiple rather than single services. For example, returning to the Thailand case study, it is well known that both coral reefs and sea grasses complement the role of mangroves in providing both the habitat-fishery and storm protection services. Thus full modelling of the integrated mangrove–coral reef–sea grass system could improve measurement of the benefits of both services. As we learn more about the important ecological and economic role played by such services, it may be relevant to develop multi-service ecosystem modelling to understand more fully what values are lost when such integrated coastal and marine systems are disturbed or destroyed.

Discussion

Carlo A. Favero
IGIER, Bocconi University and CEPR

The objective of the paper is to apply a production function (and expected damage) approach to 'valuing the environment as input', with an application to a mangrove ecosystem in Thailand. I shall concentrate my discussion only on the production function approach, but the main methodological points raised are naturally extended to the expected damage function approach.

An environmental good or service essentially serves as a factor input into production that yields utility. The fundamental problem of the empirical application is the evaluation of the following value function:

$$V_t = E_t \sum_{j=0}^{T} \frac{B_{t+j}}{(1+r)^j}$$

where B is the social benefits in any time period of the mangrove ecosystem, and r is the discount rate.

There are two fundamental questions:

1. What is the appropriate discount rate?
2. How to evaluate B?

The first question is not explicitly addressed and different scenarios on the discount rate are adopted; the production function approach is the answer to the second question.

In theory the production function approach can be described as follows:

- Specification of a dynamic intertemporal optimization problem, where one of the constraints is the production function relating the input of interest to the measurable output.
- Solution of the model.
- Identification and estimation (or, whenever estimation is not possible, calibration) of the technology and preference parameters of the model and of the auxiliary parameters.
- Dynamic stochastic simulation of the model to derive $E_t B_{t+j}$ and the associated confidence intervals.

In practice two alternative approaches are considered: a static one and a dynamic one. I shall not comment on the static approach because I find this inappropriate to the very nature of the problem at hand, which is, by definition, dynamic.

In the dynamic approach a model is postulated to determine the dynamics of the stock of fish measured in biomass units, X_t, the fishing effort, E_t, the landed fish price per unit harvested, p, and the harvest, h. The adopted model is described as follows:

$$X_{t+1} - X_t = F(X_t, S_t) - h(X_t, E_t)$$

$$E_{t+1} - E_t = \phi[p_t h_t - w_t E_t]$$

$$F(X_t, S_t) = rX_t \left[1 - \frac{X_t}{\alpha \ln S_t}\right]$$

$$h_t = qX_t E_t$$

$$p_t = kh_t^\eta$$

where $F(X_t, S_t)$ is biological growth in the current period, which is a function of S_t, the mangrove area, $h(X_t, E_t)$, harvesting is a function of the stock as well as fishing effort, E_t. Fishing effort is modelled as a partial adjustment model in which the equilibrium value is determined by fish price per unit harvested and the unit cost of effort, w.

The model is estimated and then simulated keeping w exogenous and taking alternative scenarios for S, that by consequence is taken as exogenous. Using some assumption for the discount rate the present value of a reduction in the mangrove area is then computed.

The results are interesting but there are a number of important questions that the modelling strategy leaves open:

- In the dynamic model S is exogenous and no law of motion for S is specified. The model is not capable of explaining the reduction in S that we observe in the data. In fact, if agents were acting following this model we would have never observed a reduction in S, because a reduction in S has only costs and no benefits. Macroeconometricians might see the applicability of the Lucas critique to this model as an immediate consequence of the assumption of exogeneity of S.
- Expectations do not explicitly enter the model.
- What are the costs incurred in omitting from the model the dynamics of w?
- What is the performance of this model when evaluated in sample by dynamic simulation?
- How is uncertainty added for estimation and more importantly for dynamic simulation? The result reported in Table 4 seems to take account of only coefficient uncertainty while, given the modelling choices, the fluctuations in the relevant variables not explained by the adopted model are likely to be the main source of uncertainty.

I think that the answer to this set of open questions could further enhance the potential of the interesting methods for valuing ecosystem services very well discussed in this paper.

Omer Moav

Hebrew University, University of London Royal Holloway, Shalem Center, and CEPR
Edward Barbier demonstrates how basic micro theory can be implemented to estimate the value of ecological services for human welfare. In particular, two methods are developed: the production function approach and the expected damage function approach. Both methods utilize exogenous variation in the size of the ecosystem service, such as the size of a mangrove forest, on a beneficial outcome. According to the former the outcome is welfare gained from the decline in the price of a consumption good, such as fish, that utilizes the ecosystem as an input in its production process. In the latter it is the economic value of the reduction in damage, arising, for instance, from storms, that is reduced by a larger ecosystem.

The theory is rather straightforward. It is the availability of the data that the estimation depends on, and it is not clear that for most practical problems there exists sufficient exogenous variation in the ecosystem, allowing for a reliable assessment. Nevertheless, Barbier convincingly illustrates that despite the difficulties, these methods have the potential to provide important information about the value of the ecosystem and thereby the value of preventing its disappearance. This information can become critical for policymakers, and might, even if only in marginal cases, generate the crucial political force to reverse processes of natural habitat destruction.

The value of the functions of the ecosystem include, as stated by Barbier, 'climate stability, maintenance of biodiversity and beneficial species, erosion control, flood mitigation, storm protection, groundwater recharge and pollution control'. This statement reveals another limitation of the estimation methods. It focuses on a limited set of benefits, implying a potentially huge underestimation of the value of the ecosystem. First, due to information problems regarding most functions, it is difficult to identify the size of the impact and/or its welfare value. For instance, most likely exogenous variety in the ecosystem is not sufficient to estimate its effect on climate stability, and the welfare value of biodiversity is a question hard to answer.

Second, the cost of preserving the ecosystem – giving up the benefits of its alternative use – is paid by the local population, while many of its services extend beyond that. As is well known, preserving natural ecosystems is a problem with large externalities that go beyond borders. In other words, who cares? Do we expect the poor fisherman in Thailand, or their government, to allocate a significant weight in its welfare function to biodiversity? In fact, it is the population of the developed world that cares, and this population's willingness to pay a compensating price, could be above and beyond the benefit of the ecosystem to the local population.

A more technical comment on the estimation process regards the open access assumption and, in particular, the implicit assumption that changes in the habitat are sufficiently small, relative to the economy, such that the producer's surplus is unchanged. Welfare gains from a larger ecosystem emerge only from the reduction in consumer goods prices. This assumption adds to the bias in the estimation, reducing the value of the ecosystem. To see this point, suppose that prices of the consumption good are also given (traded good in an open economy). In this case there is zero welfare gain from preserving the environment.

A final comment about the estimation method regards the implicit assumption of stability of the steady-state equilibrium. However, non-monotonic convergence to the steady state might characterize the dynamics of the ecosystem. For instance, the population of a species might converge to its steady state in oscillations, implying that a negative shock to the ecosystem might, once it is sufficiently fragile, result in extinction of a species rather than a proportional reduction in the size of the natural population.

Beyond the problems of estimating the direct value of the ecological services for human welfare, lies a somewhat deeper question regarding the long-run effects of the utilization of natural resources for the benefit of mankind in the production process. Maintaining natural habitats and benefiting their production services, or destroying them and benefiting from their alternative land use for agriculture, might have different long-run consequences on demographic variables, institutional development, and, in particular, human capital promoting institutions (e.g., public schools, loans, and child labour regulation), and the resulting accumulation of human capital.

Natural resources, according to many studies, are a hurdle for the process of development, in particular the accumulation of human capital. (e.g. Gylfason, 2001). But to the best of my knowledge, we do not know yet how to make a distinction in that regard between an open-access preserved ecosystem and agricultural land. Therefore, depleting resources or increasing the size of agricultural land on the account of the ecosystem, could have a significant impact on the economy.

Moreover, the transition from an open access ecosystem into private owned farmland might have an impact on wealth inequality, in particular inequality in the ownership of such land. Deninger and Squire (1998) show that inequality in land ownership has a negative impact on economic growth. Engerman and Sokoloff (2000) provide evidence that wealth inequality, brought about oppressive institutions (e.g., restricted access to the democratic process and to education). They argue that these institutions were designed to maintain the political power of the elite and to preserve the existing inequality. Galor *et al.* (2005) provide evidence that inequality in the ownership of agricultural land has a negative effect on public expenditure on education, and argue that the elite of landowners might prevent public schooling, despite the support of the owners of capital and the working class.

On the other hand, if the destruction of the ecosystem increases farmland and thereby possibly promoting industrial development, and if the process does not generate large wealth inequality, the return to human capital will most likely rise. This could trigger a process of development stemming from reduced fertility and increased investment in education. This brings us back to the main problem of preventing the distractions of an ecosystem: the externality. Each small economy might be better-off destroying the ecosystem, giving rise to an inefficient equilibrium. The analysis suggested by Barbier, could, at least, highlight the benefits of preserving natural habitats for the local economy.

APPENDIX: APPLICATION TO THAILAND CASE STUDY

This appendix outlines the econometric estimations for valuing habitat-fishery linkages and the storm protection service of mangroves in the Thailand case study of Section 4.

A1. Static valuation of habitat-fishery linkage

To apply the static analysis of habitat-fishery linkages of Section 3.3.1 to the Thailand case study, it is necessary to estimate the unknown parameters (A, a, b) of the log-linear version of the Cobb–Douglas production function:

$$\ln h_{it} = A_0 + a \ln E_{it} + b \ln M_{it} + \mu_{it} \qquad (A1)$$

where $i = 1, \ldots, 5$ zones, $t = 1, \ldots, 14$ years (1983–96) and $A_0 = \ln A$.

Equation (A1) was estimated using the pooled data on demersal fisheries, shellfish and mangrove area from Barbier (2003). These were the data on harvest, h_{it}, and effort, E_{it}, for Thailand's shellfish and demersal fisheries, as well as mangrove area, M_{it} across the five coastal zones of Thailand and over the years1983–96. Various regression procedures for a pooled data set were utilized and compared, including: (i) ordinary least squares (OLS); (ii) one- and two-way panel analysis of fixed and random effects; and (iii) a maximum likelihood estimation by an iterated generalized least squares (GLS) procedure for a pooled time series and cross-sectional regression, which allows for correction of any groupwise heteroscedasticity, cross-group correlation and common or within-group autocorrelation. Table A1 indicates the best regression model for the shellfish and demersal fisheries respectively, and the relevant test statistics.

For demersal fisheries, the preferred model shown in Table A1 is the GLS estimation allowing for groupwise heteroscedasticity and correcting for both cross-group and common autocorrelation. For the panel analysis of the demersal fisheries, the likelihood ratio tests of the null hypothesis of zero individual and time effects across all five zones and fourteen time periods were significant, thus rejecting the null hypothesis. In addition, the Breusch–Pagan Lagrange multiplier (LM) statistic was also significant at the 95% confidence level for both the one-way and two-models, which suggests rejection of the null hypothesis of zero random disturbances. The Hausman test statistic was also significant at the 99% confidence level, suggesting that the fixed effects specification is preferred to the random effects. However, in both the one- and two-way fixed effects model the t-test on the estimated parameter for a in Equation (A1) was insignificant, suggesting the null hypothesis that $a = 0$ cannot be rejected. As indicated in Table A1, from the pooled time series cross-sectional GLS regression for demersal fisheries, the likelihood ratio (LR) test statistic of the null hypothesis for homoscedasticity based on the least squares regression was computed to be 24.64, which is statistically significant. Although not shown in the table, the alternative Wald test for homoscedasticity is also statistically significant and confirms rejection of the null hypothesis. Thus the GLS model with correction of groupwise heteroscedasticity is preferred to the OLS regression. The LM statistic of 14.43 also reported in Table A1 for demersal fisheries is a test of the null hypothesis of zero cross-sectional correlation, which proves to be statistically significant. Although not indicated in the table, the LR test statistic for groupwise heteroscedasticity as a restriction on cross-group correlation was estimated to be 23.26, which is also statistically significant. Thus the null hypothesis of zero cross-group correlation in the demersal fisheries regression can be rejected. The common autocorrelation coefficient across all five zones was estimated to be 0.484, and as shown in Table A1, once the GLS model for demersal fish was corrected for this common autocorrelation, the null hypothesis that the coefficient a = 0 is now rejected.

For shellfish, as indicated in Table A1 the preferred estimation of Equation (A1) is the GLS estimation allowing for groupwise heteroscedasticity and correcting for cross-group correlation, with A_0 restricted to zero. For the panel analysis of shellfish, the likelihood ratio tests and Breusch–Pagan LM tests of the null hypothesis of no individual and time effects were significant, thus rejecting the null hypothesis. The

Table A1. Estimates of Equation (A1) for Thailand's shellfish and demersal fisheries

Coefficient	Demersal fishery[a]	Shellfish fishery[b]
A_0	11.213 (24.568)**	–
A	0.341 (4.992)**	1.688 (38.254)**
B	0.100 (2.763)**	0.196 (3.693)**
Log-likelihood[c]	5.401	−71.517
Likelihood ratio statistic[d]	24.643**	35.076**
Lagrange multiplier statistic[e]	14.426*	21.304**

Notes: *t*-statistics are shown in parentheses.
[a] Preferred model is groupwise heteroscedastic and correlated GLS, corrected for common autocorrelation.
[b] Preferred model is groupwise heteroscedastic and correlated GLS, with A_0 restricted to zero.
[c] In the demersal fishery regression, correction of cross-group correlation $Cov[e_{it}, e_{jt}] = \sigma_{ij}$ leads to a positive log-likelihood.
[d] Tests the null hypothesis of homoscedasticity based on OLS.
[e] Tests the null hypothesis of zero cross-group correlation based on OLS.
* Significant at 95% confidence level.
** Significant at 99% confidence level.

Sources: Author's estimations.

Hausman test statistic was significant, suggesting that the fixed effects specification is preferred to the random effects. However, in both the one- and two-way fixed effects model the *t*-test on the estimated parameters for a and b in Equation (A1) was insignificant, suggesting the null hypothesis $a = b = 0$ cannot be rejected. As indicated in Table A1, from the pooled time series cross-sectional GLS regression of shellfish, the LR test statistic of the null hypothesis for homoscedasticity based on the least squares regression is 35.08, which is statistically significant. Although not shown in the table, the alternative Wald test for homoscedasticity is also statistically significant and confirms rejection of the null hypothesis. Thus the GLS model with correction of groupwise heteroscedasticity is preferred to the OLS regression. The LM statistic of 21.30 also reported in Table A1 for the shellfish regression is a test of the null hypothesis of zero cross-sectional correlation, which proves to be statistically significant. Although not indicated in the table, the LR test statistic for groupwise heteroscedasticity as a restriction on cross-group correlation was estimated to be 43.90, which is also statistically significant. Thus the null hypothesis of zero cross-group correlation in the shellfish regression can be rejected. As shown in Table A1, once the GLS model of shellfish was corrected for groupwise heteroscedasticity and correlation, the null hypotheses that $a = 0$ and $b = 0$ are now rejected.

The estimations of Equation (A1) for Thailand's shellfish and demersal fisheries were used in conditions (5) and (6) to calculate the welfare impacts of mangrove deforestation over 1996–2004 on Thailand's artisanal fisheries. The analysis uses the same iso-elastic demand function as in Barbier (2003), with a demand elasticity, ε, of −0.5. The results are reported in Table 3, which shows welfare calculations for both the point estimates and upper and lower bounds on these estimates based on the standard errors of the regression coefficients reported in Table A1.

A2. Dynamic valuation of habitat-fishery linkage

The dynamic habitat-fishery modelling approach to valuing the habitat-fishery link-age is outlined in Section 3.3.2. The main difficulty in applying this approach to valuing mangrove-fishery linkages in Thailand is that data do not exist for the bio-mass stock, X_t, of near-shore fisheries. Thus the appropriate system of equations to estimate comprises (10) and (11). Because E_t and c_t are predetermined, both of these equations can be estimated independently (Homans and Wilen, 1997). For both the shellfish and demersal fisheries, the estimated equations are:

$$E_{it} = a_0 + a_1 R_{it-1} + a_2 E_{it-1} + \mu_{it-1} \tag{A2}$$

$$\frac{c_{it} - c_{it-1}}{c_{it-1}} = b_0 + b_1 \frac{c_{it-1}}{\ln M_{it-1}} + b_2 E_{it-1} + \mu_{it-1}, \tag{A3}$$

where $i = 1, \ldots, 5$ zones, $t - 1 = 1, \ldots, 13$ years (1983–95), $R_{it-1} = k h_{it-1}^{1+\eta}$, $a_1 = \phi$, $a_2 = (1 - \phi w)$, $b_0 = r$, $b_1 = -r/\alpha q$ and $b_2 = -q$. Both equations were estimated using the pooled data on demersal fisheries, shellfish and mangrove area from Barbier (2003). These were the data on harvest, h_{it-1}, and effort, E_{it-1}, for Thailand's shellfish and demersal fisheries, as well as mangrove area, M_{it-1} across the five coastal zones of Thailand and over the years 1983–96. In addition, to calculate R_{it-1} from h_{it-1} the elasticity $\eta = 1/\varepsilon = -2$ was assumed as in the static analysis. Various regression procedures for a pooled data set were utilized and compared, including: (i) OLS; (ii) one- and two-way panel analysis of fixed and random effects; and (iii) a maximum likelihood estimation by an iterated GLS procedure for a pooled time series and cross-sectional regression, which allows for correction of any groupwise heteroscedas-ticity, cross-group correlation and common or within-group autocorrelation. Tables A2 and A3 indicate the best regression models of Equations (A2) and (A3) for the shellfish and demersal fisheries respectively, and the relevant test statistics.

For demersal fisheries, the preferred model for the effort equation (A2) is the GLS estimation allowing for groupwise heteroscedasticity and corrected for common autocorrelation. For the panel analysis, the likelihood ratio and Breusch–Pagan LM tests of the null hypothesis of no individual and time effects were not significant; thus, the null hypothesis cannot be rejected. However, as indicated in Table A2, from the pooled time series cross-sectional regression of Equation (A2) for demersal fisheries, the LR test statistic of the null hypothesis of homoscedasticity based on the OLS regression is computed to be 93.22, which is statistically significant. Although not shown in the table, the alternative Wald test for homoscedasticity is also statistically significant and confirms rejection of the null hypothesis. Thus the GLS model with correction of groupwise heteroscedasticity is preferred to the OLS regression. The test statistics for the null hypothesis of zero cross-group correlation are mixed. The LM statistic of 12.24 indicated in Table A2 is significant, whereas the LR test statistic of 12.56 is not. When the GLS regression is corrected for groupwise correlation, however, the constant term a_0 is no longer significant. The common autocorrelation coefficient across all five zones is estimated to be 0.242, and although slight, correction of this autocorrelation improved the overall robustness of the GLS estimation.

As shown in Table A2, the preferred model for the effort equation (A2) for shellfish is the one-way random effects estimation corrected for heteroscedasticity. The LR and Wald tests of the pooled time series cross-sectional regressions of Equation (A2) for shellfish indicated that the null hypothesis of homoscedasticity can be rejected. Thus the GLS model with correction of groupwise heteroscedasticity is preferred to the OLS regression. However, in all versions of the GLS regression the coefficient a_1 was negative and statistically insignificant. The LR test for the presence of individual effects is statistically significant, thus rejecting the null hypothesis of no such effects, and although not shown, the equivalent F-test of the null hypothesis is also statistically significant. Neither the Breusch–Pagan LM test of the null hypothesis of random provincial-level disturbances nor the Hausman test of the random versus the fixed effects specification is statistically significant. Although these results are somewhat contradictory, they suggest that, if individual effects are present, they are likely to be random. The LR test and F-test of the presence of time effects is not significant, suggesting that the one-way is preferred to the two-way specification. Correction of heteroscedasticity improves the robustness of the one-way random effects estimation

Table A2. Estimates of Equation (A2) for Thailand's shellfish and demersal fisheries

Coefficient	Demersal fishery[a]	Shellfish fishery[b]
a_0	22.365 (2.254)*	808.720 (2.661)**
a_1	0.00004 (4.375)**	0.000003 (0.233)
a_2	0.84855 (21.703)**	0.70470 (8.183)**
Log-likelihood	−380.903	−520.513
Likelihood ratio statistic for homoscedasticity[c]	93.223**	−
Likelihood ratio statistic for correlation[d]	12.552	−
Lagrange multiplier statistic[e]	12.241*	−
Likelihood ratio statistic for individual effects[f]	−	16.285**
Breusch–Pagan Lagrange multiplier statistic[g]	−	0.04
Hausman test statistic[h]	−	1.88

Notes: t-statistics are shown in parentheses.
[a] Preferred model is groupwise heteroscedastic GLS, corrected for common autocorrelation.
[b] Preferred model is one-way random effects corrected for heteroscedasticity.
[c] Tests the null hypothesis of homoscedasticity based on OLS.
[d] Tests the null hypothesis of zero cross-group correlation based on OLS.
[e] Tests the null hypothesis of zero cross-group correlation based on OLS.
[f] Tests the null hypothesis of zero individual effects.
[g] Tests the null hypothesis of zero random disturbances based on OLS.
[h] Tests the null hypothesis of correlation between the individual effects and the error (i.e. random effects is preferred to fixed effects estimation).
* Significant at 95% confidence level.
** Significant at 99% confidence level.

Sources: Author's estimations.

without affecting the parameter estimates. Although not shown in the table, the preferred model displayed a very low estimated autocorrelation of 0.022.

As indicated in Table A3, the preferred model for the growth in catch per unit effort equation (A3) for demersal fisheries is the GLS estimation allowing for group-wise heteroscedasticity. For the panel analysis, the LR and Breusch–Pagan LM tests of the null hypothesis of no individual and time effects were not significant; thus, the null hypothesis cannot be rejected. However, from the pooled time series cross-sectional regression, both the LR and Wald test statistics of the null hypothesis of homoscedasticity are also statistically significant. Thus the GLS model with correction of groupwise heteroscedasticity is preferred to the OLS regression. The test statistics for the null hypothesis of zero cross-group correlation are mixed. The LM statistic of 11.03 indicated in Table A3 is significant, whereas the LR test statistic of 18.56 is not. However, correcting the GLS regression for groupwise correlation does not affect the estimation significantly. Although not shown in the table, the preferred model displayed a very low estimated autocorrelation of −0.006.

Table A3 displays the preferred model for the growth in CPE equation (A3) for shellfish, which is the GLS estimation allowing for groupwise and correlated hetero-scedasticity and corrected for common autocorrelation. For the panel analysis, the LR and Breusch–Pagan LM tests of the null hypothesis of no individual and time effects were not significant; thus, the null hypothesis cannot be rejected. However, from the pooled time series cross-sectional regression, both the LR and Wald test statistics of the null hypothesis of homoscedasticity are also statistically significant. Thus the GLS model with correction of groupwise heteroscedasticity is preferred to the OLS regression. Although the LR and LM test statistics for the null hypothesis

Table A3. Estimates of Equation (A3) for Thailand's shellfish and demersal fisheries

Coefficient	Demersal fishery[a]	Shellfish fishery[b]
b_0	0.4896 (2.908)**	0.2997 (2.371)*
b_1	−0.000187 (−2.368)*	−0.000201 (−2.354)*
b_2	−0.000204 (−2.637)**	−0.000060 (−2.007)*
Log-likelihood	−22.337	−30.350
Likelihood ratio statistic for homoscedasticity[c]	24.627**	109.342**
Likelihood ratio statistic for correlation[d]	18.235	11.434
Lagrange multiplier statistic[e]	11.026*	8.491

Notes: *t*-statistics are shown in parentheses.
[a] Preferred model is groupwise heteroscedastic GLS.
[b] Preferred model is groupwise heteroscedastic and correlated GLS, corrected for common autocorrelation.
[c] Tests the null hypothesis of homoscedasticity based on OLS.
[d] Tests the null hypothesis of zero cross-group correlation based on OLS.
[e] Tests the null hypothesis of zero cross-group correlation based on OLS.
* Significant at 95% confidence level.
** Significant at 99% confidence level.

Sources: Author's estimations.

of zero cross-group correlation are not significant, correcting the GLS regression for groupwise correlation improves the significance confidence level of the estimated parameter b_2 from 90 to 95%. The common autocorrelation coefficient across all five zones is estimated to be 0.147, and although slight, correction of this autocorrelation improved the overall robustness of the GLS estimation.

Using the estimated parameters for Equations (A2) and (A3) for Thailand's shellfish and demersal fisheries allows simulation of the welfare impacts of mangrove deforestation over 1996–2004 on Thailand's artisanal fisheries. Again, the same demand function with elasticity of −0.5 as in Barbier (2003) is employed. The results are reported in Table 3, which shows welfare calculations for both the point estimates and upper and lower bounds on these estimates based on the standard errors of the regression coefficients reported in Tables A2 and A3.

A3. Expected damage function valuation of storm protection service

As discussed in Section 3.5, the key step in applying the expected damage function approach to valuing the storm protection service of a coastal wetland such as mangroves is to estimate how a change in mangrove area influences the expected incidence of economically damaging natural disaster events.

Suppose that for a number of coastal regions, $i = 1, \ldots, N$, and over a given period of time, $t = 1, \ldots, T$ the ith coastal region could experience in any period t any number of $z_{it} = 0, 1, 2, 3 \ldots$ economically damaging storm event incidents. A common assumption in count data models is that the count variable z_{it} has a Poisson distribution, in which case the expected number of storm events in each region per period is given by:

$$E[z_{it}|S_{it}, x_{it}] = \lambda_{it} = e^{\alpha_i + \beta_s S_{it} + \beta' x_{it}}, \quad \frac{\partial E[z_{it}|S_{it}, x_{it}]}{\partial S_{it}} = \lambda_{it}\beta_s \tag{A4}$$

where as before, S_{it} is the area of wetlands, x_{it}, are other factors, and α_i accounts for other possible 'unobserved' effects on the incidence of disasters specific to each coastal region. Estimation of β_s, along with an estimate of the conditional mean λ_{it}, allows $\partial Z/\partial S$ in Equation (13) to be determined. One drawback of the Poisson distribution (Equation (A4)) is that it automatically implies 'equidispersion', that is, the conditional variance of z_{it} is also equal to λ_{it}. To test whether this is the case, the Poisson method of estimating (A4) should be compared to other techniques, such as the Negative Binomial model, which do not assume equidispersion in the variance of z_{it}.

For the Thailand case study, the estimation of (A4) is:

$$\ln E[z_{it}|M_{it}, x_{it}] = \ln \lambda_{it} = \alpha_i + \beta_s M_{it} + \beta' x_{it} + \mu_{it}, \tag{A5}$$

where $i = 1, \ldots, 21$ coastal provinces, $t = 1, \ldots, 18$ years (1979–96). The EM-DAT (2005) International Disaster Database contains data on the number of coastal disasters occurring in Thailand since 1975 and the approximate location and date of its impacts. From these data it is possible to determine z_{it}, the number of economically damaging coastal natural disasters that occurred per province per year over 1979–96. Mangrove area, M_{it}, is measured in terms of the annual mangrove area in square kilometres for each of the 21 coastal provinces of Thailand over 1979–96. Two control variables were included as the additional factors, x_{it}, which may explain the incidence of economically damaging coastal disasters, the population density of a province and a yearly time trend variable. The inclusion of the population density variable reflects the prevailing view in the natural disaster management literature that 'hazard events that occur in unpopulated areas and are not associated with losses do not constitute disasters' (Dilley *et al.*, 2005, p. 115).[11] The yearly time trend was included as a control because the number of coastal natural disasters seems to have increased over time in Thailand (see Figure 5).[12]

Various regression procedures for a panel data set for count data models were utilized and compared, including: (1) Poisson models assuming equidispersion, i.e. equality of the conditional mean and the variance; (2) maximum likelihood estimation of Negative Binomial models allowing for unequal dispersion; and (3) comparing provincial to zonal fixed effects. Table A4 reports the best count data model for estimating Equation (A5) and the relevant test statistics.

As shown in Table A4, the preferred specification of the count data model is the Negative Binomial model with zonal fixed effects. In both the Poisson and Negative Binomial panel models, the zonal fixed effects specification (with coastal zone 5 as the default) is preferred to individual province effects, which is verified by LR tests of the two specifications. Although the parameter estimates for the zonal fixed effects are not shown, these estimated effects were significant at the 95% or 99% confidence levels. As indicated in Table A4, two standard tests were employed for the null hypothesis of equidispersion of the conditional mean and variance of the Poisson specification of the count data model (Cameron and Trivedi, 1998; Greene, 2003). Both the LM statistic and the *t*-test for equidispersion based on the residuals of the Poisson regression are significant, indicating that the null hypothesis can be rejected, and the Negative Binomial model that does not assume equidispersion is preferred to the Poisson specification. The LR statistic reported in the table tests the null hypothesis that the coefficients of the regressors are zero; as the statistic is significant, the hypothesis is rejected.

The results displayed in Table A4 for the preferred model show that a change in mangrove area has a significant influence on the incidence of coastal natural disasters in Thailand, and with the predicted sign. The point estimate for β_8 indicates that a 1 km^2 decline in mangrove area increases the expected number of disasters by 0.36%.

---

[11] This view is also reflected in the criteria used in the International Disaster Database to decide which hazard events should be recorded as 'natural disasters'. In order for EM-DAT (2005) to record an event as a disaster, at least one or more of the following criteria must be fulfilled: 10 or more people reported killed; 100 people reported affected; declaration of a state of emergency; call for international assistance. The simple correlation between population density and mangrove area for the sample is relatively low (−0.389).

[12] This is a procedure recommended by Rose (1990), when such a trend effect is suspected.

Table A4. Negative binomial estimation of Equation (A5) with zonal fixed effects

Variable	Parameter estimate[a]	Marginal effect[b]
Mangrove area (M_{it})	−0.0036 (−4.448)**	−0.0031 (−2.745)**
Population density $(POPDEN_{it})$	−0.0005 (−1.079)	−0.0004 (−0.894)
Annual time trend $(YRTRN_{it})$	0.0781 (5.558)**	0.0669 (2.615)**
Dispersion parameter (α_{it})	0.0001	
Estimated conditional mean (λ)	0.8559	
Log-likelihood	−373.66	
Lagrange multiplier statistic[c]	39.967**	
Regression t-test[d]	−5.385**	
Likelihood ratio statistic[e]	74.919**	

Notes: t-statistics shown in parentheses.

[a] Parameter estimates for the zonal fixed effects are not shown. Zone 5 is the default and the fixed effects for zones 1 to 4 were negative and significant at the 95% or 99% confidence levels.

[b] Estimate of $\lambda_{it}\beta_3$ (see Equation (A4)).

[c] Tests the null hypothesis of equidispersion in the Poisson model.

[d] A regression-based test of the null hypothesis of equidispersion in the Poisson model.

[e] Tests the null hypothesis that the restricted regression without the explanatory variables M_{it}, $POPDEN_{it}$ and $YRTRN_{it}$ is the preferred Negative Binomial model with zonal fixed effects.

* Significant at 95% confidence level.

** Significant at 99% confidence level.

Sources: Author's estimations.

It is likely that the mangrove loss in Thailand, especially since the mid-1970s (see Figure 4), has increased the expected number of economically damaging coastal natural disasters per year. The estimated marginal effect corresponding to β_S of a change in mangrove area on coastal natural disasters (−0.0031) can be employed to estimate the resulting impact of mangrove deforestation over 1979–96 in Thailand on expected damages of natural coastal disasters. This is described further in Section 4.3 and shown in Table 4.

As discussed in Section 3.5, an underlying hypothesis of the expected damage function methodology is that, if coastal wetland loss increases the incidence of natural disaster per year, then wetland loss is also associated with increasing storm damages. However, under certain circumstances the results of a count data model could provide a misleading test of this null hypothesis. For instance, suppose a loss in wetland area is associated with a change in the incidence of storms from one devastating storm to two relatively minor storms per year. The count data model would then be interpreted as not providing evidence against the null that the change in the wetland area increases expected storm damages, when what has actually happened is that total storm damages have declined over time with wetland loss. This suggests the need for a robustness check on the count data model, such as Equation (A5) in the Thailand case study, to ensure that such situations do not dominate the application of the EDF approach.

One possible robustness check is to test the null hypothesis directly; that is, are total damages from storm events increasing with coastal wetland loss? In the Thailand case study, the relevant estimation is

$$D_{it} = \alpha_i + \beta_S M_{it} + \beta' x_{it} + \mu_{it} \qquad\qquad (A6)$$

where the dependent variable, D_{it}, is total real damages from all storm events per province per year over 1979–96. The EM-DAT (2005) database provides data on the total economic damages per province per year in Thailand, and these data were deflated using the 1996 GDP deflator. The standard regression procedures for the panel analysis of Equation (A6) were performed, including comparing OLS with fixed and random effects. Table A5 reports the OLS and random effects specifications for the preferred version of Equation (A6).

The preferred model in Table A5 is the pooled weighted least squares estimation with correction for heteroscedasticity. The LR test of the null hypothesis of zero individual effects across all 21 provinces is not statistically significant. Although not shown in the table, an alternative F-test of the null hypothesis is also not significant. Neither the Breusch–Pagan LM test of the null hypothesis of random provincial-level disturbances nor the Hausman test of the random versus the fixed effects specification is statistically significant. These tests confirm that in the panel analysis of Equation (A5) of the weighted OLS regression is more efficient than either the random or fixed effects models.

The weighted least squares regression in Table A5 indicates that, over 1979–96 and across the 21 coastal provinces of Thailand, total real storm damages increased with mangrove loss. The point estimate suggests that a 1 km^2 decline in mangrove area increases real storm damages by around \$52 per province per year. The regression also confirms that, for the Thailand case study, the null hypothesis that storm damages increase with mangrove loss cannot be rejected.

Table A5. Panel estimation of Equation (A6) for total storm damages, Thailand

Variable[a]	Pooled OLS[b]	Random effects[b]
Mangrove area (M_{it})	−51.527(−1.976)*	−52.378(−1.563)
Population density ($POPDEN_{it}$)	−12.896 (−0.343)	−18.723(−0.395)
Annual time trend ($YRTRN_{it}$)	965.325 (2.058)*	983.653 (2.100)*
Constant	1 3748.820 (1.275)	1 4728.707 (1.153)
Log-likelihood	−4598.425	
Likelihood ratio statistic[c]	14.173	
Lagrange multiplier statistic[d]		2.24
Hausman test[e]		1.04

Notes: t-statistics shown in parentheses.
[a] Parameter estimates for the zonal fixed effects for Zone 1 and Zone 4 are not shown. Although neither parameter was statistically significant, their inclusion improved the robustness of the overall regression.
[b] Weighted least squares with robust covariance matrix to correct for heteroscedasticity.
[c] Tests the null hypothesis of no fixed provincial effects.
[d] Tests the null hypothesis of no random provincial effects.
[e] Tests the null hypothesis that the random effects specification is preferred to the fixed effects. Test was performed excluding the zonal fixed effect for Zone 4.
* Significant at 95% confidence level.

Sources: Author's estimations.

REFERENCES

Acharya, G. and E.B. Barbier (2000). 'Valuing groundwater recharge through agricultural production in the Hadejia-Jama'are wetlands in northern Nigeria', *Agricultural Economics*, 22, 247–59.

Aksornkoae, S. and R. Tokrisna (2004). 'Overview of shrimp farming and mangrove loss in Thailand', in E.B. Barbier and S. Sathirathai (eds.), *Shrimp Farming and Mangrove Loss in Thailand*, Edward Elgar, London.

Aksornkoae, S., R. Tokrisna, W. Sugunnasil and S. Sathirathai (2004). 'The importance of mangroves: Ecological perspectives and socio-economic values', in E.B. Barbier and S. Sathirathai (eds.), *Shrimp Farming and Mangrove Loss in Thailand*, Edward Elgar, London.

Barbier, E.B. (1994). 'Valuing environmental functions: Tropical wetlands', *Land Economics*, 70(2), 155–73.

— (2000). 'Valuing the environment as input: Applications to mangrove-fishery linkages', *Ecological Economics*, 35, 47–61.

— (2003). 'Habitat-fishery linkages and mangrove loss in Thailand', *Contemporary Economic Policy*, 21(1), 59–77.

Barbier, E.B. and M. Cox (2003). 'Does economic development lead to mangrove loss? A cross-country analysis', *Contemporary Economic Policy*, 21(4), 418–32.

Barbier, E.B. and S. Sathirathai (eds.) (2004). *Shrimp Farming and Mangrove Loss in Thailand*. Edward Elgar, London.

Barbier, E.B. and I. Strand (1998). 'Valuing mangrove-fishery linkages: A case study of Campeche, Mexico', *Environmental and Resource Economics*, 12, 151–66.

Barbier, E.B., I. Strand and S. Sathirathai (2002). 'Do open access conditions affect the valuation of an externality? Estimating the welfare effects of mangrove-fishery linkages', *Environmental and Resource Economics*, 21(4), 343–67.

Bjørndal, T. and J.M. Conrad (1987). 'The dynamics of an open access fishery', *Canadian Journal of Economics*, 20, 74–85.

Boscolo, M. and J.R. Vincent (2003). 'Nonconvexities in the production of timber, biodiversity, and carbon sequestration', *Journal of Environmental Economics and Management*, 46, 251–68.

Cameron, C.A. and P. Trivedi (1998). *Regression Analysis of Count Data*, Cambridge University Press, Cambridge.

Carlsson, F., P. Frykblom and C. Lijenstolpe (2003). 'Valuing wetland attributes: An application of choice experiments', *Ecological Economics*, 47, 95–103.

Carpenter, S.R., D. Ludwig and W.A. Brock (1999). 'Management of eutrophication for lakes subject to potentially irreversible change', *Ecological Applications*, 9(3), 751–71.

Charuppat, T. and J. Charuppat (1997). *The Use of Landsat-5 (TM) Satellite Images for Tracing the Changes of Mangrove Forest Areas of Thailand*, Royal Forestry Department, Bangkok.

Check, E. (2005). 'Roots of recovery', *Nature*, 438, 910–11.

Chong, J. (2005). *Protective Values of Mangrove and Coral Ecosystems: A Review of Methods and Evidence*, IUCN, Gland, Switzerland.

Clark, C. (1976). *Mathematical Bioeconomics*, John Wiley and Sons, New York.

Dahdouh-Guebas, F., L.P. Jayatissa, D. Di Nitto, J.O. Bosire, D. Lo Seen and N. Koedam (2005). 'How effective were mangroves as a defence against the recent tsunami?' *Current Biology*, 15(12), 443–47.

Daily, G. (ed.) (1997). *Nature's Services: Societal Dependence on Natural Ecosystems*, Island Press, Washington DC.

De Groot, R.S., M.A. Wilson and R.M.J. Boumans (2002). 'A typology for the classification, description and valuation of ecosystem functions, goods and services', *Ecological Economics*, 41, 393–408.

Deninger, K. and L. Squire (1998). 'New ways of looking at old issues: Inequality and growth', *Journal of Development Economics*, 57, 259–87.

Dickie, M. (2003). 'Defensive behavior and damage cost methods', in P. Champ, K.J. Boyle and T.C. Brown (eds.), *A Primer on Nonmarket Valuation*, Kluwer, Boston, MA.

Dilley, M., R.S. Chen, U. Deichmann, A.L. Lerner-Lam and M. Arnold (2005). *Natural Disaster Hotspots: A Global Risk Analysis*. Disaster Risk Management Series, Hazard Management Unit, The World Bank, Washington, DC.

Ellis, G.M. and A.C. Fisher (1987). 'Valuing the environment as input', *Journal of Environmental Management*, 25, 149–56.

EM-DAT (2005). *EM-DAT: The OFDA/CRED International Disaster Database*. www.em-dat.net, Université Catholique de Louvain, Brussels, Belgium.

Engerman, S. and Sokoloff, K.L. (2000). 'Factor endowment, inequality, and paths of development among new world economies', UCLA.

FAO (2003). 'Status and trends in mangrove area extent worldwide' (by M.L. Wilkie and S. Fortuna) Forest Resources Assessment Working Paper No. 63, Forest Resources Division, Food and Agricultural Organization of the United Nations, Rome.

Finnoff, D. and J. Tschirhart (2003). 'Harvesting in an eight-species ecosystem', *Journal of Environmental Economics and Management*, 45, 589–611.

Freeman, A.M. III. (1982). *Air and Water Pollution Control: A Benefit-Cost Assessment*, John Wiley, New York.

— (1991). 'Valuing environmental resources under alternative management regimes', *Ecological Economics*, 3, 247–56.

— (2003). *The Measurement of Environmental and Resource Values: Theory and Methods*, 2nd edn, Resources for the Future, Washington DC.

Galor, O., O. Moav and D. Vollrath (2005). 'Inequality in land ownership, the emergence of human capital promoting institutions, and the great divergence', Brown University.

Greene, W.H. (2003). *Econometric Analysis*, 5th edn, Prentice-Hall, Englewood Cliffs, NJ.

Gren, I-M., K. Elofsson and P. Jannke (1997). 'Cost-effective nutrient reductions to the Baltic Sea', *Environmental and Resource Economics*, 10, 341–62.

Gylfason, T. (2001). 'Natural resources, education, and economic development', *European Economic Review*, 45, 847–59.

Harakunarak, A. and S. Aksornkoae (2005). 'Life-saving belts: Post-tsunami reassessment of mangrove ecosystem values and management in Thailand', *Tropical Coasts*, July, 48–55.

Heal, G.M., E.B. Barbier, K.J. Boyle, A.P. Covich, S.P. Gloss, C.H. Hershner, J.P. Hoehn, C.M. Pringle, S. Polasky, K. Segerson and K. Shrader-Frechette (2005). *Valuing Ecosystem Services: Toward Better Environmental Decision Making*, The National Academies Press, Washington DC.

Hirshleifer, J. and J.G. Riley (1992). *The Analytics of Uncertainty and Information*, Cambridge University Press, Cambridge.

Homans, F.R. and J.E. Wilen (1997). 'A model of regulated open access resource use', *Journal of Environmental Economics and Management*, 32, 1–21.

Jackson, J.B.C., M.X. Kirby, W.H. Berger, *et al.* (2001). 'Historical overfishing and the recent collapse of coastal ecosystems', *Science*, 293, 629–38.

Just, R.E., D.L. Hueth and A. Schmitz (2004). *The Welfare Economics of Public Policy: A Practical Approach to Project and Policy Evaluation*, Edward Elgar, Cheltenham, UK.

Kahn, J.R., and W.M. Kemp (1985). 'Economic losses associated with the degradation of an ecosystem: The case of submerged aquatic vegetation in Chesapeake Bay', *Journal of Environmental Economics and Management*, 12, 246–63.

Kaiser, B. and J. Roumasset (2002). 'Valuing indirect ecosystem services: The case of tropical watersheds', *Environment and Development Economics*, 7, 701–14.

Kaosa-ard, M. and S. Pednekar (1998). 'Background Report for the Thai Marine Rehabilitation Plan 1997–2001', Report submitted to the Joint Research Centre of the Commission of the European Communities and the Department of Fisheries, Ministry of Agriculture and Cooperatives, Thailand, Thailand Development Research Institute, Bangkok.

Kathiresan, K. and N. Rajendran (2005). 'Coastal mangrove forests mitigated tsunami', *Estuarine Coastal and Shelf Science*, 65, 601–606.

Knowler, D., E.B. Barbier, and I. Strand (2001). 'An open-access model of fisheries and nutrient enrichment in the Black Sea', *Marine Resource Economics*, 16, 195–217.

Krutilla, J.V. and A.C. Fisher (1985). *The Economics of Natural Environments: Studies in the Valuation of Commodity and Amenity Resources*, Resources for the Future, Washington, DC.

Lynne, G.D., P. Conroy and F.J. Prochaska (1981). 'Economic value of marsh areas for marine production processes', *Journal of Environmental Economics and Management*, 8, 175–86.

Mardle, S., C. James, C. Pipitone and M. Kienzle (2004). 'Bioeconomic interactions in an established fishing exclusion zone: The Gulf of Castellammare, NW Sicily', *Natural Resource Modeling*, 17(4), 393–447.

Massel, S.R., K. Furukawa and R.M. Brinkman (1999). 'Surface wave propagation data in mangrove forests', *Fluid Dynamics Research*, 24, 219–49.

Mazda, Y., E. Wolanski, B. King, A. Sase, D. Ohtsuka and M. Magi (1997). 'Drag force due to vegetation in mangrove swamps', *Mangroves and Salt Marshes*, 1, 193–99.

McConnell, K.E. and I.E. Strand (1989). 'Benefits from commercial fisheries when demand and supply depend on water quality', *Journal of Environmental Economics and Management*, 17, 284–92.

Michener, R. and C. Tighe (1992). 'A Poisson regression model of highway fatalities', *American Economic Review*, 82(2), 452–56.

Millennium Ecosystem Assessment (2003). *Ecosystems and Human Well-being: A Framework for Assessment*, Island Press, Washington DC.

Mitsch, W.J. and J.G. Gosselink (1993). *Wetlands*, 2nd edn, Van Norstrand Reinhold, New York.

Myers, R.A. and B. Worm (2003). 'Rapid worldwide depletion of predatory fish communities', *Nature*, 423, 280–83.

Naylor, R. and M. Drew (1998). 'Valuing mangrove resources in Kosrae, Micronesia', *Environment and Development Economics*, 3, 471–90.

Olson, M.K. (2004). 'Are novel drugs more risky for patients than less novel drugs?' *Journal of Health Economics*, 23, 1135–58.

Pagiola, S., K. von Ritter and J. Bishop (2004). *How Much is an Ecosystem Worth? Assessing the Economic Value of Conservation*, The World Bank, Washington DC.

Parks, P. and M. Bonfaz (1997). 'Nonsustainable use of renewable resources: Mangrove deforestation and mariculture in Ecuador', *Marine Resource Economics*, 9, 1–18.

Ready, R.C. (1995). 'Environmental valuation under uncertainty', in D.W. Bromley (ed.), *The Handbook of Environmental Economics*, Blackwell Publishers, Cambridge, MA, pp. 568–93.

Ricketts, T.H., G.C. Daily, P.R. Ehrlich and C.D. Michener (2004). 'Economic value of tropical forest to coffee production', *Proceedings of the National Academy of Science*, 101(304), 12579–82.

Rodwell, L.D., E.B. Barbier, C.M. Roberts and T.R. McClanahan (2002). 'A model of tropical marine reserve-fishery linkages', *Natural Resource Modeling*, 15(4), 453–86.

Rose, N.L. (1990). 'Profitability and product quality: Economic determinants of airline safety performance', *Journal of Political Economy*, 98(5), 944–64.

Sathirathai, S. and E.B. Barbier (2001). 'Valuing mangrove conservation in Southern Thailand', *Contemporary Economic Policy*, 19, 109–22.

Schnute, J. (1977). 'Improved estimates of the Schaefer Production Model: Theoretical considerations', *Journal of the Fisheries Research Board of Canada*, 34, 583–603.

Settle, C. and J.F. Shogren (2002). 'Modeling native-exotic species within Yellowstone Lake', *American Journal of Agricultural Economics*, 84(5), 1323–28.

Shabman, L.A. and S.S. Batie (1978). 'Economic value of natural coastal wetlands: A critique', *Coastal Zone Management Journal*, 4(3), 231–47.

Sugunnasil, W. (1998). 'Fishing communities and coastal resource management in Southern Thailand', mimeo, Department of Social Sciences, Prince of Songkla University, Pattani, Thailand.

Sumaila, U.R. (2002). 'Marine protected area performance in a model of a fishery', *Natural Resource Modeling*, 15(4), 439–51.

Swallow, S.K. (1994). 'Renewable and nonrenewable resource theory applied to coastal agriculture, forest, wetland and fishery linkages', *Marine Resource Economics*, 9, 291–310.

UNEP (United Nations Environment Program) (2005). *After the Tsunami: Rapid Environmental Assessment Report*, UNEP, Nairobi, 22 February; www.unep.org/tsunami/reports.

Valiela, I., J.L. Bowen and J.K. York (2001). 'Mangrove forests: One of the world's threatened major tropical environments', *BioScience*, 51(10), 807–15.

Wattana, S. (1998). 'Fishing Communities and Coastal Resource Management in Southern Thailand'. Mimeo. Department of Social Sciences, Prince of Songkla University, Pattani, Thailand.

Wetlands International (2005). *Natural Mitigation of Natural Disasters*. Assessment Report to Ramsar STRP12, Wetlands International, Jakarta, 2 February.

Winkelmann, R. (2003). *Econometric Analysis of Count Data*, 4th edn, Springer-Verlag, Berlin.

World Conservation Monitoring Centre (WCMC) (1992). 'Wetlands', in WCMC (ed.), *Global Biodiversity: Status of the Earth's Living Resources*, IUCN, Gland, Switzerland.

World Resources Institute (WRI) (1996). *World Resources 1996–7*, World Resources Institute, Washington DC.

— (2001). *World Resources 2000–2001. People and Ecosystems: The Fraying Web of Life*, World Resources Institute, Washington DC.

Wu, J., K. Skelton-Groth, W.G. Boggess and R.M. Adams (2003). 'Pacific salmon restoration: Trade-offs between economic efficiency and political acceptance', *Contemporary Economic Policy*, 21(1), 78–89.

Zinn, J. (2005). *Hurricanes Katrina and Rita and the Coastal Louisiana Ecosystem Restoration*. CRS Report for Congress, The Congressional Research Service, The Library of Congress, Washington DC, 26 September.

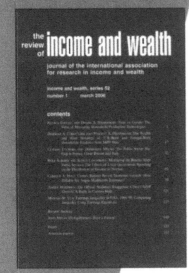